The Politics of Intersectionality

The Politics of Intersectionality series builds on the long-standing insights of intersectionality theory from a vast variety of disciplinary perspectives. As a globally utilitzed analytical framework for understanding issues of social justice, Leslie McCall, Mary Hawkesworth, and others argue that intersectionality is arguably the most important theoretical contribution of women's and gender studies to date. Indeed the imprint of intersectional analysis can be easily found on innovations in equality legislation, human rights, and development discourses.

The history of what is now called "intersectional thinking" is long. In fact, prior to its mainstreaming, intersectionality analysis was carried for many years mainly by black and other racialized women who, from their situated gaze, perceived as absurd, not just misleading, any attempt by feminists and others to homogenize women's situation, particulary in conceptualizing such situations as analogous to that of racialized others. As Brah and Phoenix point out, many black feminists fulfilled significant roles in the development of intersectional analysis, such as the Combahee River Collective, the black lesbian feminist organization from Boston, who pointed out the need of developing an integrated analysis and practice based upon the fact that major systems of oppression interlock rather than operate separately. However the term "intersectionality" itself emerged nominally from the field of critical legal studies, where critical race feminist Kimberle Williams Crenshaw wrote two pathbreaking articles, "Demarginalizing the Intersection of Race and Sex: A Critique of Antidiscrimination Doctrine, Feminist Theory and Antiracist Politics" and "Mapping the Margins: Intersectionality, Identity Politics, and Violence against Women of Color." At nearly the same time, social theorist Patricia Hill Collins was preparing her landmark work, *Black Feminist Thought: Knowledge, Consciousness and the Politics of Empowerment*, which characterized intersections of race, class, and gender as mutually reinforcing sites of power relations.

Both Crenshaw and Collins gave the name "intersectionality" to a far larger and more ethnically diverse trajectory of work, now global in nature, that speaks truth to power sited differentially rather than centralized in a single locus. What could also be called intersectional analysis was in fact developing at roughly the same time among European and postcolonial feminists, including, for example, Anthias and Yuval-Davis (1983; 1992); Brah (1996); Essed (1991); Ifekwunigwe (1999); Lutz (1991); Meekosha, and Min-ha (1989). Indeed it seems, in a manner parallel to that which Sandra Harding characterizes the evolution of standpoint theory, that intersectionality was an idea whose time had come precisely because of the plethora of authors working independently across the globe to make vastly similar sets of claims. Around the world, those interested in a more comprehensive and transformative approach to social justice—whether sociologists, legal scholars, feminist theorists, policy makers, or human rights advocates—have used the language and tenets of intersectionality to more effectively articulate injustice and advocate for positive social change.

The books in this series represent an interrogation of intersectionality at various levels of analysis. They unabashedly foreground the politics of intersectionality in a way that is designed to both honor the legacy of earlier scholarship and activism as well as to push the boundaries of intersectionality's value to the academy and most importantly to the world. We interpret the series title, The Politics of Intersectionality, in two general ways:

First, we emphasize the politics of intersectionality, broadly conceived; that is to say we include debates among scholars regarding the proper conceptualization and application of the term "intersectionality" as part and parcel of the series' intellectual project. Is intersectionality a paradigm? Is intersectionality a normative political (specifically feminist) project? Is it a method or epistemological approach? Is it (merely) a concept with limited applicability beyond multiply marginalized populations? Our own idiosyncratic answers to these questions are far less important than the open dialogue we seek by including them within the scholarly discourse generated by the series.

What this means pragmatically is that rather than dictatorially denote an extant definition of intersectionality and impose it on every author's manuscript, as series editors our task has been to meaningfully push each author to grapple with their own conceptualization of intersectionality and facilitate their interaction with an ever-growing body of global scholarship, policy, and advocacy work as they render such a conceptualization transparent to readers, reflexive as befits the best feminist work, and committed to rigorous standards of quality no matter the subject, the method, or the conclusions. As editors we have taken such an active role precisely because grappling with the politics of intersectionality demands our adherence to the normative standards of transparency, reflexivity, and speaking to multiple sites of power for which intersectionality is not only known but lauded as the gold standard. It is our honor to build this area of scholarship across false boundaries of theory and praxis; artificially distinct academic disciplines; and the semipermeable line between scholarship and activism.

No less importantly we emphasize politics to mean, well, *politics*, whether everyday senses of justice; so-called formal politics of social movements, campaigns, elections, policy, and government institutions; or personal politics of identity, community, and activism across a broad swath of the world. While this general conceptualization of politics lends itself to the social sciences, we define social sciences in a broad way that again seeks to unite theoretical concerns (whether normative or positive) with interpretive and empirical approaches across an array of topics far too numerous to list in their entirety.

The second way we interpret the series title—simultaneously, as one might expect of intersectionality scholars—is with an emphasis on the word intersectionality. That is, the books in this series neither depend solely on 20-year-old articulations of intersectionality, nor do they adhere to one particular theoretical or methodological approach to study intersectionality; they are steeped in a rich literature of both substantive and analytical depth that in the twenty-first century reaches around the world. This is not your professor's "women of color" or "race-class-gender" series of the late twentieth century. Indeed an emphasis on up-to-date engagement with the best and brightest global thinking on intersectionality has been the single most exacting standard we have imposed on the editing process. As series editors we seek to develop manuscripts that aspire to a level of sophistication about intersectionality as a body of research that is in fact worthy of the intellectual, political, and personal risks taken by so many of its earliest interlocutors in voicing and naming this work. We thus relate to intersectionality as both methodological and analytical tools that are firmly rooted in the epistemological tradition of the feminist situated gaze but do not necessarily prioritize discussion of gender relations over other cross-cutting social, economic, and political power relations.

Series Editors:

Ange-Marie Hancock, University of Southern California
Nira Yuval-Davis, University of East London

Also in the series:

Solidarity Politics for Millennials
Ange-Marie Hancock

Social Change and Intersectional Activism: The Spirit of Social Movement
Sharon Doetsch-Kidder

Urban Black Women and the Politics of Resistance
Zenzele Isoke

Gender Equality, Intersectionality and Diversity in Europe
Lise Rolandsen Agustín

Situating Intersectionality: Politics, Policy, and Power
Edited by Angelia R. Wilson

SITUATING INTERSECTIONALITY
POLITICS, POLICY, AND POWER

Edited by
Angelia R. Wilson

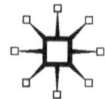

SITUATING INTERSECTIONALITY
Copyright © Angelia R. Wilson, 2013.
Softcover reprint of the hardcover 2013 978-1-137-02511-1

All rights reserved.

First published in 2013 by
PALGRAVE MACMILLAN®
in the United States—a division of St. Martin's Press LLC,
175 Fifth Avenue, New York, NY 10010.

Where this book is distributed in the UK, Europe and the rest of the world, this is by Palgrave Macmillan, a division of Macmillan Publishers Limited, registered in England, company number 785998, of Houndmills, Basingstoke, Hampshire RG21 6XS.

Palgrave Macmillan is the global academic imprint of the above companies and has companies and representatives throughout the world.

Palgrave® and Macmillan® are registered trademarks in the United States, the United Kingdom, Europe and other countries.

ISBN 978-1-349-43876-1   ISBN 978-1-137-02513-5 (eBook)
DOI 10.1057/9781137025135

Library of Congress Cataloging-in-Publication Data is available from the Library of Congress.

A catalogue record of the book is available from the British Library.

Design by Newgen Knowledge Works (P) Ltd., Chennai, India.

First edition: September 2013

10 9 8 7 6 5 4 3 2 1

For my students in their designer French outfits, their faded jeans, their actually-scruffy-not-trendy-clothes, their hijabs, brown skin, white skin, black skin, Irish green eyes, girly make up, comfortable middle-class smiles, covered in buttons against war, for human rights, unions, and Gay Pride, with defiant, rebellious voices in Swedish/Mauritian/Australian/Spanish/ American/Mancunian accents, who inspire me to think about differences—and about values worth sharing.

Contents

Series Introduction: The Politics of Intersectionality   xi

Acknowledgments   xiii

Introduction   1
Angelia R. Wilson

1   Intersectionality from Theoretical Framework to Policy Intervention   11
Wendy G. Smooth

2   Intersectional Advances? Inclusionary and Intersectional State Action in Uruguay   43
Erica E. Townsend-Bell

3   ID Cards as Access: Negotiating Transgender (and Intersex) Bodies into the Chilean Legal System   63
Penny Miles

4   International Adoption as Humanitarian Aid: The Discursive and Material Production of the "Social Orphan" in Haitian Disaster Relief   89
Kate Livingston

5   Gendered Subjectivity and Intersectional Political Agency in Transnational Space: The Case of Turkish and Kurdish Women's NGO Activists   107
Anil Al-Rebholz

6   Gender Variance: The Intersection of Understandings Held in the Medical and Social Sciences   131
Ryan Combs

7 Intersectional Analysis at the Medico-Legal Borderland: HIV Testing Innovations and the Criminalization of HIV Non-Disclosure   157
   Daniel Grace

8 Crossroads or Categories? Intersectionality Theory and the Case of Lesbian, Gay, and Bisexual Equalities Initiatives in UK Local Government   189
   Surya Monro and Diane Richardson

Notes on Contributors   209

Index   213

Series Introduction: The Politics of Intersectionality

Currently intersectionality scholarship lacks a meaningful clearinghouse of work that speaks across (again false) boundaries of a particular identity community under study (e.g., black lesbians, women of color, environmental activists), academic disciplines, or the geographical location from which the author writes (e.g., Europe, North America, Southeast Asia). For that reason we expect that the references of the chapters will be almost as helpful as the chapters themselves, particularly for senior professors who train graduate students and graduate students seeking to immerse themselves broadly and deeply in contemporary approaches to intersectionality. We are less sanguine, however, about the plethora of modifiers that have emerged to somehow modulate intersectionality—whether it be intersectional stigma, intersectional political consciousness, intersectional praxis, post-intersectionality, paradigm intersectionality, or even Crenshaw's original modes of structural and political intersectionality. Our emphasis has been on building the subfield rather than consciously expanding the lexicon of modes and specialities for intersectionality.

In the fifth book in this series, *Situating Intersectionality: Politics, Policy and Power*, editor Angelia Wilson has curated a set chapters from a successful conference of the same name in the United Kingdom, and marks several firsts in our Politics of Intersectionality series. Wilson turns our attention for the first time outside of the United States, exploring the constructions of intersectionality and their applications in the European Union, the UK, Uruguay, Turkey, and elsewhere. This edited volume is thus an important consideration of the geographical dispersion of the term intersectionality and also a recognition of overlapping considerations among policy practitioners and scholars with questions of inclusion, social movements, and representation around the world. The ongoing need to render the invisible "visible" is as true in the global context as it is in the United States.

Second, Wilson's effort marks the first edited volume of our series—a notoriously difficult type of project, due to the efforts required to herd overcommitted academics to meet deadlines, respond to a variety of comments and revisions, and to do so in a timely manner. Wilson's yeoman effort allows us to explore grounded answers to two key questions: How can intersectionality help us articulate, listen to, and understand individual experiences of politics and policy? What does this teach us about political strategizing and the possibility, or not, for political solidarity? These questions remain critical in the twenty-first century, and are part of a long-standing set of questions activists, policy practitioners, and scholars must grapple with across dimensions of marginalization. As always, we welcome additional submissions for future installments of The Politics of Intersectionality series as it enters its third year as a site for groundbreaking contributions to intersectional scholarship and activism.

Acknowledgments

This collection emerged from an international conference, Situating Intersectionality, sponsored by the Women and Politics Specialist Group of the Political Studies Association (UK). The event was hosted by the Politics Department of the University of Manchester. All of the contributors to this collection would like to thank them for that support, particularly the hard work of Rainbow Murray. In addition, I would like to thank Wendy Smooth, Paisley Currah, Cynthia Burack, and the Politics of Intersectionality series editors, Ange-Marie Hancock and Nira Yuval-Davis, who offered commentary on chapters and provided clarity and direction to the themes explored here. Finally, for endless cups of tea and patiently listening to me "pip on" about this project, I would like to thank my partner, Sarah, and our kids, Joe and Grace.

INTRODUCTION

Angelia R. Wilson

Situating Intersectionality brings together academics working in the discipline of politics who are employing the analytical lens of intersectionality to articulate specific ways in which political institutions, policies, and political engagement define, marginalize, and (dis)empower. In the context of political science, an intersectional analysis can bring a nuanced understanding to the particularities of policy outcomes and to discussions of structural and political dynamics of power. According to Kimberle Crenshaw, such nuance can be lacking, for example, in analytical approaches framed in identity politics: "the problem with identity politics is not that it fails to transcend difference...but rather the opposite, that it frequently conflates or ignores intragroup difference...ignoring difference within groups contributes to tension among groups" (1991, 1242). Crenshaw warns that intersectionality is not being offered "as some new, totalizing theory of identity" (1991, 1244). Instead, intersectionality offers an analytical frame that focuses clearly on the dynamics of power. Her empirical work delineates three different aspects of intersectionality: structural intersectionality, political intersectionality, and cultural intersectionality (1991, 1254–1282). The first recognizes that the embodiment of, and relations between, multiple identities as defined in sociopolitical categories results in very different individual experiences. Individuals locate themselves, and are located, in relation to the intersections of various structural definitions of "identity" and the resulting experiences can engender diverse outcomes regarding, for example, politics and policy. Second, political intersectionality refers to the ways in which different categories of citizens engaged in identity politics may disempower and marginalize each other, perhaps unintentionally. Finally, representational intersectionality notes how cultural constructions can disempower and reproduce, for example, racial and gender hierarchies.

In her article "Multiple Inequalities, Intersectionality and the European Union," Mieko Verloo reflects on Crenshaw's distinctions. Concentrating on the first two she notes that "structural intersectionality occurs when inequalities and their intersections are directly relevant to the experiences of people in society," and political intersectionality indicates "how inequalities and their intersections are relevant to political strategies" (2006, 213). She laments that much of the academic discussion about intersectionality has focused on the former: "strikingly, almost no reference is made to the concept of political intersectionality...very little attention is paid to both structural and political intersectionality in policy-making" (2006, 214). The contributions here speak to this gap and draw upon the wealth of academic discussion that has developed since Crenshaw's initial conceptualization. As political science academics, two key concerns emerge from the authors in this collection: How can intersectionality help us articulate, listen to, and understand individual experiences of politics and policy? What does this teach us about political strategizing and the possibility, or not, for political solidarity? In this brief introduction, I want to call attention to some of the literature addressing these two questions.

First, how can intersectionality help us articulate, listen to, and understand individual experiences of politics and policy? Answers to this question often imply a direct comparison, that is, "better than identity politics" or "better than a class analysis." Unsurprisingly then, some express concern that intersectionality may obfuscate the distinctive dynamics of power in relation to, and within, different identity categories (Skeggs, 2006 as noted in Phoenix and Pattynama, 2006). However, as Ange-Marie Hancock explains in *Solidarity Politics for Millennials*, identity politics conceptualizes, for example, race and gender as parallel phenomena and this can lead to an *oppression olympics* with groups competing for the title of being the most oppressed in order to gain political support of dominant groups (2011). But these *olympics* leave the overall system of structural inequality unchanged. Likewise, a multiple, or additive, approach leads to "competition rather than coordination among marginal groups" rather than transforming the logic of distribution (2007, 70). Intersectionality, Laurel Weldon clarifies, focuses on the interaction of different structures of inequality resulting in a more developed picture of oppression and discrimination (2008). The intent is not to homogenize the experience of inequalities or marginalization but to widen the possibilities to articulate fluidity, political, and temporal specificity. In terms of an analysis of politics, policies, and political movements, it is important then to envision the relationship between intersectionality and identity politics not as an "either/or" but working in "conjunction with" in order to map the dynamics of power.

Intersectionality keeps the analytical gaze steadily on the *dynamics* of structural power: mapping the fluidity and temporality of identity construction resulting from the fluidity, temporality, and adaptability of that power. Johanna Kantola and Kevät Nousiainen note that "intersectional approaches explore the ways in which domination, subordination and subjects are constructed in particular locations and contexts" (2009, 462). For example, categories of inequality differ regarding "dimensions of choice... visibility...and change" (Kantola and Nousiainen, 2009, 468; see also Hancock, 2007, 63–70). For Gill Valentine the appeal of intersectionality is in "the emphasis it places on the complexity of and fluidity in the ways that identities are unmade as well as made, and undone as well as done" (2007, 18). In *Intersectionality and Beyond*, the authors conceptualize intersectionality as offering an understanding of how inequalities are "routed through one another and which cannot be untangled to reveal a single cause" (Grabham et al., 2009, 1). In this collection, Smooth explains that intersectionality not only "troubles" essentializing notions of identity but it also enables a recognition of the ways in which identities shift and change over time just as the institutions delineating them shift and change. This emphasis on particularity within a context of various power structures facilitates a detailed understanding of political outcomes. Nira Yuval-Davis notes: "in specific historical situations and in relation to specific people there are some social divisions which are more important than others in constructing specific positionings" (2006, 199). To this end, the contributions in this collection deploy intersectionality in order to map specificities of experiences resulting from the dynamics of structural and political power.

This brings us to the second thematic question underpinning this collection: What does this teach us about political strategizing and the possibility, or not, for political solidarity? Psychologist Erica Burman observes: "abstracting any single dimension of 'difference' as a focus of concern or intervention is inevitably—conceptually, politically and therapeutically—inadequate" (2003, 297). For Burman, the invidious modality of identity politics "divides and fragments so as to render alliance and coalition nigh on impossible." Without an intersectional frame, political strategies may be built upon inaccurate maps of power or, at least ones lacking indications of potential pitfalls or opportunities for allegiances and collaboration. Verloo points out that "different inequalities are dissimilar because they are differently framed" and therefore it is crucial to "ground policy strategies not only in the similarity, but also in the distinctiveness of inequalities" (2006, 221). Continuing she argues that identity politics or additive approaches are "in danger of ignoring differences in the political goals at stake, because they tend to conflate social position and identity with political position and opinion...they pay almost no attention to existing power struggles within organizations, and thereby make these struggles opaque and dangerous to the democratic process" (2006, 222). This overlooks the "political dimension of equality goals" (2006, 223). For example, those working the context of the European Union have argued that gender mainstreaming and any subsequent additive approach to the equalities agenda ignore the complexities of identities (see articles in Egeland and Gressgård, 2007). Kantola and Nousiainen call for close examination of the political processes underpinning such "intersectional discrimination" where several grounds of discrimination "interact with each other simultaneously" (2009, 468). Their argument resonates closely with Hancock's analysis that the governance structures that led to the gender mainstreaming establish hierarchies of inequalities and competition for scarce financial resources and political goodwill. Because of this additive approach, Verloo argues, more attention "to structural mechanisms and to the role of the state and the private sphere in reproducing inequalities is much needed" (2006, 211). Continuing she details the political agenda:

> The fact that inequalities are dissimilar means that such "equality" mainstreaming cannot be a simple adaptation of current tools of gender mainstreaming. Whether one thinks of checklists, training, impact assessment or expert meetings, a clear conceptualization

of how intersectionality operates, a theory of the power dynamics of a specific inequality, as well as a choice for a clear political goal will be needed. Moreover, the fact that multiple inequalities are not independent means that such "equality" mainstreaming cannot be a simple extrapolation of gender mainstreaming. If intersectionality is at work in strategies against inequalities, then new and more comprehensive analytical methods are needed and methods of education, training and consultation will have to be rethought. (2006, 222)

Whether or not one adopts this particular political agenda, it serves as a testament to the necessity for an intersectional analysis highlighting the dynamic relationship between political structures, identity formation, and policy outcomes. A new generation of political science scholars, comfortable employing intersectional analysis, are framing the particularities of individual experiences within the complexity of policy making in an increasingly small, technologically connected, and ideologically nuanced public square. This collection gives voice to these scholars whose empirical research spans the Welsh countryside, the Turkish hinterland, the streets of Chile, Uruguay, Poland, Spain, England, and the great (political) state of Ohio.

Wendy Smooth, in chapter 1, calls for political scientists to "operationalize intersectionality" in order to disrupt identity categories and staid methods of categorizing and quantifying procedures that define identities and experiences. For Smooth, intersectionality is concerned with "the systems" that give identities meaning. Political science can bring "clarity to the conversation and the processes by which multiple identities are constituted" and how they evolve and "interact with political institutions, structures and movements." Deployed in conjunction with other methodological tools, intersectionality complements, disrupts, and enhances our understanding of politics, political activism, and "hidden power differentials" of governance through legislative and judicial action (Hancock, 2007). In opening this collection, Smooth establishes the "core foundations" of intersectionality by drawing upon her own extensive research regarding the experiences of African American women legislators who face a "matrix of domination" (Collins, 1991). These core foundations sit at the heart of the conceptualization of intersectionality informing the remaining chapters.

Throughout this collection, authors draw upon an intersectional analysis to make sense of the diversity of activism appearing as various populations respond to influences from identity politics of race, feminism, and LGBT movements. Erica Townsend-Bell considers how we identify intersectional advances to assess "whether states act intersectionally and the conditions under which they might do so." Through her research in Uruguay, she identifies differences between activism that leads to intersectional outcomes and activism that leads to only inclusionary outcomes. In doing so, she establishes conditions for intersectional outcomes. For her, a crucial key to securing intersectionality-based policies is for activists, working together, to learn to make coherent intersectional demands in a language understood by the institutions of the state.

The articulation of intersectional goals, as each author here notes, is difficult as activism stretches across essentialized identity categories. Some voices may be heard while others are not. Penny Miles considers how judicial activism—or activism via litigation—can undermine intersectional understandings of identities and structures of oppression. Taking the requirement of ID cards in Chile as a starting point, Miles shows how media representations perpetuate cultural normativity that privileges some transgender citizens over others. Despite moments where intersectional outcomes fall short of desired goals, some discussion in the public square of transgender issues has facilitated a broadening of issues and the emergence of professional expertise in legal as well as activist circles.

Media and political discourses are at the heart of the intersectional analysis offered in chapter 4 by Kate Livingston. Focusing her analytical lens on the language and power informing "disaster relief," Livingston argues that in the context of the 2010 earthquake in Haiti, one can trace the construction of the "social orphan" through expedited international adoption as a form of humanitarian aid. Her fascinating account of this discourse demonstrates "how this political category is produced by raced, classed and gendered processes that engender and maintain hierarchical relationships among groups." This construction perpetuated and promoted institutional policies that maintain international systems of inequality and ignored possibilities of strengthening internal capacities within Haiti.

In chapter 5, Anil Al-Rebholz raises questions about the role of nongovernmental organizations (NGOs) in importing and defining feminism in Turkey. The original empirical data considered by Al-Rebholz tells a story about the nature of solidarity within feminist activism and about the dynamics of transnational feminism. Listening to the voices of Kurdish and Turkish women working in NGOs, she draws attention to the institutionalization of feminism via transnational interventions or, in her words, the "NGOisation of the movement." However, another theme emerges as she lifts up the stories of how Kurdish women understand their relationship with Turkish feminists. While Western-educated Turkish feminists have imported feminist ideas, Kurdish women charge that they have only told part of the story: the story of white, liberal American feminism. In response, Kurdish women have appropriated the ideological and political positioning of African American feminists such as Angela Davis and bell hooks. As one interviewee notes, while Turkish feminism focuses on gender identity, "we think…feminism is more than this." Using the work of Yuval-Davis, Al-Rebholz gives a compelling account of "multiple intersecting sources of subordination" embedded in hegemonic power relations, including those found within the production of feminist knowledge.

Over the last 20 years, the UK has developed a raft of equalities policies. In the wake of what appears to be commitment to equality in the public square, those directives are beginning to filter into the social practices affecting every citizen. It is in these moments, where the rubber meets the road, that one can see how policy implementation attempting to facilitate inclusion has struggled precisely because it emerged from a politics based on essentialized conceptualizations of identity. As Ryan Combs demonstrates in chapter 6, at the intersection of medical and social science discourse on gender variance, multiple constructions of identities often have to give way to pragmatic negotiations within established policy parameters. "Ambiguity makes policy making difficult" and because of this Combs sees a need for persistent reflective analysis regarding how policy articulations effect individual constructions of identity. He argues against rationalization or resignation in the face of complexity but challenges policy makers and the medical community to be more open to dialogue that rejects essentialism, listens to variation, and is more open to critical examination of structural issues such as rationing medical services.

In chapter 7, Daniel Grace employs Intersectionality-Based Policy Analysis (IBPA) to better understand the complexity between medical technologies and policy outcomes framing work around HIV/AIDS prevention in Canada. He outlines the particular difficulties at the intersection of criminal laws to prosecute alleged cases of HIV non-disclosure and of medical technologies encouraging early stage detection. The IBPA methodological approach allows policy analysts to detail clearly the problems at such an intersection and, in doing so, it illuminates possible ways through such policy difficulties. In Grace's own words, intersectionality requires "that complex, historically situated factors" including "principles of equity, power and social justice" be integrated meaningfully as part of any response to HIV as a public health issue.

In the final chapter, Surya Monro and Diane Richardson offer a detailed analysis of lesbian, gay, and bisexual equalities initiatives in UK local government. Given the significant extension of equalities policies across the UK, it is important to take stock as to how these are implemented, what effects they have on embodied citizens, and importantly what service providers think they are doing when they "do equality" at the coalface. For anyone, in any country, thinking ideologically or concretely about desired equalities policies, Monro and Richardson's robust analysis of UK policy outcomes offers substantial fodder for contemplation. As Townsend-Bell noted, it is important for activists to demand intersectionality if we desire outcomes that reflect this ideal. Returning to the challenge set by Wendy Smooth to think about the interaction between intersectionality and political science, Monro and Richardson's contribution details a balanced methodological approach that calls for "attention to specific categories...as a means for achieving depth of analysis and as a way of developing intersectionality into something that can be applied at the institutional level." Alongside this, they note that there should be "attention to the interstices...[as] it enables sensitivity to other social characteristics, such as the material, ability, faith, and age" in order to give a more complete picture of social forces routed through each other.

The voices in this collection provide informed, empirically grounded answers to the key questions: How can intersectionality help us articulate, listen to, and understand individual experiences of politics and policy? What does this teach us about political strategizing and the possibility, or not, for political solidarity? The researchers here carry a methodological toolbox in which intersectionality has become a familiar implement for helping understand the fluid, interlocking world around them. In addition, the global nature of this research testifies to the adaptability and usefulness of this tool. The application and usage may itself change over time and the tool may wear at different points from the variety of deployments in culturally and disciplinary specific contexts. Nevertheless, intersectionality facilitates a nuanced articulation of the specificities of individual experiences of politics and policy, and in doing so it can aid us in refining political strategies and in discerning possibilities, or not, for political solidarity.

References

Burman, Erica. 2003. "From Difference to Intersectionality: Challenges and Resources." *European Journal of Psychotherapy & Counselling* 6(4): 293–308.
Collins, Patricia Hill. 1991. *Black Feminist Thought Knowledge, Consciousness, and the Politics of Empowerment.* New York: Routledge.
Crenshaw, Kimberlé. 1991. "Mapping the Margins: Intersectionality, Identity Politics, and Violence Against Women of Color." *Stanford Law Review* 43(6): 1241–1299.
Egeland, Cathrine, and Randi Gressgård. 2007. *Nordic Journal of Women's Studies* 15(4): 207–209.
Grabham, Emily, with Didi Herman, Davina Cooper, and Jane Krishnadas. 2009. "Introduction." In *Intersectionality and Beyond: Law, Power and the Politics of Location,* edited by E. Grabham, D. Cooper, J. Krishnadas, and D. Herman. Abingdon: Routledge-Cavendish.
Hancock, Ange-Marie. 2011. *Solidarity Politics for Millennials: A Guide to Ending the Oppression Olympics.* New York: Palgrave Macmillan.
———. 2007. "When Multiplication Doesn't Equal Quick Addition: Examining Intersectionality as a Research Paradigm." *Perspectives on Politics* 5: 63–79.
Kantola, Johanna, and Kevät Nousiainen. 2009. "Institutionalizing Intersectionality in Europe." *International Feminist Journal of Politics* 11(4): 459–477.
Phoenix, Ann, and Pamela Pattynama. 2006. "Editorial: Intersectionality." *European Journal of Women's Studies* 13(3): 187–192.
Valentine, Gill. 2007. "Theorizing and Researching Intersectionality: A Challenge for Feminist Geography." *The Professional Geographer* 59(1): 10–21.

Verloo, Mieke. 2006. "Multiple Inequalities, Intersectionality and the European Union." *European Journal of Women's Studies* 13(3): 211–228.

Weldon, Laurel S. 2008. "The Concept of Intersectionality." In *Politics, Gender and Concepts: Theory and Methodology*, edited by G. Goertz and A. Mazur. Cambridge: Cambridge University Press.

Yuval-Davis, Nira. 2006. "Intersectionality and Feminist Politics." *European Journal of Women's Studies* 13(3): 193–209.

1

INTERSECTIONALITY FROM THEORETICAL FRAMEWORK TO POLICY INTERVENTION

Wendy G. Smooth

Intersectionality, the assertion that social identity categories such as race, gender, class, sexuality, and ability are interconnected and operate simultaneously to produce experiences of both privilege and marginalization, has transformed old conversations while inspiring new debates across the academy. Intersectionality encourages recognition of the differences that exist *among* groups, moving dialogue beyond considering only the differences *between* groups. Originating from discontent with treatments of "women" as a homogenous group, intersectionality has evolved into a theoretical research paradigm that seeks to understand the interaction of various social identities and how these interactions define societal power hierarchies. Intersectionality encourages us to embrace the complexities of group-based politics by critically examining the variances in social location that exist among those claiming membership in groups.[1]

At the same time that intersectionality helps to make sense of the experiences of people who find themselves living at the intersections of social identities, intersectionality also is concerned with the systems that give meaning to the categories of race, gender, class, sexual identity, among others. In other words, at the societal level intersectionality seeks to make visible the systems of oppression that maintain power hierarchies and organize society while also providing a means to theorize experience at the individual level.

Intersectionality scholarship has emerged as one of the most significant areas of research across academic disciplines. It has been considered "the most important theoretical contribution that women's studies in conjunction with related fields has made so far" (McCall, 2005, 1771). It has opened a plethora of new and exciting research questions and analyses. Viewing the world from the intersections of various social locations, including race, gender, class, ability, nationality, sexuality, among other locations, has produced an important paradigm shift in terms of how we study and approach questions of hierarchy, inequality, power, and what constitutes the just society. As Berger and Guidroz (2010, 7) argue, intersectionality represents a new "social literacy" that challenges traditional framing of research questions and methodology. Speaking to the reach of this new social literacy, they assert that to be "an informed social theorist or methodologist in many fields of scholarly inquiry, but most especially in women's studies, one must grapple with the implications of intersectionality." (Ibid.)

In this chapter, I focus largely on the developments of intersectionality from a Western, predominately US, perspective. However, as intersectionality is at its core concerned with questions of power and inequities, this discussion is applicable to wider political contexts. In fact, as more scholars engage intersectionality in their work in non-Western contexts, under differing political regimes, power hierarchies, and varied historical understandings of how difference is constituted, we are able to further our collective understandings of power and the role that institutions play in giving meaning to identities. Not all claims of intersectionality theory as constituted through a Western, specifically US, lens are applicable to non-Western, non-US contexts. As I show here, this perspective reflects particular power hierarchies predominantly, though not exclusively around race, gender, class, sexuality, and ability. Social categories do not carry the same meaning across contexts and systems of oppression operate differently according to the context. While race, gender, class, sexuality, and ability have been central to intersectionality approaches in the United States, these same categories may be less salient in other contexts where citizenship, language, and region may structure the formation of social hierarchies.[2] For example, Anil Al-Rebholz in this volume illustrates the salience of religion and culture as categories of analysis, while race is less a determinant of social hierarchies in the lives of women in Turkey.

As intersectionality is used to understand power hierarchies in spaces outside the United States, the categories of analysis must change as well. However, as intersectionality travels, some elements are so fundamental that without these elements intersectionality becomes unrecognizable and incapable of doing the political work it was designed to do. Kimberle Crenshaw, who is credited with naming the concept of intersectionality, has remarked that intersectionality often appears as a traveler who shows up at a destination without her luggage (Crenshaw, 2011). As it has traveled it is often stripped of the very elements that made it a critical theory with a social justice imperative. One of my goals in this chapter is to connect intersectionality back to its origins and in doing so equip it for future travels. This volume attests that while the categories of analysis may alter based on the political context under study, core elements of understanding engagements with power remain salient. As scholars around the world continue to contribute to the development of intersectionality as a research paradigm, we are able to develop greater specificity regarding the *processes* by which groups are privileged and marginalized in societies.

I begin this chapter by first offering a brief genealogy of intersectionality locating its origins with black feminist scholars and activists. Next, I assert a set of general principles reflected in articulations of intersectionality, noting the shifting terrain of intersectionality scholarship. Since intersectionality scholarship is understood widely as under development, I pose the question, "What do social scientists, such as political scientists and others interested in institutions and institutional processes, offer to the further development of the intersectionality paradigm?" Using my own work as an example of deploying intersectionality in the study of political institutions, I situate the types of questions political science illuminates in relation to intersectionality. I also recognize that the tensions that make intersectionality attractive to so many, may limit its advancement within political science and other social science disciplines. The paradox for social science researchers is that intersectionality exists as both a highly structured theoretical framework, yet a loosely configured research paradigm. An overemphasis on this concern, as I argue at the close of the chapter, could derail the potential advocacy and policy work scholars are poised to do in an attempt to address inequality across identity categories.

Those of us who study the manifestations of power through societies' political institutions are well positioned to push the development of intersectionality toward even greater attentiveness to the structures and institutions that give meaning to politicized identities. The legal apparatuses articulated through policies, conventions, resolutions, and institutions give individual subjects meaning by at times extending, and at others resending, rights. As well, these institutions and structures bound, direct, and order individual and group choices. These apparatuses configure prominently in determining the material consequences for individuals and condition how individuals articulate their identities. Ultimately, applying such structural analyses to intersectionality moves toward an expanded notion of what constitutes "identity politics." Such a focus on structures and institutions does the political work of troubling essentialized notions of identity and interrogates the idea of naturalized categories with distinct boundaries by understanding identity as evolving as institutions (i.e., laws, policies, and conventions) shift and change. In addition, this focus allows the foregrounding of the material consequences and implications of identity categorizations on individual life circumstances and group politics. Understanding the internal logic and organizational patterns of the structures and institutions that dictate and enforce identity hierarchies, I argue, is a critical step toward reconfiguring the effects of these structures and their role in determining individual and group circumstances.

The chapters in this volume are representative of the work political scientists and others interested in the study of institutions are contributing to deepening our understandings of how institutions and political structures give meaning to identities and structure the relationships between social identity groups. The focus on institutions and institutional behavior allows us to add clarity to the conversation on the *processes* by which multiple identities are constituted and how the salience of identity categorizations shift and evolve over time as they interact with political institutions, structures, and movements. In honing political scientists' contribution to this ongoing conversation in this way, I do not mean to undermine or limit the study of intersectionality at the analytical levels of individual subjective experience, cultural discourse, and representation for political scientists.[3] Indeed, these are all relevant levels of analysis for intersectionality research and illuminate important aspects of how identity categories intersect and how social divisions are constructed and maintained (Yuval-Davis, 2006). However, in light of the specific claims and values of political science as a discipline, we are positioned uniquely to advance thinking about the role of institutions and structures in defining and maintaining identity categories.

In other writings, I have made the case for political science and policy studies more fully adopting intersectionality as a research paradigm and how intersectionality contributes to the study of politics and policy analysis (Smooth, 2006, 2011). Here, I adopt a different approach, reflecting on what political science and policy studies offer to further develop the intersectional approach. Beyond, how do we situate intersectionality in the study of politics and policy, the question I explore in this piece is, "What specifically can political science and policy studies contribute to the study of intersectionality as a research paradigm that crosses disciplinary locations?" In other words, "What tools of analysis do we offer to the development of intersectionality as a research paradigm?" As well, I consider the importance of political science and policy scholars well versed in intersectionality and policy, structures, and institutions to the emerging policy debates that seek to utilize intersectionality.

Intersectionality and the Politics of Origin Stories

Origin stories are important in terms of locating a historical trajectory and are equally important to determining what remains at stake in our politically engaged scholarship. Therefore, I find it critically important to locate intersectionality's origins in struggles for inclusion that mark the experiences of those who first gave academic voice to the concept: black feminist theorists and activists. Intersectionality stems from investments in societal transformation, inclusion, and challenges to the status quo; therefore, in starting with this origin story I strive to maintain its critiques of durable hierarchies and privileges.

Retaining this understanding of intersectionality's origin is especially critical as it moves across disciplinary locations and expands from its roots in black feminist theory to function as a theoretical paradigm that may or may not center on negotiations of race and gender hierarchies. With this expansion, it becomes easy to separate intersectionality from its roots in black feminist theory, thereby erasing the intellectual contributions of black feminist scholars and more so their commitments to dismantling race and gender hierarchies.

As intersectionality has grown into an academic "buzzword" (Davis, 2008), it has come to operate as shorthand verbiage used to signify a host of meanings. In its status as the current "it" theory, it takes on assumptions and connotations that move away from its foundation. It has also become all too easy to gesture to intersectionality as a means of mentioning interrogations with difference and power hierarchies without substantively taking up the demands of intersectional analysis. As Knapp (2005) argues, it allows scholars to use the terminology and gesture to inclusion, while continuing to pursue research in ways that do not substantively challenge the status quo. Stephanie Shields (2008) illustrates this tendency through the use of what she refers to as the "self-excusing," often apologetic disclosure paragraph authors may include in their work. In this ceremonious paragraph, authors acknowledge the importance of intersectionality, yet absolve themselves from actually substantively including such analyses in their work (Shields, 2008, 305). In this way, scholars are credited with recognizing the significance of such an analysis and are credited with being politically and intellectually relevant, but their refusal to participate in developing the concept through empirical and theoretical analysis contributes to a stagnating process. Such treatments transform intersectionality into a signifying keyword. Keywords, as Fraser and Gordon (1994) assert, assume a taken-for-granted common-sense status that elide critical reflection. In the wake of becoming academic cache, we can too easily take for granted the historical roots of intersectionality and the politicized struggles associated with the term.

My locating and centering the origin story of intersectionality with black feminist intellectuals also represents an attempt to return attention to intersectionality's critical stance on uncovering the operation of power and privilege that render individuals and groups marginalized. This stands in contrast to deployments of intersectionality that explore how power is most familiar, or explore the compounded privileges of the powerful.[4] Intersectionality can tell us much about the ways in which intersections of privilege collide to produce greater privilege. For example, a white, Western, middle-classed, heterosexual, able-bodied man presents interlocking social identities that help to explain how he experiences the political world. Intersectionality theory is capable of shedding light on his experiences, identities, and the resulting compounded privileges. However, I maintain that intersectionality is most useful *not* when it is used to explore how power is most familiar, but when intersectionality offers us a means to make visible hidden power differentials that are naturalized through systems of inequality, or when it helps researchers disrupt dominate narratives of privilege. In such projects, intersectionality is aligned more closely with its origins and does the political work of unraveling oppressive systems of power.

A Brief Genealogy of Intersectionality

While critical race legal theorist Kimberle Crenshaw is credited with coining the term intersectionality in her writings on black women's experiences with employment discrimination (1989) and domestic violence (1991), scholars including Crenshaw acknowledge the foundations of intersectionality as emerging much earlier in the works of early black feminist intellectuals. Around the same time of Crenshaw's writings, scholarship reflecting upon oneself as belonging to multiple identity groups and understanding that identity as a qualitatively different experience was developing also beyond the United States (see, for example, Anthias and Yuval-Davis, 1992).

Crenshaw (1989) coined the term "intersectionality" as a metaphor to explain the ways in which black women under the US legal system are often caught between multiple systems of oppression marked by race, gender, and economic hierarchies without being recognized for their unique experiences at the convergence of these systems.[5] Focusing on employment discrimination cases, Crenshaw argues that dominant conceptualizations of discrimination under the law rely on determining discrimination using only a single axis framework.

Using court cases brought forth by black women, Crenshaw illustrates a repeated pattern in which black women are protected under discrimination laws only to the extent in which their experiences align with either white women or black men (Crenshaw, 1989, 143). Racial discrimination cases are thus determined by the experiences of black men, and, in sex discrimination cases, the experiences of white women are privileged. As Crenshaw shows, the courts have a history of failing to account for the lives of black women who experience the effects of discrimination injuries on the basis of both race *and* gender. As well, Crenshaw argues that discrimination law discredited black women as suitable representatives in cases of race or sex discrimination because in either context their "hybrid" identity precluded them from serving as "pure" representatives of either claim (Crenshaw, 1989, 145). In fact, their claims of belonging to both groups have been treated as a compounded discrimination that reaches beyond the intent of antidiscrimination law.

Crenshaw argues that the single axis framework articulated by the courts limits claims of discrimination as emanating from a discrete source of discrimination race *or* sex but not accounting for the experiences of those who are "mutually burdened." The intersectional metaphor is explained:

> Consider an analogy to traffic in an intersection, coming and going in all four directions. Discrimination, like traffic through an intersection, may flow in one direction, and it may flow in another. If an accident happens in an intersection, it can be caused by cars traveling from any number of directions, and sometimes, from all of them. Similarly, if a Black woman is harmed because she is in the intersection, her injury could result from sex discrimination or race discrimination. (Crenshaw, 1989, 149)

It is through this analysis of discrimination law that Crenshaw sets the parameters of the intersectionality framework. In discussing the responses of the courts, she argues that the simultaneous experience of race and sex discrimination render black women invisible by the courts. Similarly, women of color were rendered invisible through the early discursive practices of both feminist and critical race theory. While Crenshaw bases her discussion of intersectionality on the experiences of black women, scholars later extended her discussion to focus on the ways in which single-issue frameworks fail to adequately capture the experiences of a myriad of groups in society that experience marginalization along multiple axes of power.

Writing in the late 1980s, Crenshaw's work is a continuance of women of color's writings that reflect dissatisfaction with treatments of women of color's activism, writings, and lived experiences. Numerous scholars argue that women of color's contributions were suppressed through failures to recognize the convergence of identity categories or systems of oppression. The Combahee River Collective (1982 [1977]), Anzuldua (1987), Dill (1983), Moraga and Anzuldua (1984), King (1988), and Mohanty (1988), all produced pivotal writings during this period that shared in disrupting notions that the category "woman" denotes a universal, homogeneous experience. Instead, these authors asserted that race, class, and sexuality distinguish women's behavior and experiences.

These writings represent a continuance of feminist scholars of color articulating the multiplicities of their identities and the political consequences of multiple constituted identities. For centuries, women of color have articulated the conundrum that the term intersectionality represents and have articulated both a scholarly and activist tradition emanating from their social location in US society. Nineteenth-century African American scholar-activist Anna Julia Cooper recognized the unique position of African American women at the nexus of struggles for racial and gender equality. Cooper argued that the progress of African Americans rested upon the abilities of African American women to advance. She eloquently articulates that it is "when and where I enter, in the quiet, undisputed dignity of my womanhood, without violence and without suing or special patronage, then and there the whole...race enters with me" (Cooper, 1892, 31). Cooper's words were similar to other activist women of color such as Sojourner Truth and Ida B. Wells who also articulated the unique positioning of African American women. Later, groups such as the Combahee River Collective, a cadre of black lesbian feminist activists writing in the 1970s, articulated the simultaneous effects poised by race, class, gender, and sexuality.

Across social movements, women of color argued for a politics of inclusion that recognized the legitimacy of their claims based upon their needs as women of color. Many authors recognize the linkages of intersectionality to the developments in black feminist theory. Evelyn Simien (2006) situates intersectionality as growing from black women's lived experience and argues that such theorizing developed as a pragmatic response to their life circumstances. Black feminist theory remains an important theoretical home for the study of intersectionality, though more contemporary discussions of intersectionality advocate for moving away from thinking of intersectionality as a framework solely explaining the experiences of women of color to thinking in terms of how intersectionality offers more robust understandings of power differentials that exist among various groups in society (Hancock, 2007a).

As intersectionality developed, and in its earliest theorizing and application, most scholars focused on the triumvirate of oppression: race, class, and gender. These three social identities and systems of power were given primacy in light of the ways systems of racial discrimination, gender discrimination, and class oppression work in tandem to situate women of color, particularly in US society. However, as intersectionality has evolved, there is greater emphasis on the systems and processes that operate in tandem to produce various inequalities and privileges. Several chapters in this volume do this work. For example, Miles engages intersectionality as a framework to interrogate state-administered identification practices that protect state interests in maintaining a gender binary while the trans community in Chile must live between legal and lived identities that as Miles argues, "renders everyday interaction a complex, distressing and destabilizing process" (67). Miles and contributors to this volume are not only mobilizing intersectionality scholarship beyond the parameters of the United States where different systems map the basis for discrimination and inequality, but they are also placing an important emphasis on the institutions, processes, and systems that undergird systems of inequality.

Principles of Intersectionality

Intersectionality's substantial popularity is driven partially by its appeal to progressive politics exercising a practice of inclusionary politics in which marginalized groups are given voice. With the great acclaim that surrounds intersectionality, there is still much dissent surrounding its boundaries. Scholars from across disciplinary locations are engaging in further developing intersectionality by asserting new definitions, new levels of analysis, and arguing the most appropriate methodologies to capture the theoretical assertions of intersectionality. Intersectionality presents as in flux with limited distinctive boundaries, which is both inviting and problematic for scholars.

Here, I present some general premises of intersectionality as an evolving paradigm and then reflect on each in more detail. In doing so, I fully recognize that intersectionality continues to develop across disciplinary spaces; its elements are under constant negotiation and revision. Nevertheless, these principles are starting points to understanding this dynamic and complex framework. At its core foundations, intersectionality is concerned with the following:

1. *Resisting additive models that treat categories of social identity as additive, parallel categories and instead theorizes these categories as intersecting;*
2. *Antiessentialism and insists upon variation within categories of social identity;*
3. *Recognition that social identity categories and the power systems that give them meaning shift across time and geographical location;*
4. *Embracing the coexistence of privilege and marginalization acknowledging that they are not mutually exclusive;*
5. *Changing the conditions of society such that categories of identity are not permanently linked to sustained inequalities in efforts to build a more just world.*

1. Resisting Additive Models and Parallel Categories

Intersectionality has encouraged scholars to move away from models that situate categories such as race, gender, class, and sexuality as a singular axis of power. This framework staunchly resists an understanding of gender, race, class, sexuality, ability as parallel categories. Instead, what intersectionality encourages us to do is to understand the ways in which these categories are not simply parallel but intersecting categories. Intersectionality posits that race, class, gender, sexuality, ability, and various aspects of identity are constitutive. Each informs the other and taken together, they produce a way of experiencing the world as sometimes oppressed and marginalized and sometimes privileged and advantaged depending on the context.

Intersectionality requires that we pay close attention to the particulars of categories of social identity. As many have argued, it is not enough to simply "add race and stir" to include perspectives of women of color. Intersectionality requires that we recognize that systems of oppression and hierarchy are neither interchangeable nor are they identical; therefore, much is made of understanding the ways that these categories function. These social categories have differing organizing logics in that race works differently than gender, class, or sexuality. Power associated with these categories is neither configured in the same ways nor do they share the same histories therefore, they cannot be treated identically (Phoenix and Pattynama, 2006).

2. Antiessentialism and Diversity within Categories

Intersectionality takes into account that there is great variation within categories of social identity. Understanding social identities as mutually constitutive produces an array of ways of experiencing blackness, working class, or sex and sexuality. This encourages us to move away from *essentializing* or reducing experiences to "*the* Latino experience" or "*the* lesbian experience" and allows for multiple ways of experiencing these social categories as they link and are informed by other categories. Cathy Cohen (1999) argues that in doing so, we avoid producing secondary marginalization in which issues are defined based upon the needs of the more privileged of a group and not in the interests of those who are impacted by multiple systems of oppression or even less valued systems of oppression by particular communities. This reduces the lure to privilege one aspect of a person's identity at the expense of other aspects. In *Affirmative Advocacy*, Dara Strolovich (2007) shows how this secondary marginalization process happens among advocacy groups that purport to represent complex identities often marginalized in US politics. She finds that despite claims of representing the totality of their group, advocates representing marginalized groups seldom represent their constituents who are intersectionally marginalized, even among the most well-intentioned groups.

3. Power as Shifting and Changing

While intersectionality places great emphasis on understanding the means by which power is configured, it also establishes power as dynamic and shifting rather than static and fixed. As such, we cannot conclude that power operates in the same ways across contexts of time and location. Sociopolitical and economic histories figure prominently into adequately defining the power relations intersectionality seeks to make visible.

Depending upon the context, those who are marginalized and those who have power differ. Therefore, we cannot evaluate oppression and marginalization without a sense of history as well as the social, political, and economic opportunities available to various groups across history. Categories are not fixed and change over time. Their social and political meanings often change in different historical contexts, and are contested and restructured both at the level of the individual (what it means to me and my experiences) and at the societal level (what it means to society and social systems) (Yuval-Davis, 2006). The significance of geographical location to transforming the relationships between categories as well as within categories has grown as intersectionality travels across disciplinary locations and into transnational conversations. The systems of power that dictate whether that social identity is a marker of privilege or marginalization also changes according to geographical location and configurations of power in that society.

4. Privilege and Marginalization

Privilege and marginalization are central to studies of intersectionality. While many might assume that these two categories are mutually exclusive, intersectionality scholarship has focused on their coexistence. One can experience oppression along one axis and privilege along another. Intersectionality focuses on power across categories and in relation to one another understanding that power is not equal across categories. Patricia Hill Collins (1990) situates race, class, and gender as interlocking systems that create an overarching "matrix of domination" in which actors can not only be victimized by power but can also exercise power over others. Collins highlights the contradictory nature of oppression suggesting that few "pure victims" or "pure oppressors" exist. Penalty and privilege are distributed among individuals and groups within the matrix of domination such that none are marked exclusively by one or the other.

5. Changing Conditions

Julia Jordan-Zachery (2007) reminds us that from the earliest conceptualizations of intersectionality, embedded in the theory is a liberatory agency possessed by those experiencing the effects of life at the intersection. The imperative to change existing conditions and take action from their location at the intersection toward impacting the lives of those both within and between social identity categories is an important theme woven throughout. So as much as researchers categorize intersectionality as a descriptive framework or research paradigm, it is very much a political concept grounded in an emancipatory politics with social justice-based outcomes as the goal. Intersectionality is understood as rooted in efforts to change societal conditions that create and maintain oppressive power hierarchies. In addition to recognizing the differences that exist among individuals and groups, intersectionality is invested in modes of institutional change designed to remedy the effects of inequalities produced by interlocking systems of oppression.

In summary, the version of intersectionality to which I subscribe is informed by a plethora of scholarly thinking on the parameters of intersectionality. It can apply to everyone, as we all have a race, gender, sexuality, and social class, whether we experience our social locations as inequalities or privileges. However, intersectionality is at its best when used to uncover patterns of privilege and marginalization as opposed to focus on familiar understandings of privilege. Our social locations are not fixed such that we are construed permanently as oppressors or the oppressed.[6] Intersectionality is context specific; structural and dynamic (Weldon, 2006). The relevant axes of power for investigation are determined by the situation and site under study. As Hancock (2007a) surmises, the intersectional approach "changes the relationship between the categories of investigation from one that is determined a priori to one of empirical investigation" (2007a, 67). It asserts that categories are relevant and have an impact on understanding material lives and at the same time it is interested in disrupting the impetus to render categories as fixed and mutually exclusive. Intersectionality offers a means to contest the power arrangements between categories and even embraces and envisions a futuristic intellectual politics in which categories are stripped of any deterministic powers.[7]

Intersectionality, Agency, Institutions, and Institutional Processes

So, what does political science and other fields that center on institutions, institutional processes, and structures contribute to the ongoing development of intersectionality as a research paradigm? Such disciplines as political science can help intersectionality studies gain greater balance between the individual and structural levels of analysis. By virtue of intersectionality's development as a response to the law's treatment of individuals, it is borne out of a politics of recognition. As such, it demands that the law recognize the ways in which *individuals'* multiple identities matter to their treatment. While the law necessitates this focus on the individual, intersectionality theorists have pushed against the reliance on the individual as the fundamental level of analysis for intersectional analyses (Yuval-Davis, 2006; Conaghan, 2009). With such an approach, the structures, institutions, processes, and systems that generate and mediate the experiences of individuals are elided in favor of a focus on the individual or particular groups.

The potential contributions of political scientists to the study of intersectionality lie precisely in illuminating the *structural* effects and the processes by which institutions contribute to identity constructions and mobilizations. In her discussion of the salience of structure to intersectionality, political scientist S. Laurel Weldon aggressively situates structural analysis as the core of intersectionality offering that the focus on identity itself is a misguided understanding of intersectionality. She argues, "It is not often recognized that structural analysis is *required* by the idea of intersectionality. It is the intersection of social *structures*, not identities, to which the concept refers. We cannot conceptualize 'interstices' unless we have a concept of the structures that intersect to create these points of interaction" (Weldon, 2006, 239). Such considerations of structure necessitate a focus on institutions and institutional processes, necessitating engagements with the law, public policy, and governing bodies.

Rather than advocate the primacy of one level over the other, I am arguing that intersectionality scholarship has gone so far in the direction of centering its analysis at the level of the individual and the individual's agency that it overlooks the powerful role of institutions and structures in mediating the individual's behavior and structuring the range of available choices. It is from this perspective that I suggest political science's contribution to intersectionality as potentially restoring some balance and tempering the explanatory value of individual agency in intersectional analysis.

To be clear, I do not draw the types of distinctions as Baukje Prins (2006) does between an intersectionality grounded in structural analysis with subjects being constituted through static systems of domination and marginalization and a constructionist version of intersectionality in which the subject is understood as the primary factor determining identity. For Prins, the constructionists approach treats identity as more a point of narration in which the subject is "both actor in and co-author of our own life story" (2006, 281) and understands the individual's identity as a matter of choice and as constituted through the individual's "own acting and thinking" (2006, 280). In contrasts, she interprets the structural approach to treat identity as a matter of recognition, naming, and categorization that is predetermined by systems of domination and profoundly stable and predictable. Such a constructionist vision of intersectionality is deeply invested in the power of individual agency. The emphasis on the subject's free will to become a subject by their own determination, on their own terms, dismisses the myriad of ways that the "isms" (racism, sexism, heterosexism, and classism) interplay with the subject's possibilities. More so, it reflects a failure to understand the ever-evolving processes of institutions and structures. Far from static, institutions are shifting constantly, but with particular goals in mind—to protect the values of the institution, ensure its survival, and extend its values and ideas of appropriateness.

A more integrated vision of intersectionality that articulates roles for both the structure and the individual offers a closer approximation social reality. Understanding institutions and structures not as static and overly deterministic but as evolving often in relation to the resistance politics and strategies of intersectional actors, reflects the complex relationship between individual and structural levels of analysis. Resistance strategies are understood in larger contexts of institutional processes and historical events that can facilitate as well as curtail opportunities for changing categorizations and dismantling dominant frameworks. Such an integrated model appreciates the weight of institutional and structural forces as well as the transformative potential of resistance strategies employed by intersectional actors.

Intersectionality, particularly as it interfaces with other political projects that uplift individual agency, threatens a move toward suppressing the role that institutions and structures play in modifying individual behavior and ordering choices. Such approaches to intersectionality theorizing overstate the agency of individuals and their freedom to act independently with the power to shape their own political understanding of their identities. As Gill Valentine (2007) concurs, "the existing theorization of the concept of intersectionality overemphasizes the abilities of individuals to actively produce their own lives and underestimates how the ability to enact some identities or realities rather than others is highly contingent on the power-laden spaces in and through which our experiences are lived" (2007, 19).

Political scientists and others who focus on institutions such as the law, public policy, governing bodies, and social movements understand that individual agency is subject to and enacted within institutions and as such is always bounded and beholden to strong institutional forces that can render groups visible or invisible, beneficiaries or pariahs, in relation to the state. Advancing an appreciation for the role of institutions in relation to individual agency allows us to engage more fully with the political and material *implications of* multiply constituted identities, the institutional processes by which identities are made meaningful, as well as the conditions under which institutions offer to recognize identities as multiply constituted.

For an example of this kind of research approach, I turn to my own work on US state legislatures to reflect on how an attentiveness to intersectionality produces new insights on institutional processes that are unavailable through a focus on either dominant groups or through the focus on a singular axis—race *or* gender. As well, I seek to show the ways political science scholarship can contribute to extending intersectionality's reach beyond traditional identity politics.

By examining the legislative experiences of African American women, I explore the effects of race and gender on the meanings of legislative power and influence. Dominant understandings and narratives of legislative power are disrupted when viewed from an intersectionality perspective, which highlights the way in which legislative power is a deeply gendered and racialized construct. Race and gender impact the paths to power and influence available to legislators, as well as the types of influence they are even afforded in the eyes of their colleagues.

These are critical concerns as US state legislatures have become increasingly diverse. The key questions are: How are these institutions incorporating women and men of color and white women—all relative newcomers to these lawmaking bodies? How are the traditional politics of these institutions changing in light of a more diverse group of legislators? I focus on the experiences of African American women legislators, but the goal is not simply to document their experiences as African American women, though admittedly that would indeed be a contribution given the sparse research on the experiences of women of color in US electoral politics. The questions engendered from this research center on how institutions respond to difference: How do race and gender interact with commonly held assumptions about institutions and legislative behavior? Does race and gender impact the power that is commonly understood to emanate from holding positions in the legislative leadership, having seniority, and high levels of legislative activity? What happens when African American women legislators occupy the leadership positions or have the legislative attributes that traditionally confer power and influence? Are these institutional norms gendered and racialized?

The effects of race and gender on legislative power arrangements are substantial. The formal leadership structure is evidence of race and gender hierarchies in the legislature. Few African American women hold the top leadership positions or chair the powerful committees that are commonly associated with increasing a legislator's influence. Their exclusion from these leadership posts only partially accounts for their more limited influence among their colleagues. The challenge for African American women legislators is more complex than gaining access to legislative leadership positions. Their limited access to legislative power is complicated by their exclusion from informal power structures that exist in the legislature. African American women who hold positions in the formal leadership repeatedly report that they are not included among the inner circle of confidents hand selected by top party leaders, even though their positions suggest they would have access to these inner circles. This exclusion precludes them from participating in critical policy discussions that impact their constituents. Such informal circles of power become a parallel power structure that contests the power of the official party leadership structure and undermines the power of some formal leaders.

Even when African American women legislators occupy the same political spaces, share similar positions, and political titles, they are regarded differently by their colleagues. Influence that would have otherwise been associated with individual legislators in alignment with traditional institutional norms regarding the power of leadership positions is not equally conferred upon African American women. What it means to be a party leader or a committee chair is mediated by the legislator's race and gender. These traditionally powerful positions neither hold the same meaning nor do they lead to the same outcomes for African American women. African American women's legislative performances are bounded by such deeply racialized and gendered institutional processes and structures in the legislature.

My findings, along with other scholars working on race and gender in legislative institutions, are showing how gender and race problematize even the most stable categories such as party leader and committee chair.[8] What it means to hold these positions and the outcomes these positions produce differ when African American women occupy these positions. These stable categories are transformed by race and gender, producing outcomes that are, as Crenshaw argues, "qualitatively different" (Crenshaw, 1991, 1245). Gender and race are not merely identity categories, but act as mediating forces that serve to limit avenues that would lead traditionally to institutional influence. The gender and race hierarchies prevalent in US society more broadly compete with well-established norms of legislative behavior. Adherence to these power arrangements ultimately impact policy outcomes and raise questions on the quality of representation, particularly for communities of color. When traditional paths to power and influence are either unavailable to them or fail to yield the desired outcomes, African American women are forced to devise alternative strategies to remain relevant and effective representatives on behalf of their constituents.

If we were to employ only an individual level of analysis, focused on evaluating individual African American women's effectiveness, we miss the institutional norms and characteristics that structure legislative behavior. African American women's individual agency is intertwined with the formal and informal structures and processes that render some legislators influential and others less so, much on the basis of race and gender preferences and hierarchies. The presence of African American women in state legislatures challenges and expands our understandings of legislative norms and behavior. Centering their experiences counters previous studies that constructed narratives of institutional power relying solely on the experiences of white men, the dominant majority group in US state legislatures. Through examining African American women lawmakers' location within the legislative institution, we have new understandings of how power is constituted in the legislature. When we assume an intersectional vantage point that embodies both the individual and structural levels of analysis, it teaches us more regarding the full workings of institutions and forces us to reexamine traditional understandings of institutional norms, processes, and behaviors.

Unresolved Tensions

Although intersectionality presents as an exciting, groundbreaking theoretical framework and emerging research paradigm, several issues remain unresolved and can stymie the progress of intersectionality in political science and other social science disciplines. For scholars interested in applying intersectionality to empirical projects, a number of tensions emerge around methodological issues. Notably, as Kathy Davis (2008) details, the very elements of intersectionality that make it so attractive to scholars across disciplinary locations are the very issues that also make it contentious. Intersectionality lacks a clear, concise definition; it lacks parameters; it does not specify which categories should be theorized as intersecting; the relationship between the categories; how many categories can be included; and when to stop adding categories of analysis. There are no established hard and fast rules about when intersectionality should and should not be applied and there is no methodology associated with it. All the elements that make it attractive to scholars across disciplines also make for an uneasy alliance with political science and other social sciences given the dominant methodological strands in these disciplines.

These issues all reflect methodological concerns that are particularly salient for social scientists. However, we might question why these concerns move to the center when previously marginalized voices and issues are gaining traction in the academy.[9] Nevertheless, intersectionality scholars are responding to these critiques and tensions. Two issues have dominated social scientists' concerns and have limited their engagement with intersectionality.

The first issue is the uneasiness with identifying which are the appropriate categories for analysis to constitute an intersectional approach and second the quantitative methodological biases that currently dominate many social sciences and encourage scholars to become consumed with appropriate statistical models that might accurately reflect the theoretical concept of intersectionality. While these research considerations have their place, becoming mired in these debates detracts from opportunities to address the very systems of inequality that intersectionality illuminates. As the chapters in this volume attests, across geographic spaces the political moment is ripe for engaging policy frameworks that reflect intersectional solutions; however with scholars of intersectionality focused elsewhere there is a risk missing the possibilities of this policy window.

The dominant paradigms of political science methodology sit in opposition to the concerns of intersectionality as I have defined it. One of the most significant barriers to the advancement of intersectionality within political science and other social science disciplines is the appropriate methodological modeling of intersectionality (Hancock, 2007a, 2007b; Simien, 2006, 2007; Orey and Smooth, 2006; Weldon, 2006). What is most familiar to political scientists interested in speaking to the effects of race, gender, or class is to employ an additive approach, particularly in quantitative analyses. Political scientist Evelyn Simien (2007, 266) argues that adding dichotomous variables to regression models and controlling for their effects fail in relation to two aspects of intersectionality theorizing. One, in treating variables as dichotomous, it fails to capture the range of possibilities within each variable category. For example, race is conceived as black *or* white and gender is conceptualized in terms of men *or* women. So, it fails to capture the simultaneous nature of identity that intersectionality asserts. In other words, such methodological approaches fail to capture the ways gender is racialized and race is gendered. Further, such insistence on binaries limits opportunities to explore the fluidity of sexual identity that scholars in this volume, particularly Miles, Combs, Monro, and Richardson take up in relation to the state in this volume. To extend Simien's concerns, such quantitative methodologies fail to take into account how categories such as race, gender, sexual identity vary over time and across geographical location. Overall, the existing approaches most familiar to political scientists and other social scientists are not adept at capturing all the ways that intersectionality seeks to move away from static, essentialist understandings of categories.

Political scientists are not alone in raising such questions. In a special issue of the journal *Sex Roles*, guest editor Stephanie Shields writes:

> Some social sciences have been more open to the transformative effects of an intersectionality perspective than others. The intersectionality perspective has had more impact in academic specializations already concerned with questions of power relations between groups. Disciplines/specializations whose conventional methodologies embrace multidimensionality and the capacity to represent complex and dynamic relationships among variables are more open to the intersectionality perspective. (Shields, 2008, 302)

While Shields is most concerned with the field of psychology, her assessment is quite applicable to political science and other social sciences. Given the central concerns and values of political science, particularly its emphasis on discerning the operations of power in society, we might assume it to be ripe for intersectional analyses. However, Shields's fears for intersectionality's advancement in psychology parallel my own fears for its advancement in political science. The realization of intersectionality's potential is at risk of succumbing to our preoccupations with what is cast as the "methodological challenges" of intersectionality.

As much as political scientists can offer intersectionality, in return, intersectionality can offer political science an expanded appreciation for varied methodological tools and approaches. Given the critical potential of political science voices to enhancing the development of intersectionality, it is useful to challenge methodologists to become innovative in pursuit of strategies that meet the demands of complexity that intersectionality requires. To this end, Hancock (2007a) encourages an openness among intersectionality scholars to the potential innovations that quantitative scholars working with large data sets can offer the study of intersectionality. She cautions that true innovation will surface when scholars engage in data collection techniques that more fully account for the dynamism among and between categories of identity (2007a, 66). She strikes an important balance between eschewing quantitative analyses and locating intersectionality as exclusively the purview of ethnographies and other qualitative methodologies. The balance she encourages is most possible when all methodological approaches available to intersectionality scholars are valued equally. This necessitates confronting what I term the "tyranny of the quantitative" in the discipline and creating spaces for academic production open to the range of methods that allow scholars to deeply engage the political context, suspend their predetermined categorizations, and fully explore the relationships between identity categories.

SEIZING THE MOMENT: INTERSECTIONALITY AND EQUITY POLICIES

Resisting these methodological divides that stand to mire the advancement of intersectionality is especially important at this political moment. Political scientists and other scholars of policy, institutions, and institutional processes are poised to make substantial contributions toward shaping the emerging policy debates on intersectionality. Institutions of governance increasingly are expressing interests in employing intersectionality as a tool in policy making and, as I detail in this section, they benefit from engagement with scholars well versed in intersectionality as well as structures, institutions, and policy making.

National and international governing bodies including the United Nations and the European Union are turning increasingly to intersectionality approaches to articulate and develop ideal responses to concerns for equality and a more sophisticated awareness of diversities across and within identity groups. For example, the United Nations' Committee on the Elimination of Racial Discrimination (CERD) embraces Crenshaw's definition of intersectionality to articulate the nature and processes of racism. Squires (2008) identifies intersectionality debates emerging in the creation of Britain's Equality and Human Rights Commission (EHRC), noting the ways intersectionality is troubling the EHRC's approaches to inequality. The EHRC's debates between addressing inequalities along singular axis using multiple, yet separate equality laws versus more integrated approaches that address multiple forms of inequality by constructing a single policy intervention are debates that certainly reflect the essence of intersectionality's concerns. In response, intersectionality scholars are weighing in on these state posed remedies to existing inequalities (Squires, 2008; Yuval-Davis, 2006; Verloo, 2006; Lombardo and Verloo, 2009; Raj, Bunch, and Nazombe, 2002; Bassel and Emejulu, 2010).

Verloo (2006) advises, and scholars in this volume confer, that intersectionality scholars must carefully monitor and critically evaluate purported articulations of intersectionality masked as equity policies. Taking the case of intersectionality and public policies in Uruguay, Erica Townsend-Bell argues in this volume that we must distinguish between policies aimed toward fostering equity and inclusion and those calling for interventions that reflect the principles of intersectionality. She points out that states are becoming increasingly responsive to group claims and are designing affirmative action programs and gender quotas, for example as a means of addressing group claims. However, these remedies address inequality only along a singular axis. Such policies fall short of an intersectionality framework in that in addressing only a singular aspect of difference they maintain the race *or* gender approach. Rather than locate shortcomings with the state, instead Townsend-Bell finds that advocacy groups in Uruguay seldom frame issues as intersectional problems requiring intersectional solutions. Townsend-Bell's assessments make the connections between the state's actions on intersectionality and the work of advocacy groups, pointing out the interconnectedness of the two. However, as other scholars denote, advocacy and interest groups too find it difficult and politically confining to deploy intersectional frames in their work.

In studying US advocacy groups, Dara Strolovich's (2007) work further illustrates Townsend-Bell's conclusions as Strolovich makes the case that the political environment and nature of legal frameworks limit advocacy groups' embrace of intersectionality. Advocacy groups that we might imagine as best situated to represent intersectional groups and their interests actually fail to do so as these groups are organized to represent issues along a single axis. US civil rights-based groups organized to advocate around race issues, for example, find it difficult to advocate for intersectional race issues focused on race and class (welfare reform debates in the 1990s), race and gender (gender pay equity issues), or race and sexuality (marriage equality). This reality, as Strolovich argues, is not necessarily due to lack of will but more so because the political environment seldom supports organizations addressing the complexity of intersectional issues. A range of factors contribute to an environment that works against intersectional representation by advocacy groups from funding organizations casting advocacy groups in narrow terms to legal provisions that fail to acknowledge intersectional realities. Both Townsend-Bell and Strolovich's work illustrate the potential pitfalls of states adopting policies that focus on a single axis of inequality masked as intersectional frameworks. When states take such approaches, the status quo is maintained and intersectional groups and their interests continue to go unrepresented. Moreover, their work demonstrates the need to have intersectional policy advocates both inside and outside the state.

Scholars examining the deployment of intersectionality as a policy tool point to strong tendencies on the part of states to adopt equity remedies organized around a singular axis such as gender in the case of gender mainstreaming policies.[10] In addition to the arguments Strolovich and Townsend-Bell offer regarding advocacy groups failing to adopt intersectional frameworks, fundamental misunderstandings and misrepresentations of intersectionality also contribute to the insistence on singular inclusion policies. Even well-intentioned equity and inclusion policies fall short in that they so often assume all inequalities share the same ontological history and internal logic. In doing so, they violate the premises of intersectionality. Such approaches to remedying inequality and fostering inclusion ignore the historical and contextual realities that race, gender, class, and sexual inequalities emanate from different sources, produce different effects, and are understood as coconstitutive. Equality policies that favor a single-strand approach to equality reflect an assumption of virtual sameness among groups and such assumptions run counter to the scholarship on intersectionality, which asserts the varying historical roots and effects of differing types of inequality (Squires, 2008; Verloo, 2006).

These efforts to build more robust equality-centered institutions and structures using the framework of intersectionality are confronting an array of challenges. As I have discussed throughout this chapter, on some level these challenges are inherent to operationalizing the level of complexity that intersectionality demands theoretically, and in part these challenges speak to the lack of specificity associated with theoretical treatments of intersectionality. These challenges to using intersectionality are reflective of deeply entrenched, institutionalized understandings of inequality as existing along a singular axis. However, through studying structures such as the United Nations, legislatures and other governing bodies, organized advocacy and interest groups, as well as gender quotas with a focus on their internal logics and politics, we better understand the process through which they advance or curtail the adoption of intersectional policy frameworks. Combining an understanding of the internal logics of institutions with an understanding of the principles of intersectionality, we are better positioned to construct institutions, structures, and policies that actually increase equality and foster greater inclusion (Bassel and Emejulu, 2010). From the earliest assessments of intersectionality's arrival in these policy discussions, it was clear that where the voices of intersectionality scholars are absent, these debates easily stagnate or worse revert to competitive struggles between identity groups over limited resources (Yuval-Davis, 2006; Lombardo and Verloo, 2009; Hancock, 2011).

The questions and debates raised in our scholarly discussions will filter into these public policy windows of opportunity. Through increased dialogue between scholars across geographic contexts in forums such as this volume, we will be able to capitalize on the political potential of the moment and move toward the creation of public policies that more accurately reflect and address the ways that individuals and groups experience equality and inequality. This focus on the search for more equitable institutions and structures that bring recognition to those rendered invisible, those who are in need of government redress for discrimination, is reflective of intersectionality's origins that sought to articulate a means of social change that substantially challenged and transformed existing hierarchies. Those trained to study power situated in institutions are equipped to seize upon this political moment.

Notes

1. I am grateful to the Shifting Agendas conference participants who shared their thoughtful comments during my keynote address. I am also grateful to Angelia Wilson for organizing the conference and offering sage advice and feedback on this chapter. I owe a special thanks to my fall seminar students in "Operationalizing Intersectionality" at The Ohio State University, as several ideas discussed here were refined during our intense debates during the seminar. My thoughts on intersectionality are far more clear as a result

of our collective reading. Finally, elements of the sections on the principles intersectionality and the genealogy of intersectionality are detailed in W. Smooth, "Intersectionality and Women's Leadership," in *Gender and Women's Leadership: A Sage Series Handbook*, edited by Karen O'Conner (New York: Sage Publications, 2010).
2. Which categories are to be included in intersectionality analyses is a source of debate among scholars. From the onset of the terms' usage, the categories most interrogated in tandem were race, gender, and to a lesser extent, class. However, as intersectionality scholarship has evolved, categories taken as central to the intersectionality approach have more often included sexuality and ability.
3. In fact, several treatments of the intersectional realities of African American women's political representation in policy debates are illustrative of political scientists building linkages between cultural representations and policy discourse. For example see Ange Marie Hancock's *The Politics of Disgust* (2004); Julia Jordan-Zachery's *Black Women, Cultural Images and Social Policy* (2008); and Michele Tracey Berger's *Workable Sisterhood: The Political Journey of Stigmatized Women with HIV/AIDS* (2004).
4. For contrasting views on the deployment of intersectionality to study privileged groups, see: Jessica Holden Sherwood "The View from the Country Club: Wealthy Whites and the Matrix of Privilege," in *The Intersectional Approach*, edited by Berger, Michele Tracey, and Kathleen Guidroz (Chapel Hill: University of North Carolina Press, 2010).
5. In Crenshaw's writings, she is clear that intersectionality does not refer only to the categories of race and gender. See: "Mapping the Margins: Intersectionality, Identity Politics and Violence against Women" in which she explicitly states that "the concept can and should be expanded by factoring in issues such as class, sexual orientation, age, and color" (1991, 1245).
6. Jennifer Nash (2008) raises salient points regarding the coexistence of power and privilege in intersectionality scholarship.
7. McCall (2005) offers a compelling framework for understanding the range of ways intersectionality engages with categories and the range of treatments present among intersectionality scholars.
8. Similar observations are discussed regarding African American women serving in the US Congress. Mary Hawkesworth (2003) details how processes of "race-gendering" impact African American women's positions in Congress and the ways the issues to which they speak are marginalized precisely because of constructions of power in relation to the intersecting constructions of race and gender.
9. As Zuberi and Bonilla-Silva argue in *White Logic, White Methods: Racism and Methodology* (2008), prevailing notions of "white logic"

insist that in the Western imagination logic, reason, and objectivity and the tools and methods through which they are exercised are the sole purview of elite white men. Essentially, these methodological questions are deployed precisely to maintain control over established ways of knowing, who produces knowledge and who has a rightful claim to knowledge production.

10. Emanuela Lombardo and Mieke Verloo (2009) offer a detailed discussion of gender and gender mainstreaming as an entrenched institutionalized policy system in Europe. They employ a thought exercise that considers the possibilities of expanding (stretching to use their language) the gender equality policy frame to be more inclusive of different types of inequality. Across the EU states, gender mainstreaming, after much feminist activism, is the familiar frame for conceptualizing inequality, and many would argue it constitutes a primary policy frame for understanding inequality. A challenge is presented to this "gender as inequality" frame when activists and scholars interested in policy frameworks that understand and process inequalities from the perspective of intersectionality assert competing frameworks that decenter gender as the primary inequality. Lombardo and Verloo's thought exercise forces us to consider what happens when the primacy of gender is challenged with reconceptualized equality policies.

References

Anthias, Floya, and Nira Yuval-Davis. 1992. *Racialized Boundaries: Race, Nation, Gender, Colour and Class and the Anti-Racist Struggle.* London: Routledge.

Anzuldua, Gloria. 1987. *Borderlands: La Frontera: The New Mestiza.* San Francisco: Aunt Lute Books.

Bassel, Leah, and Akwugo Emejulu. 2010. "Struggles for Institutional Space in France and the United Kingdom: Intersectionality and the Politics of Policy." *Politics and Gender* (6)4: 517–544.

Berger, Michelle Tracey. 2004. *Workable Sisterhood: The Political Journey of Stigmatized Women with HIV/AIDS.* Princeton: Princeton University Press.

Berger, Michelle Tracy, and Kathleen Guidroz. 2010. "Introduction." In *The Intersectional Approach: Transforming the Academy through Race, Class, and Gender*, edited by Michelle Tracey Berger and Kathleen Guidroz. Chapel Hill: University of North Carolina Press.

Cohen, Cathy. 1999. *The Boundaries of Blackness.* Chicago: University of Chicago Press.

Collins, Patricia Hill. 1990. *Black Feminist Thought Knowledge, Consciousness, and the Politics of Empowerment.* New York: Routledge.

The Combahee River Collective. 1982 [1977]. "A Black Feminist Statement." In *All the Women are White, All the Blacks are Men, But Some of us are Brave*, edited by Gloria T. Hull, Patricia Bell Scott, and Barbara Smith. New York: Feminist Press.
Conaghan, Joanne. 2009. "Intersectionality and the Feminist Project in Law." In *Intersectionality and Beyond: Law, Power and the Politics of Location*, edited by Emily Grabham, Davina Cooper, Jane Krishnadas, and Didi Herman. Cavendish: Routlege-Cavendish.
Cooper, Anna Julia. 1892. *A Voice of the South*. Xenia, OH: Aldine Publishing House.
Crenshaw, Kimberle. 2011. "Intersectional Interventions: Unmasking and Dismantling Racial Power." W. E. B. DuBois Lecture Series. Cambridge: Lecture Delivered on February 2.
———. 1991. "Mapping the Margins: Intersectionality, Identity Politics and Violence against Women of Color." *Stanford Law Review* 43: 1241.
———. 1989. "Demarginalizing the Intersection of Race and Sex: A Black Feminist Critique of Antidiscrimination Doctrine, Feminist Theory and Antiracist Politics." *University of Chicago Legal Forum*: 139: 139–167.
Davis, Kathy. 2008. "Intersectionality as Buzzword: A Sociology of Science Perspective on What Makes a Feminist Theory Successful." *Feminist Theory* 9(1): 67–85.
Dill, Thornton Bonnie. 1983. "Race, Class and Gender: Prospects for an All Inclusive Sisterhood." *Feminist Studies* 9(1): 131–150.
Fraser, Nancy, and Linda Gordon. 1994. "Genealogy of Dependency: Tracing A Keyword of the U.S. Welfare State." *Signs* 19(2): 309–336.
Hancock, Ange-Marie. 2011. *Solidarity Politics for Millennials: A Guide to Ending the Oppression Olympics*. New York: Palgrave Macmillian.
———. 2007a. "When Multiplication Doesn't Equal Quick Addition: Examining Intersectionality as a Research Paradigm." *Perspectives on Politics* 5: 63–79.
———. 2007b. "Intersectionality as a Normative and Empirical Research Paradigm." *Politics & Gender* June 2007: 248–254.
———. 2004. *The Politics of Disgust: The Public Identity of the Welfare Queen*. New York: New York University Press.
Hawkesworth, Mary. 2003. "Congressional Enactments of Race-Gender: Toward a Theory of Raced-Gendered Institutions." *American Political Science Review* 97: 529–550.
Jordan-Zachery, Julia. 2008. *Black Women, Cultural Images and Social Policy*. New York: Routlege.
———. 2007. "Am I a Black Woman or a Woman Who is Black? A Few Thoughts on the Meaning of Intersectionality." *Politics & Gender* 3(2): 254–264.

King, Deborah K. 1988. "Multiple Jeopardy, Multiple Consciousness: The Context of a Black Feminist Ideology." *Signs* 14(1): 42–72.
Knapp, Gudrun-Axeli. 2005. "Reclaiming Baggage in Fast Traveling Theories." *European Journal of Women's Studies* 12(3): 249–265.
Lombardo, Emanuel, and Mieke Verloo. 2009. "Stretching Gender Equality to Other Inequalities: Political Intersectionality in European Gender Equality Policies." In *The Discursive Politics of Gender Equality: Stretching, Bending and Policy-making*, edited by Emanuela Lombardo, Petra Meier, and Mieke Verloo. New York: Routledge.
McCall, Leslie. 2005. "The Complexity of Intersectionality." *Signs* 30(3): 1771–1800.
Mohanty, Chandra Talpade. 1988. "Under Western Eyes: Feminist Scholarship and Colonial Discourses." *Feminist Review* 30(Autumn): 61–88.
Moraga, Cherrie, and Gloria Anzaldua, eds. 1984. *This Bridge Called My Back: Writings of Radical Women of Color*. 2nd ed. New York: Kitchen Table Press.
Nash, Jennifer. 2008. "Re-Thinking Intersectionality." *Feminist Review* 89: 1–15.
Orey, Byron D'Andra, and Wendy G. Smooth. 2006. "Race *and* Gender Matter: Refining Models of Legislative Policy Making in State Legislatures." *Journal of Women, Politics and Policy* 28(3/4): 97–120.
Phoenix, Ann, and Pamela Pattynama. 2006. "Intersectionality." *European Journal of Women's Studies* 13(3): 187–192.
Prins, Baukje. 2006. "Narrative Accounts of Origins: A Blind Spot in the Intersectional Approach?" *European Journal of Women's Studies* 13(3): 277–290.
Raj, Rita, Charlotte Bunch, and Elmira Nazombe, eds. 2002. *Women at the Intersection: Indivisible Rights, Identities, and Oppressions*. New Brunswick: Center for Women's Global Leadership, Rutgers.
Sherwood, Jessica Holden. 2010. "The View from the Country Club." In *The Intersectional Approach: Transforming the Academy through Race, Class, and Gender*, edited by Michelle Tracey Berger and Kathleen Guidroz. Chapel Hill: University of North Carolina Press.
Shields, Stephanie A. 2008. "Gender: An Intersectionality Perspective." *Sex Roles* 59: 301–311.
Simien, Eveyln. 2007. "Doing Intersectionality Research: From Conceptual Issues to Practical Examples." *Politics & Gender* 3: 264–270.
———. 2006. *Black Feminist Voices in Politics*. New York: State University of New York Press.
Smooth, Wendy. 2011. "Standing for Women—Which Women? The Substantive Representation of Women's Interests and the Research Imperative of Intersectionality." *Politics & Gender* 7: 436–441.

———. 2006. "Intersectionality in Politics: A Mess Worth Making." *Politics & Gender* 2: 400–414.
Squires, Judith. 2008. "Intersecting Inequalities: Reflecting on the Subjects and Objects of Equality." *The Political Quarterly* 79: 53–61.
Strolovich, Dara. 2007. *Affirmative Advocacy Race, Class and Gender in Interest Group Politics*. Chicago: University of Chicago Press.
Valentine, Gill. 2007. "Theorizing and Researching Intersectionality: A Challenge for Feminist Geography." *The Professional Geographer* 59: 1, 10–21.
Verloo, Mieke. 2006. "Multiple Inequalities, Intersectionality and the European Union." *European Journal of Women's Studies* 13(3): 211–228.
Weldon, S. L. 2006. "The Structure of Intersectionality: A Comparative Politics of Gender." *Politics & Gender* 2(2): 235–248.
Yuval-Davis, Nira. 2006. "Intersectionality and Feminist Politics." *European Journal of Women's Studies* 13(3): 193–209.
Zuberi, Tukufu, and Eduardo Bonilla-Silva. 2008. *White Logic, White Methodology: Racism and Methodology*. New York: Rowan & Littlefield.

2

Intersectional Advances?
Inclusionary and Intersectional
State Action in Uruguay

Erica E. Townsend-Bell

This chapter addresses the question of whether states can act intersectionally, and which social groups are most likely to push states to do so. I focus on the Uruguayan case, where I find that such action is limited to very specific instances that match the conditions required for inclusionary action: strong civil society mobilization, international pressure, party system change, and moderate- to low-cost solutions, alongside one simple, but thus far underutilized necessary condition for intersectional action: explicitly intersectional demands. I find in this case study, that women of color are more likely to engage in intersectional claims making and forward intersectional demands, while traditional feminist groups are less likely to do so.

Intersectionality is potentially at a crossroads. Whereas the basic concept has been elaborated throughout the history of black feminist thought, the specific term as introduced by Crenshaw is gaining in popularity across the feminist spectrum, taking on distinct nuances most appropriate to the particular contexts in which it is deployed. Yet, as the term gains in popularity and appeal, there is a special danger of the idea being appropriated, misinterpreted, or misapplied. Kathy Davis's (2008) coining of intersectionality as a "buzzword" is an apt description of precisely this concern. It is quite similar to the leveling effect that Rachel Luft (2009, 100) describes when she voices concern that "uniform deployment may inadvertently contribute to flattening the very differences intersectional approaches intend to recognize." This issue is raised in other ways as well; for instance, scholars have questioned why the race, class, gender trilogy is so frequently, and in some cases, uncritically adopted as the most appropriate or most comprehensive frame for analyzing intersectionality (Dhamoon, 2009; García-Bedolla, 2007; Grabham, 2009; Knapp, 2005; Nash, 2008; Weldon, 2006).

Nonetheless, recently intersectionality theory is being taken up by state and policy activists. This trend is perhaps most notable in the European context, where the European Union has pushed a more integrated approach for combating various forms of inequality. What remains at question is whether these new state attempts are intersectionality per se, or something different. Indeed, a number of recent works have indicated skepticism about such prospects, noting the shortcomings of policy and civil society attempts to enact intersectionality (Bredström, 2006; Kantola and Nousiainen, 2009; Koldinská, 2009; Lewis, 2009; Lombardo and Verloo, 2009; Luft and Ward, 2009; Manuel, 2007; Skjeie and Langvasbråten, 2009; Squires, 2008; Verloo, 2006).

These criticisms all converge around the central question of what is and is not intersectional action and whether states can perform such action. Certainly it is the case that states are paying more attention to difference, and evidence seems to indicate that they are doing so in a manner that seeks to move beyond the narrow identity politics battles of previous decades. But what exactly does that mean? Is attention to difference beyond simple identity politics the same as intersectionality? That is, are states concerned with the *full* eradication of social injustice and the fullest possible inclusion of the polity? Or are they more concerned with the still laudable, but narrower, goal of simply ameliorating injustice to some degree? Moreover, what are the conditions under which states' act might support intersectional action, what are the limits of said action, and where is this activity occurring?

One place where these developments are occurring is Latin America, a historic hotbed of class-based mobilization, and home to increasing mobilization on the basis of ethnicity, gender, and recently, sexuality, due in large part to pressures on states from social movement activists, civil society groups, and international actors concerned with gender, indigenous, and Afro-Latin inclusion. As a result of these pressures, governments have begun to respond with mechanisms for greater equality and inclusion in the form of gender quotas, autonomy agreements, and affirmative action initiatives, among other inclusionary but not necessarily intersectional mechanisms. Uruguay is a space where numerous gains for equality have been made in a short period of time, some intersectional and some not. Thus this case allows us to address the central concerns of whether states act intersectionally, and the conditions under which they might do so. As I will argue, states can act intersectionally, but often do not. In the Uruguayan case, such action has been limited to very specific instances that match the conditions required for inclusionary action: strong civil society mobilization, international pressure, party system change, and moderate- to low-cost solutions, alongside one simple, but underutilized necessary condition for intersectional action, explicitly intersectional demands.

Intersectional Advances?

The period from 2005 to 2010 ushered in a time of significant change in the Uruguayan political context. A new political coalition, the *Frente Amplio* (Broad Front), entered national government for the first time in 2005 with the stated intention of making a series of changes in Uruguay. These changes included its largest agenda item, an emergency antipoverty program designed to help with the lingering effects of a severe 2002 economic crisis that had left a significant amount of Uruguay's children and other citizens well below the poverty line. The Frente Amplio also took up a number of other issues that had previously received little traction in Uruguayan politics. In short order the parliament passed civil union legislation, becoming the first Latin American country to pass such a law at the national level (2007); legislation allowing gay candidates to enter the military (2009); adoption rights for same-sex partners in a formal civil union (2009); and legislation allowing transsexuals to have a legal sex change (2009).

In the same time span the first Frente Amplio president, Tabaré Vázquez, appointed Romero Rodríguez, then president of *Organizaciones Mundo Afro* (Black World Organizations; OMA), the largest black civil rights organization in Uruguay, as the first ever presidential advisor on racial equality. Similarly, Carmen Beramendi, director of the National Institute of Women

(Inmujeres), selected Beatriz Ramírez, cofounder of OMA and previous head of the Afro-Uruguayan Women's Support Group (GAMA), to form and head the newly created Secretariat for Afro-Descendant Women. At the same time, Alicia García, also a member of OMA and the then head of GAMA, entered the Ministry of Housing, as an assessor overseeing the occupation of a development of black female head of household apartments. And finally, the Vázquez administration signed off on the first Uruguayan gender quota law (2009), which takes effect for the 2014–2015 electoral cycle, and which requires that at least one of every three candidates for national or departmental office be a person of the opposite sex. Thus far the current Frente Amplio administration of President José Mujica (2010–2015) has been less active on issues of equality and inclusion, but given that many of the changes noted above occurred toward the end of Vázquez's administration, whether that will remain the case is yet to be seen. There has been some discussion of a debate on extending quota legislation, although no bill has yet been introduced. Nor is there a bill legalizing gay marriage. Although at the time of writing, gay marriage activists report they are working with members of the legislature to introduce such a bill. There is a bill pending for the decriminalization of abortion, similar to legislation that was vetoed by President Vázquez after achieving a majority of votes in the Chamber of Deputies and the Senate in 2008. Finally, in continuation of changes made in the previous administration, Beatriz Ramírez, the director of the Secretariat for Afro-descendant Women, has been made the director of Inmujeres, while Alicia Esquivel, an Afro-Uruguayan pediatrician, has been named the head of the Secretariat for Afro-descendant Women for the 2010–2015 period.

In sum, there have been numerous changes and advances for equality in the six-year period since the Frente Amplio has come to power. Nonetheless, the majority of these changes are clearly not intersectional, in that they do not address overlapping forms of difference in Uruguayan society. Still, it is important to understand how these changes came about and to be attentive to why the Frente Amplio has been willing to implement these varied initiatives. I discuss each of the factors that converged to promote equality changes in turn, before ending with a brief discussion of what motivates intersectional versus inclusionary state action.[1]

Mobilization from Below

Mobilization from below is a key necessary, though not sufficient, condition for both intersectional action and inclusionary action. The two groups that have been most successful in garnering concessions from the state in the last five years, Afro-descendant women and lesbian, gay, bisexual, and transgender (LGBT) actors, are also those who mobilized quite strongly in the latter half of the 2000s. Importantly, both groups significantly increased their degrees of mobilization during this period, and changed the form of their mobilizing strategies.

Afro-descendant women have been organizing in autonomous fashion since the formation of GAMA in 1993. As a result of perceived rebuffs from the broader feminist movement, black feminist organizing from the period of 1993 until roughly 2004 tended to be internally focused, dealing with the production of research documents, self-esteem and self-help training, employment initiatives, and so forth (Townsend-Bell, 2007). This reflected not just GAMA's strategy, but OMA's, a federated black organization of whom GAMA formed a part. Beginning in 2004, GAMA and OMA, recognizing the limits of this organizing schema and the limits of attempting coalition with other civil society actors who they perceived to be disinterested in such alliances, began to focus their attention on greater interaction within the governments of Montevideo and Uruguay. This new strategy reflected awareness of Uruguay's very state- and party-centered political society. In short order OMA and the Frente Amplio headed government of Montevideo established a Thematic Unit for Afro-descendant's in the municipality, to be followed by similar postings in the national Frente Amplio run government, beginning in the 2005 period. As one GAMA director noted:

> You know, before we really had a very punctual relationship [with the government]. We worked with the government in specific instances, but it was nothing very profound... The change we are making now is a structural one, designed to create more space for us in the government and based on the realization that the black collectivity have to insert ourselves, so that all entities are taken into account by the government. [The goal is to make them realize] that racism is an issue; it is not a minimal theme. (GAMA director, March 2005)

This strategy proved to be a positive move. Although, GAMA and OMA were somewhat skeptical of the governments' commitment to issues of race and gender, both the municipal and national Frente Amplio administrations proved open to creating some institutional space for Afro-descendants. Thus this move allowed activists to pursue political opportunities within the state. Moreover, it opened greater interest and space for civil society coalitions addressing race and gender, particularly between new black feminist and black interest organizations that have formed since 2006. "[Our attempt] at mainstreaming, has generated a number of possibilities; we [now] have mechanisms for inserting ourselves closer to the state in a positive way, this is a new and interesting process and, [there is] fertile ground." Nonetheless, state insertion is not a cure-all, "there is still a history of exclusion and discrimination. The fact that I am here does not negate that" (director, Secretariat for Afro-descendant Women, June 2008).

LGBT groups have a much shorter history, with the oldest and strongest of contemporary groups, *Ovejas Negras (Black Sheep)*, forming in December 2004, followed by several other groups in 2007 and 2008, including the national Uruguayan Federation for Sexual Diversity (FUDIS) in 2007. These are not the first lesbian, gay, or LGBT groups to form in Montevideo, but they do appear to have lasted longer and had a greater impact in a short time, particularly Ovejas Negras. Activists attribute this success to their forward thinking organizing strategy.

> We are very post-identity; that [an identity politics approach] is really rooted in the 1990s when mainstreaming of politics was not the norm. Those that have adopted the new method [of mainstreaming] have been more successful. Those that are too traditional, insisting that everything be designed, instituted, and directed by them have not been effective. We [the LGBT movement] have matured. Our major goal was and is to coalesce with other organizations as the most effective strategy. It was us who started the LGBT coordination [FUDIS] two years ago, and then abandoned it, because we really have to follow the trajectory [of working with strong organizations]. Many of those groups [other LGBT groups] are two persons, they are not even groups, much less organizations. Our allies can be in other sectors. (Ovejas Negras members, October 2010)

LGBT activists, particularly members of Ovejas Negras, felt that the most effective strategy would be to form alliances with other civil society actors, particularly feminist groups, who could function as their allies and help to provide them with a form of political capital that could result in positive changes, particularly in the form of legislation. For LGBT activists this meant, primarily, aligning with feminists and with making a case for how sexuality and gender discrimination are overlapping issues, and thus of interest to feminists.

Importantly, according to contemporary LGBT activists, earlier and more fleeting gay and lesbian groups had not taken this approach, leaving them disengaged from potential allies. Contemporary LGBT activists argue that earlier LGBT organizing attempts were unsuccessful because they did not act strategically, by helping feminists and other potential allies to make these connections. They argue that earlier activists should have taken a similar approach, not because it was the "right" or most ideologically consistent approach, but because it was the most politically effective. As one activist noted, "Even today there is no lesbian movement because of feminist unwillingness to recreate itself philosophically...[So what] we have done is to really emphasize post-material themes such as sexual diversity and its importance to feminism" (LGBT activist, October 2010). In essence, contemporary LGBT activists have moved beyond arguments that it should be obvious to feminists and other equality activists why sexual equality is important, or that feminists should feel responsibility for engendering all forms of equality, and moved toward what they consider the more pragmatic route of making those links for them. Like all mobilizing strategies, this approach has had consequences. "The response was timid at first; there was no place [for LGBT issues] within the liberal focus of other organizations. We are now accepted as legitimate actors, though things are still tentative and somewhat difficult" (Ovejas Negras member, October 2010).

Thus, the form in which LGBT activists mobilized varied somewhat from Afro-descendants, yet both groups' mobilizing strategies share a focus on moving away from isolationist or group-specific organizing approaches, to making links to other actors with political capital. In both cases these strategies have had their limitations, but do appear to have allowed more positive movement forward than either movement had experienced in the past.

INTERNATIONAL PRESSURE

As noted previously, Latin America in general is undergoing an intense period of change, with states, intellectuals, and civil society activists moving from staunch arguments that racial and ethnic discrimination was nonexistent in the region, and that gender discrimination could not be seen in the light of Western feminism, to formal state recognition of gender equality, and racial and ethnic diversity. Much of this change has been the hard fought result of often dangerous organizing by Latin American citizens. But these inclusionary agendas have also been informed and aided by international actors in the form of international nongovernmental organizations (NGOs), intergovernmental organizations (IGOs), and other states. Analysts describe the International Labor Organization's publication of Convention 169, the Indigenous and Tribal Peoples Convention in 1989, the UN conferences for gender equality, especially the Fourth World Conference on Women (Beijing) in 1995, and the first World Conference Against Racism (WCAR) in 2001, as invaluable mechanisms for forcing governments to take up discussions of equality previously off limits (Hooker, 2009; Wade, 2009).

Moreover, activists of all stripes describe the support of international NGOs and IGOs, ranging from the United Nations Development Fund for Women (UNIFEM) and the United Nations Development Program (UNDP) to country-specific organizations, and international governments such as the United States, Spain, and Canada as invaluable resources that allow them to fund research and advocacy projects designed, in part, to help convince domestic governments of the need for action. This has been particularly true of Uruguay, where activists do not describe a setting in which the government is forced or bullied into providing concessions to equality actors, but rather speak to the support of international entities in funding projects and providing the rhetorical support for agenda items that they want to move forward, including projects promoted and run by the municipal and national governments, but funded by international actors.

For instance, Afro-descendants speak of the rhetorical space that the WCAR provided as especially important for allowing them to broach the previously taboo topic of racism in Uruguay. Though activists had managed to convince the government to perform a special housing census in 1996 that counted people by race for the first time since the 1800s, they reported numerous barriers to analysis or action on racism at the public level (GAMA members, August 2003). Activists indicate that it was only after the WCAR that they began to get real traction on issues of racism and racial equality, including perhaps the most far-reaching and intersectional project thus far, three housing developments for black female heads of household living under the poverty line (OMA director, July 2003).

GAMA activists describe this long requested form of affirmative action and reparation for forced removal of black communities from their traditional neighborhoods during the dictatorship as a political nonstarter prior to the WCAR. "One of the points of the UN Durban conference given to the state was to make reparations to the black community for the dislocations from barrios Sur, Palermo, and the Cordón. It was really as a result of the UN Recommendations that we finally achieved this demand" (GAMA director, May 2008). Afro-descendants, particularly GAMA, made a successful argument that because more than half of black citizens are women, and because traditional black neighborhoods were also poor and working-class neighborhoods, these reparations should take the form of housing for Afro-descendant female heads of household below the poverty line. Though progress on the housing had been made under previous governments, the process was slow and uneven until the Frente's election in 2005. The first phase of the housing development was completed finally in early 2010.

International support has a direct impact on equality actors' ability to mobilize. Activists note that the increased isolationism of the United States in regard to Latin America, "almost killed the black movement…[Fortunately] the UN and Spain appeared; Spain in particular gave a lot of money, although it is less now" (Afroasamblea activist, October 2010). Funding from the Spanish government and other entities has helped fund government-supported projects, such as a soon to be finished National House of Afro-Uruguayan Culture, alongside surveys and outreach materials publicizing civil unions and gender quotas.

In addition, regional relationships have been quite important, especially for LGBT and feminist groups, who have used a rhetoric of what peer countries are or are not doing to good effect. Activists describe this strategy as particularly effective when they can make comparisons between Uruguay and Argentina, using LGBT, feminist, or general human rights legislative initiatives in Argentina to make an argument for what Uruguay should be doing (Paulón, 2010; Ravecca, 2010).

Party System Change, Low-Cost Solutions, and Intersectional Demands

Thus far I have emphasized the importance of mobilization from below and international pressure, which I will tentatively delineate respectively as a necessary and a sufficient condition, as conditions creating the possibility for inclusionary and intersectional action. Party system change has been an important sufficient condition for inclusionary and intersectional action. This has occurred alongside two additional necessary conditions: low-cost solutions and intersectional demands from activists. The Frente Amplio coalition's achievement of an outright majority of votes for the legislature (55.09%) and, for the first time in recent Uruguayan history, the executive (51.67%), was the culmination of a significant shift in one of the oldest two party systems of the Americas. The Frente's 2004 victory left the historically dominant Colorado party with only 10.6 percent of parliamentary seats, potentially reconfiguring the electoral landscape to a new two-party system made up of the Frente Amplio and the historic opposition party, the National, or Blanco, party. The Frente Amplio coalition retained its majority in the 2009–2010 elections, although not with the same degree of dominance as was the case for the 2004–2005 election. The Frente Amplio coalition currently holds 51.9 percent of legislative seats, while current president José Mujica won 47.96 percent of the vote in the first round of presidential elections, prompting a run-off election and resulting in a final vote total of 52.39 percent for Mujica. Thus it is as yet unsettled whether Uruguay is most accurately described as a two-party system or a two-and-a-half-party system. What is certain is that the Frente Amplio is institutionalizing and gives the appearance that it will continue to be a significant force in Uruguayan politics, while the fortunes and viability of the historically dominant, centrist Colorado party remain unclear. In sum, Uruguay has undergone a significant, if still potentially unfinished, party system change in recent years.

The rise of a leftist party is a crucial part of the explanation of why Uruguay has seen such rapid movement on issues of equality. It is worth considering briefly why the Frente Amplio has been willing to support these kinds of changes. While it is a leftist, or what some would call simply a progressive, government that is no reason to suspect that it would be any more open to issues of equality, diversity, and the like than any other type of government. Indeed, the Frente Amplio consistently has made clear that class equality is its central concern. The first administration's attention centered primarily on reducing poverty rates and assuaging the negative and lingering impacts of the 2002 economic crisis when it assumed power in 2005. Thus support for the changes mentioned above was far from guaranteed.

Yet, some have argued that it is the Frente Amplio's own history that paved the way for greater attention to difference. Many of its members, including President Mujica, were jailed either for participation in the 1970s urban guerilla movement, the Tupamaros, or under suspicion of treason or other equally trumped-up charges that were brought as a way to quell the fast rising popularity of an outsider party that managed to claim some 18 percent of the vote in its first electoral showing in 1971. Although elections were suspended as a result of dictatorial rule beginning in 1973, said suspension did not prevent further arrests, torture, or, for the lucky ones, exile. As one Uruguayan political scientist has noted, "It's important that the Frente Amplio suffered so much in the 1970s, because they [the members of the Frente Amplio] really understand the idea of human rights, it's not just an abstract concept" (Ravecca, 2010). Equality activists make a similar argument:

> It cost them [society] a lot to recognize other types of discrimination; for so many years it was all about poverty, that was the only type of discrimination that anyone recognized. Only recently has this changed. [Why?] Because of the new government primarily. It has helped many to realize that that there are many different types of discrimination. But the process has been slow, even within the government. It costs them a lot to understand the need. To understand the difference between discrimination and racism. Discrimination occurs to everyone—women, indigenous people, homosexuals, etc. Racism is just an issue of Afro-descendants. (OMA Member, Member of Government; May 2008)

Thus it appears that the government is committed to implementation of what it considers human rights initiatives, although this process has been somewhat uneven, reflecting achievement of some demands and setbacks on others. Said differently, party system change offered a new window of opportunity for social activists, with state actors showing commitment to some of the demands introduced, and not others. There has been important variation in the types of legislation, policy solutions, and other initiatives sought, with only a small number of those positive changes mentioned above, specifically, state action regarding women of color, falling under the category of intersectional change. There are a number of reasons for these variations, chief among them (1) how costly the suggested solutions are (2) and what kinds of solutions were demanded.

Activists argue that the Frente Amplio has been more responsive to what might loosely be called "human rights initiatives." However, it is the case that some legislative initiatives and policy solutions have come to fruition while others, particularly feminist movement initiatives like abortion and gender quotas, have failed or have been watered down significantly. Given that the sexual education and reproductive rights bill, including abortion, passed both houses of the legislature in 2008, and that the president vetoed only that part of the bill regarding the decriminalization of abortion, it may be reasonable to say that that result was the idiosyncratic outcome of one President Vázquez's (or as some argue, his very Catholic wife's) moral and religious preferences. But gender quotas, though they did pass, did not fare a much better outcome. As mentioned, the quota requires that candidates of both sexes be represented in every three places on the electoral list for both houses, through at least the first fifteen places. Where only two seats are contested, then two sexes shall be represented, and lists that fail to comply will be rejected by the Electoral Court. Yet, the law is only applicable to the 2014–2015 period, with no guarantee of renewal.

Thus, both the longevity and impact of the law are unresolved questions. Even the formal promoters of the law, the women's caucus of the Uruguayan Parliament express mixed feelings regarding the need for and the potential impact of the legislation. One supporter affirmed, "It is a very timid law, but it was the only consensus possible," while another indicated her opposition to the legislation, "I have my own value, my own worth. I don't need to be here just because of some rule that says I have to be here. And what happens now? Right now I am here on my own merit, but after they will say, 'well we had to.' Women have to want to be here. There is no need for a quota, women just have to work harder and want it...At times we women assassinate ourselves" (Member of Parliament, October 2010; Member of Parliament, October 2010). Similar concerns about whether gender quotas were the right strategy were echoed in the floor debates. There were numerous arguments against the legislation, but only two senators voted against the bill in the end. According to Niki Johnson and Verónica Pérez (2010, 36), this was not because they had changed their positions, but because they felt it was the "politically correct" thing to do, and because the commitment is of a very limited nature.

In sum, the gender quota bill seems to have created a dilemma for the Frente Amplio. The party wants to appear progressive and forward thinking on issues of equality, but, unlike the other advances mentioned above, the legislation of gender quotas requires a significant change in the rules regarding candidate selection, and ultimately seat apportionment and power distribution. To put it bluntly, gender quotas are very costly, particularly given that Uruguay has historically never claimed more than 15 percent women represented in Parliament.[2] This is the sense in which the Member of Parliament argued that the quota legislation achieved was "the only consensus possible;" an unpopular and otherwise unpassable bill was successful because it was introduced as one-time experiment that could, but would not necessarily be, extended, and that would not be immediately applicable.

Language legislating rights for LGBT citizens may be considered quite costly as well, and it is reasonable to argue that this would be true for much of Latin America. However, the Uruguayan case presents a number of caveats that appear to have made this legislation less politically risky than might be assumed. First, although the Catholic church does hold sway in Uruguayan society, it is still the case that Uruguay is and has been staunchly secular since the early twentieth century. Indeed, analysts have long described Uruguay as the most secular country in Latin America (Loveman, 1998). Moreover, the Frente Amplio does not identify as a party with any religious attachments, while it does identify as a party very interested in the promotion of human rights. Nonetheless, there was definitely opposition from the church and other conservative actors in society, as well as minority opposition within legislature. But the Frente Amplio's legislative majority was sufficiently large that minority party opposition was not sufficient to overcome an affirmative vote. Similarly, the church's lobbying efforts and sway in society was not significant enough to create major opposition within the electorate. Thus Frente members were free to vote their conscience on these issues without worry of major backlash from the electorate. Importantly, the Frente Amplio's factions routinely suspend party line voting requirements on "conscience issues" such that individual members who were not in favor of such legislation were equally free to vote their preference without fear of political repercussions.

Indeed as one LGBT activist noted, "No one changes their vote because of social themes. The only thing that makes people switch their votes here is economic redistribution...[and remember] these are only formal rights" (Ovejas Negras member, October 2010). In fact, activists argued that it was, in part, because of the lingering effects of the economic crisis that they were able to secure this legislation, in that one result of the crisis was an even greater inattention to social issues than normal. Moreover, LGBT activists indicate that they are well aware of the limits of formal rights, both in pushing larger cultural change, and in terms of how well they are enforced. Activists report that there needs to be much more emphasis in actual implementation of the laws, areas in which the government has been much less supportive. This has been especially true for the most controversial of the laws, the legal sex change registration. Activists report that it was much harder to find the votes for that law, among the Left as well as the Right. There was no public debate on that law, but it was still very controversial, and the law remains inoperative while the government creates a commission of experts from the Ministries of Health and Culture to whom those who want to change their sex would have to go and make their case. Indeed, activists indicate that they see this commission as a smokescreen meant to stall the effectuation of the law indefinitely (Ovejas Negras member, October 2010). In sum, the laws are paradoxically far-reaching but also limited both in their scope and execution. It would be inaccurate to argue that this legislation is simply symbolic, but it may be equally inaccurate to argue that such legislation required a significant expenditure of political capital on the part of state actors.

Similarly, the naming of women and men of color to various posts in government, and the designation of black female head of household developments are no small feat in a country that continues to identify itself as homogeneous and European, and which was quite hostile to public discussions surrounding race for the majority of history. Nonetheless, it is difficult to argue that these changes required much in the way of real concessions from the Frente Amplio. In one case, the position of special advisor to the president, the position was really subject to the whim of presidential interests; it was not renewed under current president José Mujica.

In regard to the housing developments, the original agreement calls for some 90 apartments, only 36 of which have been completed as of early 2011. Moreover, though the municipal and national government have supported the development of the apartments, it was always agreed that the women themselves would be responsible for the majority of the construction, which increases potential residents' investment in their homes, but which also limits the symbolic and financial commitment of the governments. Finally, in a move that makes this project arguably more intersectional, if less an affirmative action project, the housing is officially designated as a black female head of household development, and the majority of the owners are Afro-descendant women. But there is no questionnaire or affidavit requiring women to claim their blackness for admission to the apartments. In reality any woman who meets the economic qualifications can apply for the housing (Assessor, Ministry of Housing, May 2008).

The naming of a Secretariat for Afro-descendant women, and the later appointment of an Afro-descendant woman as director of Inmujeres, is as equally far-reaching as the LGBT legislation and other achievements listed above, and as with said legislation, the positive (and negative) unintended consequences of such changes remain to be seen. Nonetheless, without minimizing the progression represented, it is necessary to note that the secretariat is still just one among several themes within Inmujeres. As the director noted in 2008, "It is a complex process, but it is fertile. We are closer. I cannot make decisions but the closeness [to decision makers] offers possibilities as well" (June 2008). Inmujeres, like many such examples of state feminism, is not a ministry, does not claim its own budget, and has little decision-making power. Moreover, while the naming of Ramírez as director is a clear reflection of Inmujeres' commitment to working with Afro-descendant women, this does not usurp her primary role as director of the National Institute for *Women*.

Conclusion

Consequently, the convergence of several conditions was required for inclusionary and intersectional action in Uruguay. Strong mobilization from below, and low- to moderate-cost demands appear to have been necessary for forward movement of all kinds, while party system change and international pressure were important sufficient conditions for such progress. Finally, it appears that one additional necessary condition was required for explicitly intersectional action. This was simply that groups *sought* explicitly intersectional action. Afro-descendant women tied their demands to race, gender, and, in a more implicit fashion, class, and were successful in pushing forward their claims.

The Uruguayan case points to an emerging conclusion in other locales; states are primarily in the business of promoting inclusionary action, not intersectionality (Manuel, 2007; Squires, 2008). This is not necessarily a critique of states. Scholars are right to point out that even where states have attempted intersectional action, they have often failed to meet the bar (Kantola and Nousiainen, 2009). But what is apparent in the Uruguayan case is that though there may be a constituency who would like to see states do more, or perform better in this regard, there is larger constituency that has not expressed such interests. This second category includes groups like the general Uruguayan electorate who was not particularly concerned about concessions granted to LGBT and black women activists, opposition groups expressly opposed to even traditional inclusionary approaches, and the very civil society groups who did not demand intersectional solutions. Arguably, such proposals may have been political nonstarters in most cases. But as the black female head of household development indicates, such outcomes *are possible* even if very infrequent.

A larger group of positive cases and more analysis is needed to know whether there are additional necessary or sufficient conditions for intersectional action by the state besides those addressed here, but certainly a minimally necessary condition is that such action is requested. This may be so simple a condition as to seem obvious, but the fact remains that no one besides the black women activists made such requests or integrated such analysis into their political appeals. Quotas were so costly that significant compromise (or even failure according to some respondents) was likely under any circumstances, but to what extent concerns about a wave effect (e.g., if we give women quotas who else will demand them) could have been addressed by integrating some form of racial or at least class analysis into the appeal is an open question. Not only was black female (and male) support of quotas very tepid because such issues were not addressed, but the Frente Amplio's concern with class and the lack of attention to that as a central issue may well have diluted the proposal's likelihood of passage in its original form, whether because some Frente members' only qualm was the lack of a class analysis, or because party members would have felt it too politically costly to vote against a proposal that addressed what they claimed to be an issue of primary importance.

The lack of intersectional analysis did not seem to harm LGBT activists (and may well have hurt them) but what is striking is that most of the concessions gained, and all of those that have actually been implemented, were primarily for the lesbian and gay members of their constituency. There has been much less attention to bisexual, and especially to transgender members, although activists routinely emphasize greater rights for transgender individuals as one of their major priorities.

So can states act intersectionally? Yes. But they frequently do not. Is attention to difference beyond simple identity politics the same as intersectionality? No. But that is not necessarily a critique. Inclusionary action is important too and in the Latin American context, where the existence of any significant differences beyond class were routinely denied even some 10 or 20 years ago, it is a great step forward. Moreover, as I have argued here, where states do not claim to be engaging in such action, and where no one is demanding it, then the lack of intersectional activity is unsurprising.

Notes

1. Inclusionary action can refer to a variety of things but most frequently means a traditional equality approach. That is that particular

homogeneously defined groups not be excluded from the rights and responsibilities that other citizens have. Specifically, inclusionary action can take unidimensional form, as just described, in which one dimension of difference: race, class, sexuality is addressed, or multidimensional form, in which at least two, but less than the full class of important differences in a society are addressed, and in which such differences are addressed in a manner that assumes each difference to have a discrete effect.

2. Currently the Chamber of Deputies has 15 female members, which translates to 15.2 percent.

References

Bredström, Anna. 2006. "Intersectionality: A Challenge for HIV/AIDS Research?" *European Journal of Women's Studies* 13(3): 229–243.

Davis, Kathy. 2008. "Intersectionality as a Buzzword: A Sociology of Science Perspective on What Makes a Feminist Theory Successful." *Feminist Theory* 9(1): 67–85.

Dhamoon, Rita. 2009. *Identity/Difference Politics: How Difference Is Produced, and Why It Matters*. British Columbia: University of British Columbia Press.

García-Bedolla, Lisa. 2007. "Intersections of Inequality: Understanding Marginalization and Privilege in the Post-Civil Rights Era." *Politics & Gender* 3(2): 232–248.

Grabham, Emily et al. 2009. *Intersectionality and Beyond: Law, Power, and the Politics of Location*. New York: Routledge-Cavendish.

Hooker, Juliet. 2009. *Race and the Politics of Solidarity*. New York: Oxford University Press.

Johnson, Niki, and Verónica Pérez. 2010. *Representación (s)electiva: una mirada feminista a las elecciones uruguayas*. Montevideo: UNIFEM.

Kantola, Johanna, and Kevät Nousiainen. 2009. "Institutionalizing Intersectionality in Europe." *International Feminist Journal of Politics* 11(4): 459–477.

Knapp, Gudrun-Axeli. 2005. "Race, Class, Gender: Reclaiming Baggage in Fast Travelling Theories." *European Journal of Women's Studies* 12(3): 249–265.

Koldinská, Kristina. 2009. "Institutionalizing Intersectionality." *International Feminist Journal of Politics* 11(4): 547–563.

Lewis, Gail. 2009. "Celebrating Intersectionality? Debates on a Multi-Faceted Concept in Gender Studies: Themes from a Conference." *European Journal of Women's Studies* 16(3): 203–210.

Lombardo, Emanuela, and Mieke Verloo. 2009. "Stretching Gender Equality to Other Inequalities: Political Intersectionality in European Gender Equality Policies." In *Discursive Politics of Gender Equality:*

Stretching, Bending and Policy-making, edited by Emanuela Lombardo, Petra Meier, and Mieke Verloo, 68–85. New York: Routledge.
Loveman, Mara. 1998. "High-Risk Collective Action: Defending Human Rights in Chile, Uruguay, and Argentina." *American Journal of Sociology* 104(2): 477–525.
Luft, Rachel E. 2009. "Intersectionality and the Risk of Flattening Difference: Gender and Race Logics, and the Strategic Use of Antiracist Singularity." In *The Intersectional Approach: Transforming the Academy through Race, Class and Gender*, edited by Michele Tracy Berger and Kathleen Guidroz, 100–117. Durham: University of North Carolina Press.
Luft, Rachel E., and Jane Ward. 2009. "Toward an Intersectionality Just out of Reach: Confronting Challenges to Intersectional Practice." In *Perceiving Gender Locally, Globally, and Intersectionally*, edited by Vasilikie Demos and Marcia Texler Segal, 9–38. Bingley, UK: Emerald Publishing Group.
Manuel, Tiffany. 2007. "Envisioning the Possibilities for a Good Life: Exploring the Public Policy Implications of Intersectionality Theory." *Journal of Women, Politics, and Policy* 28(3): 173–203.
Nash, Jennifer C. 2008. "Re-Thinking Intersectionality." *Feminist Review* 89: 1–15.
Paulón, Estéban. 2010. "Gay Marriage in Argentina." Talk presented at the Annual Meeting of the Latin American Studies Association, Toronto.
Ravecca, Paulo. 2010. " The Case of Civil Unions in Uruguay." Talk presented at the Annual Meeting of the Latin American Studies Association, Toronto.
Skjeie, Hege, and Trude Langvasbråten. 2009. "Intersectionality in Practice?" *International Feminist Journal of Politics* 11(4): 513–529.
Squires, Judith. 2008. "Intersecting Inequalities: Reflecting on the Subjects and Objects of Equality." *The Political Quarterly* 79(1): 53–61.
Townsend-Bell, Erica. 2007. "Identities Matter: Identity Politics, Coalition Possibilities, and Feminist Organizing." PhD diss. Washington University in St. Louis.
Wade, Peter. 2009. *Race and Sex in Latin America*. London: Pluto Press.
Weldon, S. Laurel. 2006. "The Structure of Intersectionality: A Comparative Politics of Gender." *Politics & Gender* 2(2): 235–248.
Verloo, Mieke. 2006. "Multiple Inequalities, Intersectionality and the European Union." *European Journal of Women and Politics* 13(3): 211–228.

3

ID CARDS AS ACCESS: NEGOTIATING TRANSGENDER (AND INTERSEX) BODIES INTO THE CHILEAN LEGAL SYSTEM

Penny Miles

I decided to enroll in another college. I put on my tracksuit trousers, tied my hair back. This was back in 1999. I arrive for enrolment, I take a number, and after a while I am called. "Take a seat please, miss." Me, with my certificate in my hand, my certificate with a man's name on it... I sat down, he asked me why I had left my previous college if I had such good grades... He is about to register me, [so] I tell him, "there's a problem." I told him to look at the name on the certificate... He said, "if you're going to bring a false certificate, you should at least bring one with a woman's name on it, why on earth did you bring one with a man's name on it?" I replied, "It's not false, it's mine." So I took out my ID card and passed it to him. He recoiled... he recoiled and then he said, "No, no, no, there's not going to be any registration today." And I said, "What do you mean, there'll be no registration today. Five seconds ago there was, and now there isn't?"[1]

(Mariana, trans activist, May 2009)

Mariana's narrative presents just one example of the complexities of going about daily life as a transgender or intersex person in Chile contemporary. In a society where identity (ID) cards are central to accessing most services, from public health to the labor market, the incongruence between self-presentation and official identification serve to perpetuate the discriminatory practices directed toward transgender[2] and intersex individuals. This frequently results in the denial of access to basic rights. These are seen as part of a vicious circle. Not having a legal identity congruent with the person's adopted gender essentially implies exclusion from education, employment, and health. Such a scenario has encouraged some to seek legal change to gender and name status as a means of ameliorating their inclusion in society. However, in order to do so, individuals need sufficient financial resources to undergo surgery and hormonization in a costly, privatized health service. Though gender identity is not currently regulated by law, a gap in the law has thus far been exploited in order to allow individuals to "re-sex" their transgender bodies. However, this has occurred predominantly in the cases of "the post-surgical body" (Sharpe, 2002, 3). Since 2007, there has been an increasing tendency to present more "transgressive" (Roen, 2002) petitions that seek gender recognition for preoperative[3] transsexuals and transgendered people.

This chapter focuses on transgender activism in Chile. Given the extent of social exclusion for members of these communities, the legal processes to achieve gender recognition, has become a central feature of that activism. "Gender recognition" refers to the demands presented by transsexual and transgender individuals who wish to have their adopted gender identity recognized, where it differs from the sex they were assigned at birth. I focus on both the direct and indirect outcomes of such legal action in Chile in the late 2000s, as a number of these cases have been supported by lawyers working in the public interest who are seeking not only legal change, but who also use litigation as the basis for political and social change (Sarat and Scheingold, 1998). Based on ethnographic research conducted in Chile between 2008 and 2010, my analysis explores the processes and outcomes of this legal action for the trans community. In order to make these realities comprehensible for the reader, I firstly introduce some trans narratives. The purpose of these narratives is to illustrate how difficult it is to negotiate daily life with an identity card that is incompatible with one's adopted gender identity. Yet this must be understood in a context where your ID card is central to carrying out the most menial of tasks, such as depositing a check in a bank, visiting a doctor, enrolling on a college course. I touch briefly on the inaccessibility of the Chilean legislature in dealing with matters of sexual diversity, before discussing the pursuit of litigation as a means of effecting legal change. In particular, I address how the increase in litigation has been mirrored by an emergent trans male movement. In addition, the coming together of the diverse actors necessary to mount such legal challenges, which encompass medical and legal professionals, also points to the increased potential for intersectional activism. As such the chapter considers the interaction between legal mobilization and social movement activism (McCann, 1994, 2006). In addition, it examines the complexities and heterogeneity of the trans community through the legal solutions sought and obtained.

My research draws upon over 20 transgender cases in which I conducted interviews, or of which I gained reliable secondhand knowledge. While I am able to refer to a transgender community in Chile, I am not yet able to do so for intersex populations. During the research, I came across only two cases that sought recognition for intersex individuals, only one of which I was able to access personally. The extent of the invisibility of the former is such that it does not feature in Chilean LGBT[4] activism. Currah, Juang, and Minter note that "while transgender and intersex politics refer to different constituencies and have significant differences in their goals, [they]...nonetheless grapple with questions of autonomy and gender self-determination" (2006, xv). My decision to include only a brief discussion of intersex cases below is as a consequence of that invisibility but also speaks to the relevance of some of the same legal process.

ID Cards: Denial of Access

Mariana's case illustrates just one of the many instances that respondents recalled when describing how the excessive reliance on ID cards to go about daily activities exacerbated the levels of exclusion and discrimination that they faced. The following excerpts were recorded with Emmanuel and Mauricio, two trans males. They were in the latter stages of transition, having started hormonization and undergone some surgical processes. Emmanuel demonstrates the problems associated with the ambiguity that arises between his legal identity (female), as recognized on his ID card, and his adopted gender identity (male). The excerpt highlights one of the many frustrations he faced when he tried to convince others that he was legally female. He describes below how that impacted on his ability to resolve his own monetary problems:

> I was trying to sort out my debt. The person that worked in the office didn't understand that it was me on the [ID] card...She said, "sir, you can only come and do this paperwork on her behalf with a letter from the solicitor." She never understood that it was my card. I couldn't do anything. I wasn't sure whether to laugh or cry, it was such a strange feeling, they just kept on saying "No" and that I wasn't the person that appeared on the ID card. (Emmanuel, May 2009)

Mauricio's extract, in turn, illustrates the constancy with which trans people are forced to expose and explain themselves:

> The other day I had to go and pay a fine. I went to talk to the judge. He asked for my ID card and for me to fill in a form. Then he came to me and said, "this bike is in someone else's name." I said, "it's in my name." He replied, "no, this name…" So I whispered to him that I was undergoing a sex change. "Oh," he said, "I'd never have noticed." I asked him if he could ask his secretary to call me by my adopted [masculine] name. "What is it?" he asked…Later the secretary came out and calls "Mauricio, Mauricio," and I go into the judge's office. (Mauricio, May 2009)

Given the ethnographic nature of my research, on occasions I witnessed how this experience of negotiating identity in relation to the ID card was actually lived. The instance that I describe below actually relates to an intersex case, but it exemplifies the complexity of negotiating identity in public, and resonates with the transgender experience. Juliana, who is intersex, had arranged to meet the judge presiding over her case in person, in the hope of persuading him to rule in her favor, and agree to change the legal name and gender assigned to her at birth. I was accompanying Juliana on that visit to the courts. This visit, however, then led to a trip to the hospital as more medical tests were deemed necessary. The dearth of information on intersexuality in Chile meant that the judge was relying heavily on medical evidence on which to base his ruling, as he later relayed to me in conversation. In practice, this meant frequent visits to hospitals, the Medical Legal Service[5] and private clinics for Juliana. When we arrived at the hospital, Juliana herself spoke to the receptionist, given that her expertise on the matter far outweighed that of her lawyer. When the receptionist asked if "Julio Moreno" (Juliana's legal name) was among us, Juliana—dressed in black heels, a smart black trouser suit, with long dark wavy hair, French-manicured nails—answered that he was not. I gleaned that from the ease and speed with which she responded, that she had learnt to rebuff such questions as a means of personal survival. This reliance on ID cards, and the resulting frequency of such interactions, therefore renders everyday interaction a complex, distressing, and destabilizing process, as individuals such as Juliana attempt to negotiate the dominant discourses that stigmatize them as deviant. Taking an interactionist perspective, Rubington and Weinberg note that it "focuses on...how people typify one another; how they relate to one another on the basis of these typifications; and the consequences of these social processes" (1996, 1).

Similarly, Erving Goffman analyzes stigma and social identity in relation to its social setting and concludes that "society establishes the means of categorizing persons and...social settings establish the categories of persons likely to be encountered there" (1963, 11–12). He adds that stigma is perceived through interaction when "not all undesirable attributes are at issue, but only those which are incongruous with our stereotype of what a given type of individual should be" (1963, 13). He defines stigma more directly as "an attribute that is deeply discrediting" or "an undesired differentness from what we had anticipated," which is not possessed by the "normals" (1963, 13, 15). In this instance, therefore, identities that do not conform to the gender binary are viewed as "deeply discrediting," as evidenced in the interactions illustrated above. The impact of this scenario certainly served to increase the sense of urgency that Mauricio, Emmanuel, and Juliana all experienced in needing to remedy this incongruence between legal and lived identities.

Why Litigation?

In the legislative climate in Chile, moral conservatism has prevailed vis-à-vis gender and sexuality rights since democratization in 1990 (Blofield, 2001; Htun, 2003; Miles, forthcoming). Divorce was not legalized until 2004 and reproductive rights remain highly contested, as illustrated by extensive debates and mobilization around issues such as the morning-after-pill since 2008. An antidiscrimination bill, which proposes protection on the basis of gender and sexual orientation, languished in Congress from 2005, only being approved in November 2011. Opposition to the inclusion of protections on the very basis of sexual orientation and gender were the principal cause for its lack of progress. Fransisco Estévez, sociologist and head of the Division of Social Organizations (DOS) between 2006 and 2010, attributes this slow passage of the bill through Congress to the weighty opposition of both the more established Catholic Church and the emergent Evangelical Church.

> The sector linked to the Evangelical Church believes that homosexuality is a sin...and so they cannot support a law that respects sexual diversity because that means supporting something sinful. And on the other hand, the Catholic Church is questioning the law because it argues that it will facilitate more legislation being passed; on adoption by same-sex couples, gay marriage, or same-sex unions, etc., even though this law does not cover that. They think that if is this law is passed, that the rest will follow more quickly. (Fransisco, May 2009)

Vaggione concurs that across Latin America,

> the Catholic Church's hierarchy continues to be the main political opponent to securing legislation and policy that favors the articulation of sexual and reproductive rights. The legitimacy of the Catholic Church and its representatives...limit the autonomy of the governing classes and legislators...who seek support in the Catholic hierarchy...Lobbying by representatives of the Catholic Church with legislators and judges is an important obstacle to seeking change in the legal system and jurisprudence which institutionalizes a traditional conception of the family. (2008, 14)

This traditional conception of the family encourages an adherence to binary gender roles and heterosexual sexual relations. In 1999, the Chilean legislature did actually decriminalize sodomy for males engaging in same-sex practices over the age of 18, as activists and sympathetic politicians were able to capitalize on some opportune political opportunities (Miles, 2004). However, the legislature has comprised almost equal representation of members of the opposing centrist left and right coalitions since 1990, and it does not lend itself to favoring legislation pertaining to LGBTI (Lesbian, Gay, Bisexual, Transgender, and Intersex) rights or other matters that challenge the "moral" agenda. In one interview, a left-wing deputy, María Antonieta Sáa, aptly remarked that the Chilean population was being held "hostage to a conservative elite" (María Antonieta, April 2010).

Consequently, legal mobilization strategies, or the use of litigation to advance or uphold one's rights (Zemans, 1983), have been increasingly used in recent years as a means of achieving social and legal change by social movement and legal activists. Human rights lawyers have been at the forefront of pushing for such change, and these challenges now include transgender rights. In this specific instance, litigation has been used with the intention of securing legal recognition of name and gender change for transsexual, transgender, and more recently, for intersex individuals. Though such legal processes have been occurring since the 1980s at least, recent petitions have both become more visible and more "transgressive" (Roen, 2002) in their demands, especially since 2007. Employing Bornstein's language, Roen defines this transgression as "subversive crossing, public and politically strategic transgendering" (Roen, 2002, 502–503 quoting Bornstein, 1995). Petitions are increasingly being presented where individuals have not undergone genital reassignment surgery (GRS). As I detail more fully in the following section, transgression is evident as such cases move into the public arena, instigated by trans and LGBTI activists.

Making the Legal Case

As the recognition of transgender, transsexual, and intersex identities falls outside existing legal frameworks in Chile, lawyers have had to be creative in their interpretation of the law. Law 17.344 allows individuals to solicit changes to their forenames and surnames in accordance with Article 1. This states that when these names are considered to cause "moral harm" and "when the petitioner has been known for more than five years, with reasonable motives, with names or surnames, or both, different to their own," voluntary petitions can be filed to have such changes recognized.[6] Lawyers have thus argued that "moral harm" and "reasonable motives" are justified in the cases of trans people where the official gender identity and name assigned to the individuals at birth contradicts the individual's adopted name and gender identity. Greenberg's observation that "traditionally, a person's legal sex is established by the sex that the birth attendant places on the birth certificate" rings true in the Chilean case (2006, 52). Lawyers were able to illustrate such moral harm and argue for reasonable motives by citing the extreme marginalization and stigmatization that members of these populations face as a consequence of existing outside the gender binary. As this legal process is subject to interpretation by judges (and lawyers), the paperwork demanded by judges in order to assess the case can vary. Some might ask for reports from the Registry Office, psychological and/or psychiatric reports, and often, physical examinations. The same office has recorded the instances where name and gender change have been granted, though these were granted usually only where GRS had been performed.

Since 2007, however, petitions have been presented when individuals have not undergone GRS, thus attempting to break with the equating of gender identity with genitalia (Sharpe, 2002). In May 2007, Andrés Rivera, president of the Organization of Transsexuals for the Right to Dignity (OTD), became the first known transsexual man to achieve legal recognition of his adopted name and gender without undergoing GRS. The judge who presided over the civil court in Rancagua based the ruling on the psychological exams as proof of Andrés's gender identity not on his genitalia. It must be noted that other such cases may well have been passed prior to Andrés's. However, the invisibility surrounding such cases, exacerbated by the strength of sociocultural sanctions for those that openly question the gender binaries in Chilean society, have limited access to such cases.

Media Dissemination and Trans (Male) Organizing

The importance of media dissemination through various means had been central to raising both trans (particularly male) identity awareness and associated rights consciousness (Miles, 2011), and expanding the realms of what is legally possible. As Andrés himself notes that "the problem is that transsexuals are the invisible among the invisibles, we are like the sub-minority within the minority groups" (October 2008). The OTD has concentrated efforts on dissemination and sensitization around trans issues through carefully selecting a number of documentaries to appear in. It was through this means that Emmanuel first got to know about other cases of male transsexualism, as he recounts below:

> I saw a program on television... and it was the first time that I had seen cases of male transsexualism... it was the first time that I realized that it wasn't my fault that I had been born this way... I got in touch with Andrés and went to see him... For the first time I felt understood, I met someone like me. Because most of the time you feel that you are the only one. (Emmanuel, May 2009)

Others, such as Mauricio, arrived by a similar means and trans male organizing thus emerged very tentatively in 2004 and 2005. As Emmanuel indicates above, awareness of trans male identities was practically nonexistent prior to this epoch, to such an extent that Andrés adds:

> We frequently assume lesbian identities as a means of protecting ourselves. I would much rather say that I was lesbian than say that I was a man, because otherwise your whole world will fall on you, lesbians don't have their worlds fall on them. (Andrés, October 2008)

Andrés, and others since, have appeared in other selected documentaries. He notes that more individuals have approached the organization through this means than through any other. For example, he compares this to the number of people arriving through the Internet. He reported OTD membership rising from 4 or 5 individuals in 2004–2005 to more than 31 in 2008 with numbers continuing to grow:

> About 3 months ago I appeared on a television program. I always appear on medical programs, as I'd never wanted to be interviewed on sensationalist programs. But analyzing the situation with my partner, we realized that there was a segment of the population that we hadn't reached, because young people don't watch medical programs. Among those programs that were calling me, was one called "Night Owl" [*Animal Nocturno*]. It's a very popular program and after that show 7 trans people got in touch with me.

So we realized that effectively there were people that we still hadn't reached. And, of course, I will have to appear again. (Andrés, October 2008)

Though political objectives are clearly inherent in trans male organizing, many of those who arrive are seeking support, practical help, comprehension, and a space to share experiences, as Emmanuel indicates previously. Another activist, Nadia, also remarked on the impact that the first meeting had on new members as they expressed their incredulity that they were not the "only ones" to be living that "experience" (Nadia, November 2008) when they first joined OTD and came to share their lived experience.

Closely tied to the transition process that many then decide to undertake, through hormonization and/or surgical procedures, is the associated legal process. Much of the engagement with the movement for each individual therefore relates to the importance of being able to access services that facilitate the physical and legal transition of adopting a new gender identity. Lukas Berredo, of Trans Male Support Group (GAHT), and the president of the Gender Dysphoria Support Group (AADGE), both confirmed that many members of their organizations were interested in achieving legal change. For both GAHT and OTD the need for a change in the law that facilitates gender recognition is central to their political agenda as a consequence of the centrality of the ID card in regulating everyday interaction in Chilean life.

Trans female organizing has had a broader activist agenda in contrast to the recently emerged trans male movement in Chile. Trans women began organizing in the 1990s, at first, affiliated to the two main umbrella LGBT[7] organizations, Homosexual Liberation Front (MOVILH) and the Movement for Unified Minorities (MUMS). These emerged after the transition to democratic rule. They then formed their own group in 2000, firstly through Traves Chile, and later through other organizations, such as the Amanda Jofre Syndicate. Cristina López, activist with both organizations, though affiliated to the latter since 2003, differentiates trans female organizing from other LGBT and even trans male organizing:

> It's about gender, massively about gender. It's incredible. Imagine that Andrés gets his legal documents in just two years, he practically gets married in the public eye, everyone knows about him

and he doesn't care...But it's also about how you run an organization. Trans men deal with their personal objectives, which are to deal with their transsexualism, then they leave activism. They work alone. It's a matter of gender. Here, all the girls work together. We estimate that there about 400 or 500 trans women in the metropolitan region, and of those, 150 are registered with the organization. But we attend to all of those in the metropolitan region...If we hand out condoms, we go to Vivaceta, Puente Alto, Independencia, Macul. If a girl dies, we organise the funeral...If one has been attacked, we put her in the case and take her to hospital...we also attend to the foreigners because they are much more vulnerable. (Cristina, June 2009)

López attributes this difference to the greater vulnerability of trans women in Chilean society and how they must deal with the everyday difficulties associated with extreme social and economic marginalization from education, employment, and health spheres, which has forced many into prostitution as a means of survival. Female trans organizing has therefore centered around the practical concerns of dealing with life on the streets and the vulnerabilities which extend from that. Though the very incongruence between official and adopted gender identity as indicated on their ID cards is also central to such marginalization, the difficulties with dealing with basic everyday survival has meant that less attention has been paid to attempting to advance the legal agenda, though a number of trans women have either name and/or gender recognition.

In the majority of cases the latter has only occurred where genital reassignment surgery has been performed. As Cristina notes in more straightforward terms: "you have to get a certificate from the Medical Legal Service which says that you no longer have a penis, and that you have a vagina. And as you have a vagina, you argue that you can no longer be called Juanito and so you call yourself Juanita" (Cristina, May 2009. When trans women trade their masculinity for feminity, the costs are very high in a society that privileges notions of hegemonic masculinity (Connell, 1995). Both financial and symbolic consequences result from the complex reordering of gender relations that transgenderism and transsexualism imply in this context. One of the principal reasons behind these petitions being presented without GRS is the financial implications of undergoing surgery.

Returning to the transgender divide, when conversing with trans women, I noted more skepticism as regards the possibilities that they would have been able to achieve legal change without gender reassignment surgery. But there was also a sense that the legal process was futile, given that of those that had secured their legal change, some had fallen back into the same vicious circle. Even securing the ID card had not enabled trans women to be able to integrate into society in the same way that trans men had. However, this could be related to the stage at which trans men had embarked on their transition process. Most trans women reported falling out of the education stage at an earlier age due to fact that they adopted their gender identity often in secondary school. In contrast, most men that I spoke with had begun to transition in their twenties or thirties, and in some instances, in their forties. By which time some had secured a decent education and had engaged in professional activities. One taught in university, another was an engineer, and another was a music teacher. Of the trans women who had presented petitions, one had worked her way up through the council to work as a secretary, and another worked in her friend's Internet café and another was studying. However, the majority of the others drifted in and out of the informal economy and prostitution.

Connell's "patriarchal dividend" (1995, 80–82) recognizes women's subordination even by those males unable to realize the hegemonic ideal of masculinity. The differentiated access to education, qualifications, and employment noted above, indicates that even where dominant notions of masculinity are transgressed when females transition to males, that notions of patriarchy prevail. The interplay of gender and class are also relevant in these cases, as the masculinities framework suggests. Two of the four males who achieved both name and gender recognition both distanced themselves from the respective groups they were affiliated to during their transitioning process. AADGE also suffered a similar fate when the president, after having achieved his change after winning a unique legal battle to secure a free GRS operation, stopped being active. As the driving force of AADGE, without his activism the group became redundant. The cases he was involved with are, however, still being represented by the Human Rights Office of the Legal Aid Corporation. MOVILH president, Rolando Jiménez recognized the tendency of individuals to distance themselves from the organization once their legal or other issue had been resolved. Alternatively, Cristina understands the need for continued action for trans women even after achieving recognition through the courts due to the continued difficulties in accessing those dividends such as employment and education. In contrast, trans men become increasingly more autonomous in their actions and associations, as they are now able to access the material and symbolic conditions that had previously been denied them.

Direct Outcomes

In his work on legal mobilization, McCann (1994, 2006) argues that litigation can facilitate social movement development and consolidation. He contends that this can be achieved directly through securing favorable rulings or indirectly through associated processes that occur as a consequence of undertaking legal action, though the latter have played a greater role in movement consolidation. Drawing upon his categories, the case of trans male movement development particularly, and in trans movements more generally, both direct and indirect outcomes have played a significant role in the development of trans organizing within the broader LGBTI movement in Chile.

In examining the jurisprudential outcomes of the cases that I accessed during fieldwork, two key trends emerge.[8] The first refers to the increasing disparity in judicial sentences pertaining to name and gender recognition. The second relates to the gendered nature of that disparity. A pattern of differentiated citizenship is emerging as a consequence of the decision to present petitions where GRS has not been performed and where the scope for legal interpretation is apparently broader where genitalia do not coincide with the adopted gender identity. In some cases both name and gender change are agreed by judges, and in others, only name changes are granted (and sometimes only petitioned for as AADGE president noted). In the worst-case scenario, both are rejected.

From my case studies, OTD had secured name and gender changes for three trans men and had supported a name change that had occurred in the north of Chile, while GAHT had secured one more in January 2010. AADGE had supported a number of cases where name changes only had been granted, though more petitions are being contested in the civil courts currently. Of the six petitions presented by MOVILH and the public interest litigation clinic affiliated to the Diego Portales University (UDP), all four cases that were completed were rejected in the lower courts. Only one case won on appeal, and only then was the name change granted. The other cases were rejected on appeal. The UDP reported that it intended to continue with the cases and as of April 2010 it was discussing possible strategies. This differentiated citizenship therefore seemingly has a gendered dimension to it. It reaffirms Julie A. Greenberg's assertion that "the law's role in gender assignments is multifaceted and contradictory" (noted in Currah, Juang, and Minter 2006, xviii). At least one outcome of this disparity in judicial sentences is the emergence of different possible paths to some modicum of legal recognition.

Though some petitions only seek name change and as a consequence could be considered as actively seeking a level of differentiated citizenship, Lukas Berredo of GAHT clarified this as "being better than nothing," and that it would allow many "to get by" (Lukas, April 2010). He believed that the name on the ID card was more salient in negotiating everyday interaction. He contended that fewer people actually focused on the gender. However, accepting this second-best result is indicative of the lack of belief in the system and being able to achieve a fuller sense of citizenship, equality, and integration. This has been facilitated by the fact that individuals are now able to appear in their ID photos in accordance with their adopted gender identity. Before, trans women were forced to appear with short hair and adopt a masculine appearance that coincided with their name. As Mariana notes:

> We have achieved changes to the photos that the Registry Office are willing to accept [on our ID cards]. Before, they insisted that we transsexuals had to disguise ourselves as men in order to get our ID card. We had to modify our aesthetics, in other words, tie our hair back, take our make up off, and dress like a man just to have our photo taken for the ID card. But we challenged that, and now that's not necessary. You can have your photo taken however you want, with your hair down. (Mariana, May 2009)

A second outcome can be read as arising from this disparity. When questioning the gender dimension to this differentiated citizenship, however, all trans activists concurred that one group took a "step up" the social hierarchy, and the other took a "step down." They argued that female-to-male trans people achieved the former, and that the latter referred to male-to-female trans people. In Latin American societies, where patriarchy continues to prevail, gender equality remains highly underdeveloped in both law and practice, and is manifest in societal relations through machismo. This second theme emerging from the legal disparity is reinscribing gender binaries where those transitioning to males can be seen as benefiting from Connell's patriarchal dividend.

This reinscription undermines the possibility of capitalizing on direct outcomes because dominant social discourse has encouraged "assimilationist" over "transgressive" responses. Even where name and gender changes have been achieved in the case of the four trans men I mentioned, only Andrés declared the outcome publicly by putting his face to the cause. Whilst the others were willing to allow their cases to be published on the respective websites, and conceded interviews and so forth, they did not do visibly. Of the one trans female case that it is known about where name and gender recognition were achieved without undergoing GRS, the individual also refused to go public. Prior to presenting the six petitions in June 2007, MOVILH came across the said case and approached her to see if she would support the case by coming out. In public interest litigation strategies, it is believed that the impact of the case is more potent when the public is exposed to the individual case, and that the media responds well to testimony. Mariana, in her activist role noted:

> The girl from the north who got a favorable ruling didn't want to "come out." She's not interested, she's got her life, it's also understandable that she doesn't want to come out to the press...and that she doesn't want people to know who she is. It's also counterproductive for us. If you are transsexual and you want to "pass" as a normal woman, you also have to live anonymously. If you appear on television, they say "ah, there she is, the one that had that operation, that famous trans woman"...Sometimes I question this...I don't know if it's going to help me, but I do know that it will help others, those that are coming behind us. (Mariana, May 2009)

In other words, even despite her political drive and her acknowledgment of the need for change and that few others were willing to undertake such a stance for fear of being ostracized, she wished to be able to "pass." Her instinctive response was to want to conform to the dominant norms of society, not challenge them on a personal level. It points to what the costs of "coming out" mean to her. Stychin (1998) has remarked on the paradox of members of LGBTI communities in having to come out in order to challenge one's rights and raise awareness.

Both Emmanuel and Mauricio favored "passing," which was not just driven by financial reasons, but was related to wanting to reject the past and begin a "new life." Emmanuel goes so far as to consider the ability to access a new ID card as official recognition of his "rebirth" (Emmanuel, May 2009). Living as an openly trans person in the Chilean society of the late 2000s and questioning the gender binaries was precisely the situation that they were trying to avoid by securing an ID card that represented their adopted gender identity. Having been excluded by and discriminated against in the workplace, education establishments, banks, hospitals, and so on, on the basis of crossing and challenging the gender binary, the pressure to conform from society becomes an influential determinant in wanting to conform to the dominant norms. So while the judicial rulings themselves may be transgressive, the outcomes do not necessarily reflect that transgression. The direct benefits of legal change for some may not lead to direct benefits for a more transgressive gender politics.

Despite this, a third direct benefit of legal change can be identified in the increased volume of petitions and activism. Media dissemination has served to expand trans male organization membership and to give exposure to what is legally possible in relation to achieving gender recognition. The visibility of Andrés's case, not least within the broader LGBTI community, served as the impetus for another organization, the Homosexual MOVILH to sponsor, cojointly with the UDP's public interest litigation clinic six such petitions for trans women in June 2007. Further such petitions have been presented through splinter groups formerly incorporated into the OTD, the GAHT, and AADGE. AADGE sought legal representation through the Human Rights Office affiliated to the state-sponsored Legal Aid Corporation, and GAHT pursued one case in conjunction with a lawyer hired privately, but has since associated itself with the legal clinic based at the University of Chile. In all of those petitions presented, either name or gender and name changes are sought where GRS has not been performed.

In some instances, it is the centrality of the legal action that has become the main focus of activism.

Whilst Andrés's case was given exposure through the OTD website, MOVILH took a more direct approach with the media and was able to draw on its already established links with both print and visual media. As a consequence of the petitions presented by MOVILH and the UDP, both MOVILH activists and UDP lawyer, Mayra Feddersen, reported having been approached by individuals and lawyers wishing to undertake the same legal process. Some sought legal counsel and others just sought information regarding the necessary steps to take. It was through the same mechanisms that the intersex cases came to light. One individual was directed to the Human Rights Office affiliated to the Legal Aid Corporation by the UDP. Ironically, she was initially a former UDP law student who had worked in the public interest litigation clinic. Consequently, she decided to use and adapt the same format that the clinic had applied in the transgender cases. Juliana's case, a part of this research project, was taken by the UDP between 2008 and 2009. Lawyers' willingness to embark on such courses of action, and in this case, often in the public domain, has played a central role in facilitating a more concerted level of legal activism.

The media attention achieved in certain cases, either in relation to the legal action brought, such as in the MOVILH/UDP sponsored petitions, or the actual outcomes, such as those publicized through OTD and GAHT websites, has facilitated activists' ability to secure legal representation necessary to taking further legal action. Furthermore, it has prompted others to present similar cases. One important outcome of the rise in such petitions being presented has been the growth and consolidation of actors involved in mobilizing the petitions. Below I examine the increasingly intersectional nature of activism in this context. Not only does the legal process itself require the involvement of a number of actors, such as psychologists, doctors, and lawyers, but as a consequence of this heightened awareness of cases, more actors become involved in the legal process. A greater number of lawyers have been willing to take on cases, and different universities have been willing to support these cases. In 2008, when this research began, the UDP was the principal institution supporting more diverse human rights issues, such as transgender rights. The same cause has been taken up by the University of Chile since 2010.

Indirect Outcomes

I turn now to what McCann termed as the "indirect" outcomes of legal action. He refers to these as the "centrifugal" or "radiating" effects of legal mobilization or litigation strategies (1994). The indirect outcomes have been important in enabling a more concerted litigation agenda in pursuing legal change for trans people in Chile. For example, at the time of my fieldwork, of all cases pertaining to LGBTI rights, by far the most numerous cases were transgender petitions for legal recognition. At least one indirect outcome of which was the growth in networks of knowledge and legal support. These networks, or "associative capacity" (Gloppen, 2006), have been consolidated between claimants, movement activists, and legal representatives. This has been central to pursuing a litigious agenda in relation to trans identity rights.

As I argue elsewhere (Miles, 2011), the impediments to accessing the legal resources for members of LGBTI populations, and especially trans populations, has been severely curtailed by the dominance of stigma and deviancy discourses associated with sexual orientation and gender identity that divert from the heterosexual norm or cross the gender binary. Until recently, lawyers were fearful of the "stigma contagion" (Kirby and Corzine, 1981) if seen to represent members of these communities. In an interview, Cristina López exemplifies the difficulties in securing legal representation in the case of a trans woman found dead at a well-known chemist's apartment in Santiago in 2002:

> We didn't have a lawyer. Such is the extent of their vulnerability, that not even human rights lawyers, or at least back then, were able to take on a case of this magnitude, because there is always the issue that people want to read in between the lines, or you're a client, or your like trans, or there's something wrong with you, so, you can't be normal. So we didn't have a lawyer. One person had offered to help from the Humanist Party, but then he let us down so then we didn't have one. (Cristina, June 2009)

Her emphasis on human rights lawyers taking on such cases relates to the fact that most cases dealt with here and in my research more generally have been undertaken by human rights lawyers intent on questioning and broadening the concepts of democracy and citizenship in their gendered, ethnic, class, and sexual biases. The language of human rights has been a significant tool in advancing the rights agendas of disenfranchised groups across Latin America. In the aftermath of many brutal dictatorships experienced continent-wide, it became a unifying language of struggle (Brown, 2002; Robles, 2008) and the means through which transitional justice processes have been implemented across the region. The legal processes studied here are a product of the advances made in both the political and judicial arenas, largely in the era following the Pinochet arrest in 1998, which sparked international and national debate concerning impunity for dictators and retribution for victims of mass-perpetrated state abuse. Prior to his arrest, judicial responses to such crimes seemed a distant reality. Domestically, the result of the "Pinochet Effect" (Roht-Arriaza, 2006) saw a convergence of political and judicial will to address the past human rights abuses. Such developments have since paved the way for expanding the remit of human rights into disability rights, LGBTI rights, gender rights, migrant rights, among other issues (Richards, 2004; Robles, 2008). They are in their incipient stages of contestation, however, and challenging the corporatist, hierarchical, conservative judicial realm (Hilbink, 2007) is far from a rapid process.

In this context, therefore, claimants and movement activists have sought legal representation with lawyers intent on advancing the human rights agenda. GAHT has links with progressive lawyers in the University of Chile. Nadia, one of the lawyers there, insisted that she was prepared to "take on any case that they need me to take on" (Nadia, April 2010). The relationship between MOVILH and the UDP has a long history and has covered legal issues from across the LGBTI spectrum, though more recent cases have seen better responses from the judiciary. OTD has taken cases in conjunction with a local lawyer hired privately, and AADGE has taken its cases to the Human Rights branch of the Legal Aid Corporation. The willingness of these networks to work together has facilitated the presentation of further petitions for those trans individuals undergoing transition and seeking to acquire the legal recognition of their adopted gender.

Furthermore, as the relations become more established, lawyers' expertise in the area increased. There is a greater willingness to undertake more extensive research on the area, which has led to more innovative petitions being presented, such as those presented by the University of Chile who seek to achieve the petitions without individuals being subjected to degrading examinations at the Medical Legal Service. In maximizing the petitions presented, judges are asked increasingly to respond to the problem at hand. This serves to sensitize members of the judiciary to trans issues and to question the prevailing legal culture.

This growth in associative capacity extends to professionals from psychological and psychiatric backgrounds expanding their expertise in the area of transgenderism and to sensitizing medical doctors to treating patients with dignity. In Rancagua, Andrés has gone through the process of securing doctors to perform mastectomies or hysterectomies, or to provide the necessary hormones, and psychologists to provide reports that confirm transsexualism. This has meant that he has helped create a network of professionals that other members of OTD are able to draw on when they come to undergo transitions. In a similar manner, UDP lawyer, Mayra Feddersen and MOVILH president, Rolando Jiménez, challenged the practices of medical doctors at the Medical Legal Service requested by judges to perform physical examinations of claimants, given the extremely degrading circumstances to which the latter were subjected. Though it seems that practices did not change even following a response from the Service's director, at least the initiative brought these practices to light.

This shift from individually held resources to maximizing the collective potential by increasing networks into multiple domains, such as medical, legal, and activist has emerged in parallel to the growth and consolidation of trans (male) groups. During fieldwork it became apparent that parallel processes were occurring as each group created its own legal documents and strategies in isolation from other groups. Claimants and groups might well have benefited from combining both legal and practical strategies, such as using testimony with judicial officials. Some of these parallel processes existed in part due to the personal, political, and ideological antagonisms of those that comprised the trans movement in Chile. For example, some lawyers were not inclined to approach other lawyers or other trans organizations regarding strategy-sharing even to maximize understanding or expertise levels. These counterexamples appeared to be in the minority and from the evidence presented above, one clear indirect benefit of litigation has been an increasing capacity of building and working across networks that have contributed to the development of the LGBTI movement in Chile.

Conclusions

The legal mobilization strategies being employed by trans and LGBTI activists are beginning to challenge the extensive exclusion and marginalization faced by Chilean trans populations. This search for social justice has been forced through necessity as a means of remedying the divergence between legal and lived identities. The excessive reliance on ID cards in regulating Chilean daily life—in education, banks, employment, and so forth—has led an increasing number of trans men and women to seek gender recognition through the courts. Legal mobilization strategies are concerned with both direct and indirect outcomes, and in this instance, these differing sets of outcomes are interlinking. The direct outcomes are impacting on the indirect outcomes, with multiple repercussions at individual and collective levels.

Direct outcomes essentially equate to the favorable rulings achieved. This chapter focuses on those obtained since 2007, as they have recognized trans identities without individuals having to undergo gender reassignment surgery. Andrés Rivera's landmark case, which achieved name and gender recognition without undergoing sex change surgery, set a precedent that uncoupled gender recognition from the body. As a consequence, more individuals have attempted to present similar petitions to the courts, as awareness regarding what is legally possible for transgender populations regarding recognition increases. There has been a clear departure from the past in these new petitions. Whereas previously cases would only be presented where GRS had been performed, access is now widening to those who have not necessarily undergone this surgery. This has financial and political implications. These legal proceedings were only essentially open to those with the financial resources and personal inclination to undergo genital reassignment surgery. By reducing the financial burden and increasing the diversity of demands that can be presented, such as for name change only, or by attempting to secure both name and gender changes without recourse to GRS, the possibilities have expanded greatly for trans populations in Chile.

However, these cases are being contested in courts in a civil law system where precedents are not officially recognized, and where cases are subject to legal interpretation. The variance in outcomes of rulings have meant that a situation is emerging of differentiated citizenship, as different trans individuals are obtaining differentiated access to name and/or gender change. The gendered nature of that divide is clear, as trans men more readily access a greater level of legal entitlement in relation to recognition. Although both populations are far from embodying Chilean notions of hegemonic masculinity, trans males are able to capitalize on the patriarchal dividend (Connell, 1995, 80–82), which facilitates a greater level of insertion into Chilean society post-transition. The transgressive potential implicit in the actual jurisprudence is rarely lived out in practice, as in the case of Andrés. Most who obtain favorable rulings prefer to pass and reaffirm the gender binaries, such is the pressure from Chilean society to conform to the male/female binary.

However, indirectly these legal mobilization processes have been highly influential for trans movement consolidation, and for more concerted intersectional activism. The requirements of these legal cases calls for the participation of a number of key actors, such as lawyers and legal scholars, medical and health professionals, to a greater or lesser degree. The fact that some of these cases have been pursued in the public interest by lawyers and academics involved in public interest litigation strategies has also placed great emphasis on the role of the media. It, therefore, has played a central role in this process in both raising awareness around trans male identities principally and also in disseminating notions of what is legally possible in relation to trans recognition. Such visibility has increased trans organization membership and has prompted the subsequent expansion and diversification of the trans male groups and has reinforced a more concerted focus on litigation as a means of advancing trans rights in Chile.

This points to the role played by actors outside of the trans and LGBTI movement and the intersectional nature of activism pursued in this context. Not only have lawyers have been instrumental to ensuring that petitions can be presented with sufficient frequency and expertise, but medical professionals must also negotiate the stigma contagion to deal effectively and sensitively to these cases. As the piece intimates, overcoming such stigmatizing discourses is not a straightforward process in those areas of law and medicine where concepts of hegemonic masculinity will be more closely played out. The growth of these networks then provides a stronger platform from which to continue the legal strategies to effect yet greater outcomes. One other important outcome, which is touched upon in this chapter, is that the same legal framework is being applied to intersex cases.

Overall this discussion, which centers on the growth of transgender petitions for recognition and the resulting differentiated levels of citizenship, which are emerging as a consequence, points to the need for effective policy in this area (Universidad Diego Portales, 2009, 2010). The expanding expertise on the subject matter in legal and medical domains, more expansive jurisprudence on recognition, and examples of gender recognition laws, such as the Uruguay 2009 law, all serve as points of departure for a more considered approach to the issue in Chile. The recognition of gender identity as a protected category in the antidiscrimination bill passed in November 2011 will go some way to providing greater leverage for legal recognition for Chilean trans people.

Notes

1. All translations are the author's own. Identities have been made anonymous, with the exception of the activists who wish to be recognized.
2. Currah, Juang, and Minter note: "Since about 2005, the meaning of *transgender* has begun to settle, and the term is now generally used to refer to individuals whose gender identity or expression does not conform to the social expectations for their assigned sex at birth" (2006, xiv). In the Chilean context, trans identities are contested personally and ideologically. At the time the research was conducted, there was a lack of consensus on the use of the term in its political sense, and self-identification varied across the trans spectrum. The term "trans," however, was more acceptable as an umbrella term in the original Spanish.
3. Preoperative refers to someone that has not undergone genital reassignment surgery, though may have undergone other surgical procedures. Postoperative transsexuals have undergone genital reassignment surgery (Sharpe, 2002).
4. Mauro Cabral's collection (2009) goes some way to opening the discussion on intersexuality in the Latin American context and in the Spanish language. I use LGBT here as opposed to LGBTI because the organizations themselves do not include the "I," and the "B" also remains invisible within the movement. I include it in my general usage so as not to contribute further to the invisibility.
5. The Medical Legal Service handles all the medical procedures required by the judiciary, such as forensics, postmortems, and so forth.

6. Ley No 17.344. Published in *Diario Oficial*, Santiago, September 22, 1970.
7. Historically, neither organization has included the "I" in the acronym. There has been a shift toward using more inclusive terminology such as sexual diversity. See www.mums.cl, www.movilh.cl.
8. During fieldwork, 2008 and 2010, given the extent of the prevailing social sanctions, accessing cases was achieved largely through word of mouth. I engaged with lawyers, movement activists, friendship networks from within the LGBTI movement in order to achieve this. I acknowledge that there may have been other similar cases that I may not have been able to access as a result. Moreover, given the highly sensitive nature of the research, accessing those that were engaging in litigation in the public domain posed fewer ethical dilemmas.

References

Blofield, M. 2001. *The Politics of "Moral Sin": A Study of Abortion and Divorce in Catholic Chile Since 1990*. Santiago, Chile: Flacso.

Bornstein, K. 1995. *Gender Outlaw: On Men, Women, and the Rest of Us*. New York: Vintage.

Brown, S. 2002. "'Con discriminación y represión no hay democracia': The Lesbian and Gay Movement in Argentina." *Latin American Perspectives* 29(2): 119–138.

Cabral, M., and Viturro, P. 2006. "(Trans)Sexual Citizenship in Contemporary Argentina." In *Transgender Rights*, edited by P. Currah, R. M. Juang, and S. P. Minter, 262–273. Minneapolis: University of Minnesota Press.

Connell, R. 1995. *Masculinities*. Cambridge: Polity Press.

Currah, P., R. M. Juang, and S. P. Minter. 2006. *Transgender Rights*. Minneapolis: University of Minnesota Press.

Gloppen, S. 2006. "Courts and Social Transformation: An Analytical Framework." In *Courts and Social Transformation in New Democracies: An Institutional Voice for the Poor?*, edited by R. Gargarella, P. Domingo, and T. Roux, 35–60. Aldershot: Ashgate Publishing.

Goffman, E. 1963. *Stigma: Notes on the Management of a Spoiled Identity*. London: Penguin.

Greenberg, J. A. 2006. "The Roads Less Traveled: The Problem with Binary Sex Categories." In *Transgender Rights*, edited by P. Currah, R. M. Juang, and S. P. Minter, 51–73. Minneapolis: University of Minnesota Press.

Hilbink, L. 2007. *Judges Beyond Politics in Democracy and Dictatorship: Lessons From Chile*. Cambridge: Cambridge University Press.

Htun, M. 2003. *Sex and the State: Abortion, Divorce, and the Family under Latin American Dictatorships and Democracies.* New York: Cambridge University Press.

Kirby, R., and Corzine, J. 1981. "The Contagion of Stigma." *Qualitative Sociology* 4(1): 3–20.

McCann, M. W. 2006. "Introduction." In *Law and Social Movements*, edited by Michael M. W., xi–xxvi. Aldershot: Ashgate.

———. 1994. *Rights at Work: Pay Equity Reform and the Politics of Legal Mobilization.* Chicago: University of Chicago Press.

Miles, P. Forthcoming. "Brokering Sexual Orientation and Gender Identity: Chilean Lawyers and Public Interest Litigation Strategies." *Bulletin of Latin American Research.*

———. 2011. "Lawyers, Legal Mobilisation and LGBTI Populations: Explorations in Chile." PhD Thesis, Cardiff University.

———. 2004. "Searching for Citizenship the Legal Way: Gay Communities in Argentina and Chile." Masters diss., Institute of Latin American Studies, University of London.

Richards, P. 2004. *Pobladoras, Indígenas and the State: Conflicts Over Women's Rights in Chile.* New Jersey: Rutgers University Press.

Robles, V. H. 2008. *Bandera Hueca: La Historia Del Movimiento Homosexual de Chile.* Santiago: Editorial Arcis/Editorial Cuarto Propio.

Roen, K. 2002. "'Either/Or' and 'Both/Neither': Discursive Tensions in Transgender Politics." *Signs* 27(2): 501–522.

Roht-Arriaza, N. 2006. *The Pinochet Effect: Transnational Justice in the Age of Human Rights.* Philadelphia: University of Pennsylvania Press.

Rubington, E., and M. S. Weinberg, eds. 1996. *Deviance: The Interactionist Perspective. Sixth Edition.* Boston: Allyn and Bacon.

Sarat A., and S. Scheingold. 1998. *Cause Lawyering: Political Commitments and Professional Responsibilities.* New York: Oxford University Press.

Sharpe, A. 2002. *Transgender Jurisprudence: Dysphoric Bodies of Law.* London: Cavendish Publishing.

Stychin, C. F. 1998. *A Nation By Rights: National Cultures, Sexual Identity Politics, and the Discourse of Rights.* Philadelphia, PA: Temple University Press.

Universidad Diego Portales. 2010. *Informe Anual Sobre Derechos Humanos en Chile 2010.* Santiago: Ediciones Universidad Diego Portales.

———. 2009. *Informe Anual Sobre Derechos Humanos en Chile 2009.* Santiago: Ediciones Universidad Diego Portales.

Vaggione, J. M. 2008. "Las Familias Mas Alla de la Heteronormatividad." In *La Mirada de los Jueces: Sexualidades diversas en la jurisprudencia latinoamericana. Tomo 2*, edited by C. Motta and M. Sáez, 13–87. Bogotá: Siglo del Hombre Editores, American University College of Law, Center for Reproductive Rights.

Zemans, F. 1983. "Legal Mobilization: The Neglected Role of Law in the Political System." *American Political Science Review* 77(3): 690–703.

4

International Adoption as Humanitarian Aid: The Discursive and Material Production of the "Social Orphan" in Haitian Disaster Relief

Kate Livingston

Scientific analyses of "natural" disasters consider the interplay of multiple relationships between ever-evolving processes: meteorological conditions, geological forces, population density, infrastructure, institutional preparedness, individual and community responses, among other factors. In order to understand natural disasters and their widespread impact, scholars in physical and social sciences utilize multiple levels of analysis to consider the ways in which natural and social landscapes are coconstructed in relation to each other. While disaster events such as earthquakes, floods, and hurricanes certainly shape the future of these landscapes, political and cultural histories also influence the way these events are experienced by individuals and communities. Intersectionality has thus emerged as an important methodological tool for exploring the social, political, and economic dimensions of these events. A critical theory concerned with illuminating the operation and production of power, intersectionality considers how identity categories are constituted through cultural discourse, institutional processes, and political structures in ways that produce inequality, privilege, and marginalization. Within an intersectional framework, identity categories are understood as constructs imbedded with discursive and material histories that reflect relationships among people and social institutions. As Wendy Smooth explains in this volume, feminist scholarship across a wide range of disciplines has long emphasized the role of intersectionality in challenging essentialized understandings of individual experience and monolithic constructions of group identity. However, Smooth argues, in chapter 1, that new uses of intersectionality in the fields of political science and policy analysis can build on these foundations to "gain greater balance between the individual and structural levels of analysis" (25). Recent studies of Hurricane Katrina in the social sciences serve as an example of new research that illustrates the particular contributions of policy studies to intersectionality scholarship. Scholars have advanced the intersectional paradigm as a way to examine how preexisting hierarchies of race, class, gender, ability, age, and sexuality produced disparate vulnerabilities and unequal outcomes for Gulf Coast communities affected by the storm (Chester and Squires, 2006; Weber and Masias, 2012). Notably, these works incorporate a structural analysis of post-Katrina disaster relief, exploring, as Smooth suggests in chapter 1, "how institutions and political structures give meaning to identities and structure the relationships between social identity groups" (14). Weber and Mesias's intersectional research on the experiences of post-Katrina recovery workers explores how the responses of government, nonprofit, and business institutions shaped the trajectory of recovery efforts along the Mississippi coast. Institutional policies and practices impacted health outcomes for recovery workers themselves, yet these volunteers also played a key role in proliferating recovery programs that ultimately produced raced, classed, and gendered health outcomes for Mississippi Gulf communities. Intersectionality is used as a framework to examine the ways in which the experiences of recovery workers and their roles in Gulf communities were constituted by government, nonprofit, and corporate responses that drew from and exacerbated preexisting hierarchies of power.

This chapter contributes to the growing body of disaster relief studies that uses intersectionality to explore the linkages between micro-level experience and institutional processes. In this project, I use an intersectional lens to examine how the push for expedited international adoption as a form of humanitarian aid functions at the discursive and material levels to construct the "social orphan" as a subject of disaster relief intervention. Whereas the popular definition of "orphan" once referred to children who had no living relatives, the category of social orphan is now defined by nongovernmental organizations (NGOs) as homeless, displaced, impoverished, and/or parentless (but not necessarily relative-less) children. Using the 2010 earthquake in Haiti as a case study, I argue that the Haitian social orphan is a political category underwritten by media representations of the Haitian body/family/country as barbaric and unsafe while contrasting Western bodies/families/countries as normative, modern, and stable. Drawing from Melissa Wright's discussion of "Third World" women and the role of myth in supporting structural gender inequalities, I suggest that the discursive construction of the Haitian social orphan facilitates the material transfer of Haitian children into a "waiting" global adoption economy. Through textual and discursive analysis of news media coverage of Haitian children in the months following the earthquake, I outline the popular push for expedited international adoption as a form of disaster "relief." I then analyze two constitutive dimensions of the social orphan category using an intersectional lens: first, the myth that Haitian youth are representative of a "global crisis in care" and second, the assertion that Haitian youth are "at risk" if they remain in their homeland. By bridging discursive and structural analysis, my goal is to demonstrate how this political category is produced by raced, classed, and gendered processes that engender and maintain hierarchical relationships among groups. Intersectionality serves as a framework for understanding how these power differentials function at the micro level to impact the experiences of individuals and groups at the same time as they operate at the macro and global levels to structure relationships between nations.

Popular Demands and Political Responses: Adoption As Disaster Relief

As the world braced for the details of the devastation caused by the massive 7.0 earthquake that shook Haiti on January 12, 2010, the international community mobilized to provide humanitarian aid to the millions of displaced citizens in and around the nation's capital of Port-au-Prince. While world leaders, NGOs, and private citizens worldwide pledged their support, the logistical challenge of implementing recovery efforts in Haiti became immediately apparent. Food and water shortages, lack of infrastructure, and the effects of a crippled national government quickly overwhelmed multilateral medical and humanitarian relief efforts. In the months that followed, Port-au-Prince's decimated urban infrastructure initially yielded a reported 230,000 casualties, and was projected to be "the most destructive natural disaster in modern times" (Lacey, "Quake," 2010).[1] Through images and narratives of Haitian survivors, the international news media aided relief efforts by raising both public awareness of the devastation and publicizing ways that the public could contribute to the effort. While news coverage of the earthquake fostered compassionate outreach via monetary and in-kind donations, these visual and narrative mediations almost immediately catalyzed a push toward a controversial approach to outreach: international adoption.

Central to the initial coverage of international adoption in Haiti were prospective adoptive parents who were already in the process of adopting children from Haiti. Within a week of the earthquake, US media began to cover story after story of prospective adoptive parents frantic to find out if "their" Haitian child had survived the earthquake.[2] As stories publicized the plight of both the *waiting* Haitian orphan and the uncertainty faced by *waiting* adoptive parents in the United States, demands for the expedited adoption of Haitian children into the United States reached a fever pitch.[3] The US Department of State and the Department of Homeland Security announced on January 18 that humanitarian parole would be extended to approximately 1,000 Haitian orphans whose adoptions were legally pending prior to the earthquake (Thomas, 2010). That same day, 53 Haitian orphans under humanitarian parole were personally accompanied by Pennsylvania governor Ed Rendell on a flight to Pittsburgh. A second major flight left Haiti for Florida three days later. Countries such as France and the Netherlands soon followed suit, expediting their international adoption processes and exporting Haitian orphans to join *waiting* adoptive families in Europe (Jordan, 2010; McKensei, 2010; Reid, 2010).

While news of international humanitarian parole implied that some Haitian orphans would be united with their *waiting* parents in the United States, questions remained about the fate of the children that remained in and around Haiti's crippled capital. Many groups argued that the devastation in Port-au-Prince might make it impossible to obtain the documentation necessary to prove that an adoption had been pending prior to the earthquake. At the request of their constituents, a bipartisan coalition of 34 senators urged Secretary of State Hillary Rodham Clinton to continue to move forward with attempts to locate pending Haitian adoptees and to allow for alternative eligibility procedures in the event of lost or destroyed adoption documentation (Menendez, 2010). News reports also cautioned that unaccompanied minors faced the threat of human trafficking into sexual slavery, black market adoption, and domestic servitude[4], leading many to argue that the international community should intensify efforts to bring Haitian "orphans" into some measure of protective custody.[5] As news coverage increasingly began to focus on the uncertain fate of the children remaining in Haiti, the US State Department, adoption facilitators, and charitable organizations were inundated with inquiries from prospective adoptive parents seeking to adopt Haitian children (Bazar and Kock, 2010). International organizations such as the United Nation's Children's Fund (UNICEF) moved quickly to oppose new adoptions on the grounds that family preservation should be the top priority of humanitarian efforts and that facilitating international adoptions in a time of crisis would expose children to an even greater risk for trafficking and exploitation (McKenzie, 2010).

The debate over international adoption as a form of humanitarian aid intensified when 10 Baptist missionaries from Boise, Idaho, were jailed by Haitian authorities for attempting to extricate 33 orphans to the Dominican Republic just three days after the Haitian government issued a moratorium on international adoptions (Kalson, 2010). The group, led by Laura Silsby, was charged with kidnapping for failing to have appropriate documentation for the children and further investigation revealed that the majority of children had living parents who were promised by Silsby that their children would be moved to safety ("Parents," 2010). However, Silsby's website stated that children rescued by her organization would "be eligible for adoption through agencies in the United States" (Lacey, "Abduction," 2010). The arrest of the missionaries thus intensified an already heated public debate over whether international adoption served the needs of the Haitian community, or simply catered to the desires of Western nations.

SOCIAL ORPHANS AND THE GLOBAL CRISIS IN CARE

News stories about Haiti's vulnerable children repeatedly cited UNICEF figures that over 380,000 orphans existed in Haiti prior to the earthquake. As the reported death toll rose to over 200,000 in the months after the quake, the implication was that Haiti's orphan population would swell exponentially. However, UNICEF's definition of social orphan encompasses children who have lost one or more parents (to desertion or death), including those that live with extended relatives (UNICEF, 2010). UNICEF acknowledges that this expanded definition (which implies 132 million orphans worldwide) may influence public policy in terms of humanitarian relief, but has cautioned the international community not to make the uncritical assumption that all persons designated orphans within its definition need new families.[6] While some reports on the Haitian disaster specified that approximately half of Haiti's reported 380,000 orphans had one living parent, others continued to proliferate the larger number without qualification (McCray, 2010; Jordan, 2010).

Coupled with the compelling images of orphans proliferated by the news media, these statistics undoubtedly created for the viewing public a crisis in care of global proportions. Indeed, as news reports proliferated, a growing concern was that Haiti's orphan population would be destined to languish in public institutions or on the streets, offending American middle-class notions of a stable childhood ("Arrests," 2010). This construction falls squarely within popular narratives of international adoption that construct the orphan as a very young, readily adoptable child threatened with institutionalization or homelessness. The assumption that millions of otherwise adoptable children might languishing in institutions due to a global crisis in care has both fueled and justified American interest in international adoption. International adoption has increased exponentially since the mid-1990s—from 22,200 in 1995 to a record of 45,000 in 2004; US adoptions consistently account for approximately half of all international adoptions each year (Graff, 2008).

However, the majority of orphans are not, in fact, very young children threatened with institutionalization. Officials from UNICEF have refuted the notion that there are large numbers of healthy infants in need of families through international adoption (Graff, 2008). In contrast, only 10 percent of the 132 million children designated orphans by the UNICEF definition have lost both parents, and most live with extended relatives. Further, UNICEF estimates that 95 percent of orphans are older than five, challenging the popular construction of the orphan as "the infant threatened with institutionalization."[7] Critics of international adoption as "humanitarian aid" have thus argued that international adoption is driven by prospective adoptive parents' demand for healthy infants, rather than the overwhelming supply-side need implied by the traditional meaning of the category "orphan."

Social Orphans "At Risk"

Just as the category of social orphan positions international adoption as a solution to a presumed global crisis in care, it similarly positions adoption as a way to "protect" children from certain forms of risk. The notion that adoption mitigates risk has a long history in the United States, as evidenced in both international and domestic adoption initiatives. Two well-documented examples, Operation Babylift and Operation Pedro Pan, were constructed in the US media as relocation efforts designed to mitigate children's risk in the face of national crisis. At the close of the Vietnam War in 1975, President Gerald Ford authorized the mass evacuation of approximately 3,000 Vietnamese children into the United States for adoption by US citizens. While there was an outpouring of interest by American families in these children, critics argued that this effort, known as Operation Babylift, amounted to no more than a publicity stunt designed to mitigate the criticisms of the Vietnam War. Later investigation revealed that the children had not been legally vetted as eligible for adoption. Indeed, many of them were not orphans (Bergquist, 2009). In Operation Pedro Pan, over 14,000 children were surreptitiously evacuated from Cuba to Miami from 1973 to 1980. A joint project between the Catholic Welfare Bureau and the US government, Operation Pedro Pan sought to mitigate the threat of communist indoctrination of Cuban youth under Fidel Castro. Cuban youth were placed in foster homes and orphanages throughout the United States. While some children were reunited with their Cuban parents within months, other parents never made it out of Cuba and were separated from their children for decades (Yanez, 2009). While these efforts demonstrate the ways in which American political institutions advance adoption as a solution for risk, this phenomenon is certainly neither limited to state actors nor is it limited to US involvement. In the 2007 case known as Zoe's Ark, an unauthorized French NGO attempted to extract 103 orphans out of wartorn Darfur for export to waiting families in France and Denmark. The group was arrested for kidnapping, but maintained they were simply fulfilling a moral imperative to rescue children from a crisis situation. Later investigation revealed that the children were not orphans, rather had been obtained from their families under false pretenses (Bergquist, 2009).

US approaches to domestic adoption echo a similar commitment to resolving risk through the adoption of children into "safer" communities. Formal legal domestic adoption as it exists today in the United States is a relatively recent phenomenon. Prior to the first state domestic adoption law in 1851, adoption existed in various informal and nonstandardized incarnations (Cahn, 2004). Historian E. Wayne Carp (1998) argues that in the mid-nineteenth century, increased immigration and industrialization in the United States resulted in social and economic changes that brought new national attention to the issue of child welfare. Growing poverty across the country contributed to a change in national sentiment that saw children's health and development as matters of public welfare and national stability, ushering in new era of legal and social welfare reform (Carp, 1998). Prior to 1850, typical approaches to child welfare involved the placement of needy children into almshouses that served to isolate a wide range of public "scourges" from society. Needy children, the elderly, mentally ill, and medically fragile persons of all ages were housed together in neglected public institutions, a practice later condemned by mid-century social reformers as barbaric, unsafe, and contributing to the degeneracy of minors (Gordon, 2001).

The first alternatives that emerged in the United States were institutions that exclusively served orphans. The period between 1800 and 1850 saw an increase of 164 orphanages in the United States, followed by an additional 75 between 1850 and 1870

(Carp, 1998). During the mid-1800s, a rapid influx of children into such institutions threatened the financial and logistical capacities of many urban centers. Historian Linda Gordon argues that many children served by orphan asylums were actually children of single mothers who turned to institutions as a foster care option in the face of poverty. While many mothers initially saw asylums as temporary relief, often they were unable to pull themselves out of poverty and left their children as permanent institutional wards (Gordon, 2001). In addition, though many children were orphaned or abandoned, new public "child-saving" discourses greatly contributed to the influx of children into the burgeoning child welfare system.

The ideological position of American social reformers such as Charles Loring Brace often conflated the tragic effects of urban poverty with those of parental neglect. Founder of New York's Children's Aid Society (est. 1853), Brace advanced a construction of child welfare steeped in the Protestant work ethic (Carp, 1998). He argued that street children were victims of not only poverty, but also of an unstructured and unstable lifestyle caused primarily by a lack of proper parenting. Such children could be reformed by bringing them into a child welfare system that would give them education, religious training, and a chance for a "normal" family life. Children's Aid Society agents routinely canvassed New York slums, seizing poor children under the auspices of "child-saving"—regardless of whether or not the children were actually orphans. Brace championed a new child welfare model that sought to both transform poor children into productive, moral citizens and alleviate the financial and logistical strain caused by the increased number of children being brought into institutional care (Gordon, 2001). The Children's Aid Society instituted a national "orphan train" that shipped thousands of urban children from the East to Protestant foster homes in the West. By 1910, Brace's orphan train had "placed out" over 110,000 children since it began in 1854 (Gordon, 2001).

Linda Gordon (2001) notes that the policies and practices of the Children's Aid Society were racist and classist in their assumptions of what constituted "proper upbringing." An Ivy-League-educated Protestant minister, Brace represented the interests of New York's Protestant elite, while the children he sought to "save" were largely from the city's growing Catholic immigrant population. New York's Catholic communities saw Brace's efforts as rooted in religious and ethnic bias, a genocidal attempt to indoctrinate working-class Catholic youth with the values of the Protestant elite. In response, Catholic religious and charitable institutions rapidly developed their own child welfare programs, including their own orphan train operations.

Similar mediations of adoption and risk can be found in American news stories after the Haitian earthquake about the particular vulnerabilities of children in and around the fault zone. Frequently reported figures estimated that approximately 2,000 Haitian children were trafficked each year into sexual slavery, black market adoption, and domestic servitude *before* the earthquake (Block and Siegel, 2010). Fears that unaccompanied children would be swept into a preexisting informal human economy alarmed an international public desperate to "rescue" these vulnerable youth. While the risk of human trafficking dominated public discourse on the risks faced by Haitian children, these narratives were bolstered by other manifestations of risk. Generalized international concern about trafficking was heightened by reports of looting. Gangs of thieves reportedly threatened to undermine orphan relief efforts by stealing supplies destined for orphanages (LaFranchi, 2010). Many reports pointed to the inability of Haitian families to care for their own children, an issue publicized by the revelation that many of the children involved in the Baptist missionary kidnapping case were handed over to the missionaries by desperate parents (LaFranchi, 2010). Still other reports advanced the notion of voluntary neglect by Haitian families. An adoption facilitator in Haiti, a proponent of international adoption, reported that children in her orphanage were initially found discarded among trash, while another child was reported disabled as a result of her birth mothers' failed abortion attempt (LaFranchi, 2010). Such coverage contrasted with reports of the white, Western families with "Haiti in their hearts," "eager to embrace" Haitian orphans and bring them into the safety of their "loving homes" (McCray, 2010; Bazar and Kock, 2010; "Arrests," 2010). Like Brace's orphan train operations, these mediations are embedded with racialized, gendered, and classed understandings of child-rearing and safety that work to categorize children with living relatives as orphans.

Constructing the Social Orphan Through Discursive Processes and Institutional Practices

Melissa Wright's (2006) work on the role of myth in maintaining structural inequalities provides a model for understanding how the category of social orphan is enabled through both discursive and institutional processes. Wright argues that a global "myth of the disposable Third World woman" works as a discursive construction that underwrites capitalist exploitation of women's labor (Wright, 2006, 1). This discursive construction is materially instructive in normalizing certain expectations for the treatment of women workers within global capitalism, despite the fact that the myth is a fictional composite character. For example, although women's labor in global factories is often highly skilled, the myth posits workers as unskilled and interchangeable. Wright suggests that the myth that workers have a natural labor life cycle affirms existing hierarchical relations of power wherein women workers are treated as disposable (2006). Thus, the myth is a discursive construction that supports classed and gendered practices to produce material inequalities. I argue that the construction of the social orphan as a political category in Haitian disaster relief discourses supports hierarchical institutional practices in much the same way as Wright's myth of the disposable woman. As a political category, the social orphan comes into view as the subject of policy intervention through political and social processes engaged by state structures, NGOs, and public discourse (Parr, 2009). Intersectional analysis enables us to trace these discursive and structural linkages to examine how state and NGOs draw from constructions of a global crisis in care and at-risk children to help mobilize the social orphan category.

Even as NGOs such as UNICEF attempted to qualify the terms of the category as inclusive of children with living parents, visual and narrative representations of social orphans continued to reinforce the myth that untold numbers of children would be consigned to a risky life of abandonment without US intervention. As seen in the prioritizing of international adoption out of Haiti by the US Department of State, political structures and institutions also engaged with these representations and mobilized relief efforts in response. Both before and after the earthquake, Haiti was represented as unable to secure the safety and stability of its children. The category of Haitian social orphan is thus reinforced by and embedded within a larger discourse on Haitian "otherness"—wherein public anxiety about Haitian children's vulnerability to human trafficking positions adult Haitian survivors as the immoral, deviant other within hegemonic discourses of Western colonial morality (Parr, 2009, 114). Public discourses on "risk" implicitly and explicitly construct Haitians as the uncivilized other "within middle-class standards of morality" (Parr, 2009, 114). News coverage characterizes the white, Western, middle-class mother/family/country as selfless, generous, and stable, while positing Haitian mothers/families/country as desperate, opportunistic, and negligent (if not murderous). Even when the integrity of the Western-as-normative construction is called into question, public discourse still leaves room for the possibility that deviation from the norm is but an aberration—a misunderstanding. For example, the ten Baptist missionaries were roundly chastised by the media; furor erupted when Laura Silsby was discovered to have a potential profit motive (she was bankrupt) and that her legal representation in Haiti was wanted by El Salvadorian authorities on charges of child sex trafficking (Lacey and Urbina, 2010). However, the news media still considered the possibility that the missionaries had simply "forgot(ten) about some requites" and that "their intentions were always to help" (Jordan and Gaulthier-Villars, 2010). Similarly, when immigration reviews revealed that many of the *orphans* on Pennsylvania governor Ed Rendell's highly publicized humanitarian parolee exodus were not actually orphans, Rendell's publicist justified the oversight as occurring within a "fog of war situation" and claimed that government officials assumed they were all orphans (Roche, 2010).

This is particularly interesting when viewed in light of the discourse on Haitian child trafficking and the practice of child domestic servitude. In addition to fears of child sexual slavery, news media focused on the plight of Haitian *restaveks*—children sold or placed into families as indentured domestic servants. While US officials designate the practice as child slavery, others argue that within the Haitian community the practice is sometimes understood as an informal foster care network. While the risk of abuse and sexual exploitation is documented, the practice is defended by some Haitians who see it as a viable option for children who would otherwise have no way to survive (Kay, 2007). The power to designate this practice as child slavery and to mitigate the actions of Americans as aberrations and mistakes reveals the extent to which the construction of *risk* works to legitimize Western colonial morality. Aside from the total foreclosure of the possibility that the practice could constitute a local structure of care, the designation of "child slavery" obscures the extent to which Americans themselves are implicated in the practice. The distinction made within the discourse between "child trafficker" and "hapless well-intentioned humanitarian" positions Haitian women/families/country as the deviant "other," while masking the inequalities produced by Western racism and neoliberalism that frame the economic conditions of Haitians that turn to *restavek* practices.

The category of social orphan signals what Adrian Parr theorizes in sustainability discourse as "the distinction between waste, recycling and downcycling...that determines whether a subject will count within the norms of a given society" (Parr, 2009, 102). If Haiti was considered dangerous and unable to secure the safety of its children, social orphans are constructed as "recyclable" children of "disposable Third World" Haitian women within disaster relief discourse. This distinction is made, in part, because of the high surplus value of Haitian children in preexisting international adoption economies, driven almost entirely by Western demand for adoptable infants. Inscribed within the terms of the category, the social orphan is represented as a symptom of a larger global crisis in care, under which the international community mobilizes to locate more children able to be "recycled" from their otherwise "disposable" women/families/countries of origin (Butler, 1993, 3). This is a discursive and institutional process that produces children for adoption as an effect of defining the social orphan. That is, racialized, classed, and gendered understandings of safe children and families are institutionalized through the political processes that give meaning to the term social orphan. This identity category is mobilized by states and NGOs through humanitarian disaster relief programs, bringing children into the domain of international adoption economies where they are removed, in the name of the social orphan, from families and countries of origin. Thus, this discourse has material effects in that it signifies Haitian children's availability for adoption by US citizens and, ironically, facilitates their trafficking as commodities within international adoption economies—albeit within a racialized child-saving moral framework.

The material, economic implications of this global discursive construction are most clearly illustrated in the investigative reporting of E. J. Graff (2008) on the case of Guatemala, the second most popular provider of adopted children into the United States from 2006 to 2007. In response to allegations of child trafficking in Guatemala, UNICEF (in conjunction with the Guatemalan government) conducted a survey of Guatemalan orphanages in 2007 that estimated the population of children within such institutions at 5,600. Only 1,000 of the population were age 3 or under, with approximately 400 children under a year old. Astonishingly, UNICEF found that over 270 Guatemalan babies (under 12 months) were being adopted into the United States *each month*. According to published reports, 1 out of 110 Guatemalan babies were exported to the United States in 2006. The high market value of healthy babies propelled an international adoption economy that was rooted in corruption, kidnapping, and coercion. The Hague Conference on Private International Law found that adoption facilitators in Guatemala could earn double the average local yearly wage for procuring just one infant for export to the United States. The situation in Guatemala is not isolated; similar findings have been reported in other countries, including Cambodia, Vietnam, and Ethiopia, which is the second-ranked child exporter to the United States in 2009 (Graff, 2008).

Intersectional analysis is useful in illuminating the ways in which political categories are constructed through discourse to privilege certain bodies, nations, groups over others—and how political institutions develop and operationalize those categories through policy responses. Embedded with raced, classed, and gendered hierarchies of power, the category of social orphan promotes institutional and state responses that prioritize "rescue" over public policies designed to strengthen internal capacities (Rai, 2002). Disaster narratives in visual and news media explored the extent to which Haiti was an "uninhabitable" space for children both *before* and *after* the earthquake. These narratives marginalize the caretaking efforts of Haiti at the local and national levels and mobilize the value-laden meanings embedded within in the social orphan identification. As government and institutional responses engage with these meanings in the constructions of disaster relief policies, international adoption emerges as an institutional policy response that promotes and maintains systems of inequality.

Notes

1. In the years following the earthquake, Haitian death toll numbers have been disputed by social science researchers as highly inflated. This overinflation supports the role of media, narrative, and myth in constructing the "social orphan" through discourses of risk. For examples of this critique see Kolbe and Hudson et al. "Mortality, Crime and Access to Basic Needs before and after the Haiti Earthquake: A Random Survey of Port-Au-Prince Households" (2010).
2. ABC's popular news magazine show *Nightline* featured the story of a white Iowa couple desperate to hear any word about Haitian girl who they were in the process of adopting. Fewer than a week after the airing of the initial episode, ABC's popular morning show *Good Morning America* reported from Haiti that they had found the young girl, safe but shaken, in her orphanage. See Emily Bazar and Wendy Kock (2010) and Hinman (2010).
3. Michelle T. Bond, US deputy assistant secretary for Overseas Citizens Services, assured prospective adoptive parents in a written interview that the US Department of State considered the interests of prospective adoptive parents with pending adoptions to be among the department's top priorities. See Interview with Michelle T. Bond (2010).
4. Melissa Block and Robert Siegel, "Examining Adoptions from Haiti," interview with Juan Forero, *All Things Considered*, NPR News, February 2, 2010.
5. *London Times* columnist Melanie Reid argued that in the midst of crisis, a moral imperative to rescue orphaned children from immediate danger might override "the sophisticated post-colonial option" of family preservation. Elizabeth Bartholet, Harvard legal scholar and well-known proponent of international adoption, argued that "Haitian authorities should be trying to help a lot of kids get out [of the country]—both the kids in the process of adoption and other that appear not to have parents or relatives able to take care of them". See "Arrests Intensify Haiti Adoption Debate" (2010); Reid, (2010); Fletcher (2010).
6. Definition of Orphan on UNICEF.org http://www.unicef.org/media/media_45279.html (accessed March 1, 2010).
7. This overstatement of the supply of children available for adoption is further illustrated by the fact that prospective adoptive parents face long waiting lists for domestic and international placements. Even in China, where restrictive population control policies have produced large numbers of girls available for adoption, the demand for healthy infants far exceeds the available supply. According to critics,

the reality of the "crisis in care" is that most children in desperate need of humanitarian assistance are older children, the disabled, and those with medical issues, demographics decidedly not sought out by prospective adoptive parents. See E. J. Graff's "The Lie We Love," *Foreign Policy*, November 1, 2008.

References

"Arrests Intensify Haiti Adoption Debate." 2010. *NBCNEWS.com*, February 1. http://www.today.com/id/35188317/ns/today-today_news/t/arrests-intensify-haiti-adoption-debate/#.URbZsKVsilY (accessed on March 5, 2010).

Bazar, Emily, and Wendy Kock. 2010. "Americans Eager to Embrace Haitian Orphans." *USA Today*, January 20. http://usatoday30.usatoday.com/news/nation/2010-01-19-haiti-orphans-americans_N.htm (accessed on March 7, 2010).

Bergquist, Kathleen Ja Sook. 2009. "Operation Babylift or Babyabduction?: Implications of the Hague Convention on the Humanitarian Evacuation and 'Rescue' of Children." *International Journal of Social Work* 52(5): 622–623.

Block, Melissa, and Robert Siegel (Interviewer) and J. Forero (Interviewee). 2010, February 2. "Examining Adoptions from Haiti." *All Things Considered* (Interview transcript), February 2. Washington, DC: NPR.

Bond, Michelle T. 2010. "Interview on the Situation in Haiti and the Adoption of Haitian Children." Interview with Michelle T. Bond, www.state.gov, January 19. Online (accessed on March 1, 2010).

Butler, Judith. 1993. *Bodies That Matter.* New York: Routledge.

Cahn, Naomi, ed. 2004. *Families by Law.* New York: NYU Press.

Carp, E. Wayne. 1998. *Family Matters: Secrecy and Disclosure in the History of Adoption.* Cambridge: Harvard University Press.

Fletcher, Martin. 2010. "Aid Agencies in Haiti Race to Save 'Orphans' from Child Traffickers." *The London Times*, January 26. http://www.thetimes.co.uk/tto/news/world/americas/article2002022.ece (accessed on March 5, 2010).

Gordon, Linda. 2001. *The Great Arizona Orphan Abduction.* Cambridge, MA: Harvard University Press.

Graff, E. J. 2008. "The Lie We Love." *Foreign Policy*, November 1. http://www.foreignpolicy.com/articles/2008/10/15/the_lie_we_love (accessed on January 27, 2010).

Hartman, Chester W., and Gregory D. Squires. 2006. *There Is No Such Thing as a Natural Disaster: Race, Class and Hurricane Katrina.* New York: Routledge.

Hinman, Katie. 2010. "Iowa Couple Travels to Haiti to Bring Home Adopted Daughter." *ABC Nightline*, January 19. http://abcnews.go.com

/Nightline/HaitiEarthquake/haitis-orphans-us-couple-haiti-bring-home-adopted/story?id=9595752 (accessed on February 22, 2010).
Jordan, Miriam. 2010. "Haiti: U.S. Speeds Up Adoption Process, and Orphans Arrive." *The Wall Street Journal*, January 24. http://online.wsj.com/article/SB10001424052748703415804575023553542296776.html (accessed on February 22, 2010).
Jordan, Miriam, and David Gaulthier-Villars. 2010. "Haiti Allows Adoptions: Queries Missionaries." *The Wall Street Journal*, February 2. http://online.wsj.com/article/SB10001424052748703422904575039761361995340.html (accessed on March 1, 2010).
Kalson, Sally. 2010. "Experts: Out of Country Adoptions Are A Last Resort." *Pittsburgh Post-Gazette*, January 27. http://www.post-gazette.com/stories/news/world/experts-out-of-country-adoptions-are-a-last-resort-230633/?print=1 (accessed on March 1, 2010).
Kay, Jennifer. "Trafficking Case Exposes Child Servitude." 2007. *FoxNews.com*, October 17. http://www.foxnews.com/printer_friendly_wires/2007Oct17/0,4675,HaitianSlave,00.html (accessed on October 18, 2007).
Kolbe, Athena R., and Royce Hudson et al. 2010. "Mortality, Crime and Access to Basic Needs before and after the Earthquake: A Random Survey of Port-Au-Prince Households." *Medicine, Conflict and Survival* (26)4: 281–297.
Lacey, Marc. 2010. "Estimates of Quake Damage in Haiti Increase by Billions." *The New York Times*, February 16. http://www.nytimes.com/2010/02/17/world/americas/17haiti.html (accessed on March 1, 2010).
Lacey, Marc. 2010. "Haiti Charges Americans with Child Abduction." *The New York Times*, February 4. http://www.nytimes.com/2010/02/05/world/americas/05orphans.html?pagewanted=all (accessed on March 1, 2010).
Lacey, Marc, and Ian Urbina. 2010. "Adviser to Jailed Americans in Haiti Is Accused of Trafficking." *The New York Times*, February 15. http://www.nytimes.com/2010/02/16/world/americas/16haiti.html?_r=0 (accessed on March 1, 2010).
LaFranchi, Howard. 2010. "Haiti Earthquake Reignites Debate Over Fast-Tracking Adoptions." *Christian Science Monitor*, January 25. http://www.csmonitor.com/World/Americas/2010/0125/Haiti-earthquake-reignites-debate-over-fast-tracking-adoptions (accessed on March 5, 2010).
Llana, Sara Miller. 2010. "US Missionaries: Lessons from Haiti Adoption or 'Child Kidnapping' Case." *Christian Science Monitor*, February 18. http://www.csmonitor.com/World/2010/0218/US-missionaries-Lessons-from-Haiti-adoption-or-child-kidnapping-case (accessed on March 5, 2010).

McKenzie, A. D. 2010. "Adoption Not the Best Choice for Quake Orphans." *Inter Press Service News Agency,* January 23. http://www.ipsnews.net/2010/01/haiti-adoption-not-the-best-choice-for-quake-orphans/ (accessed on February 22, 2010).

Menendez, Robert. 2010. "Haiti Adoptions: Menendez joined by Bipartisan Group of 33 Senate Colleagues in Asking Feds to Take Additional Steps to Expedite Orphan Adoptions." January 22. http://www.menendez.senate.gov/newsroom/press/haiti-adoptions-menendez-joined-by-bipartisan-group-of-33-senate-colleagues-in-asking-f eds-to-take-additional-steps-to-expedite-orphan-adoptions (accessed on March 3, 2010).

"Parents: All Haitian Orphans had Relatives." 2010. *NBCNEWS.com,* February 21. http://www.nbcnews.com/id/35507224/ns/world_news-haiti/t/parents-all-haitian-orphans-had-relatives/#.URbunaVsilY (accessed on March 5, 2010).

Parr, Adrian. 2009. *Hijacking Sustainability.* Cambridge: MIT Press.

Rai, Shirin. 2006. *Gender and the Political Economy of Development.* Cambridge: Polity Press.

Reid, Melanie. 2010. "The Paperwork Can Wait: Everybody Wins With Adoption." *The London Times,* January 21. http://www.thetimes.co.uk/tto/opinion/columnists/melaniereid/article1891892.ece (accessed on February 22, 2010).

Roche, Walter F. Jr. 2010. "Haitian Children in Legal Quagmire." *Pittsburgh Tribune Review,* February 25. EBSCO (March 5, 2010).

Thomas, Jeffery. 2010, January 19. "Haitians Orphans in Adoption Process Allowed to Enter U.S.," press release on www.America.gov. (accessed on February 15, 2010).

UNICEF Press Center. 2010. "Orphans." http://www.unicef.org/media/media_45279.html (accessed on February 10, 2010).

Weber, Lynn, and Deanne K. Hilfinger Messias. 2012. "Mississippi Front-Line Recovery Work after Hurricane Katrina: An Analysis of the Intersections of Gender, Race and Class in Advocacy, Power Relations and Health." *Social Science and Medicine* (74): 1833–1841.

Wright, Melissa. 2006. *Disposable Women and Other Myths.* New York: Routledge.

Yanez, Luis. 2009. "Pedro Pan Was Born of Fear, Human Instinct to Protect Children." *Miami Herald,* May 16.

5

Gendered Subjectivity and Intersectional Political Agency in Transnational Space: The Case of Turkish and Kurdish Women's NGO Activists

Anil Al-Rebholz

> Too often, Western feminists have ignored the politics of reception in the interpretation of texts from the so called peripheries, calling for inclusion of "difference" by "making room" or "creating space" without historicizing the relations of exchange that govern literacy, the production and marketing of texts, the politics of editing and distribution, and so on.
> (Caren Kaplan, 1997, 139).

> Every feminist struggle has a specific ethnic (as well as class) context.
> (Anthias and Yuval-Davis, 1983, 62).

Emerging as the first oppositional social movement in Turkish public sphere in the aftermath of Coup D'etat in 1980, second wave feminism has undergone an important transformation process in recent decades. Alongside the ideological differentiation between radical and socialist feminists toward the end of 1980s, starting with the 1990s, we can observe the widespread institutionalization and "NGOization" of the movement. The transformation can also be seen in the extensive pluralization of women's groups and organizations. The variety and multiplicity of women's organizations is accompanied by the diversification of ideologies, positions, perspectives, and traditions. In addition to ideological and organizational diversification, the 1990s witnessed the geographical diffusion of feminist movement. Thus what began in consciousness raising meetings of small groups of feminist women in the cities of Turkey (Istanbul, Ankara, and Izmir) has spread to the other places such as Diyarbakir, Bursa, Adana, Mersin, Van, Eskisehir, Gaziantep, and Samsun (Kerestecioglu, 2004, 75). This transitional period also saw the rise of local/regional feminisms. To sum up, the women's groups that are active in feminism today in Turkey include radical, socialist, egalitarian, secular or kemalist feminists, and Islamic women's groups, Kurdish women, minority women, human rights activists, as well as autonomous and institutionalized feminists and, more recently, third wave feminists.[1]

In Turkey, second wave feminism has contributed largely to the emergence of academic feminism. Most of the first protagonists of the movement were from an academic background. The foundation of women's studies centers at different universities at the beginning of 1990s has contributed to the establishment and recognition of feminist scientific approaches in academic knowledge production processes (Arat, 1993). Drawing on the works of feminist authors who analyze the constructions of gendered identities in the context of nation-state building processes in Middle East and south Asian societies (Kandiyoti, 1994; Yuval-Davis, 1997), the Turkish feminist academics and activists analyzed the construction of modern Turkish woman in the Turkish nationalist discourses—the roles and images attributed to *modern Turkish woman* by republican modernization project.[2] Academic feminism made important contributions in the deconstruction of kemalist women's image and in the critical engagement with Turkish modernization.

However, these analyses have not dealt with some very important questions regarding the variety of ways in which women from different ethnic, religious, cultural, and class origins have been influenced by, or come into contact with, the Turkish modernization project. Specific and group-related questions such as age, religious affiliation, ethnic identity, class position, or geographical location were not considered in this second wave feminist analyses. Similarly, these do not address questions regarding which kind of interaction patterns have taken place between the hegemonic Turkish modernization project and the women of other groups or, importantly, how these encounters would be processed into different subjectivities (Durakbasa, 1998, 29). In short, a differentiated approach is lacking in these analyses both with regard to examination of women's groups along axes of difference (urban/rural, secular/religious, Turkish/Kurdish/minority, lower class/middle class, educated/noneducated) as well as varying power structures and different subjectivation forms to which women are exposed.

The construction of identity cannot be examined only with reference to gender identity in case of Kurdish and Islamist activists and women of other minority groups. Other inequalities and differences (religious, ethnic, and national identity) and the interaction between these should be taken into consideration. Moreover, these should be investigated in relation to, and within the framework of, hegemonic relations both within the borders of nation-state and at transnational level. For an adequate analysis of different feminist politics and of different types of political subjectivities and their diverse knowledge projects,[3] a multiplicity of contradictory axes of subordination, which are influential at the level of state (discursive, institutional, and actor's level), within the sphere of civil society, and within family and kinship relations should be taken into account simultaneously (Yuval-Davis, 2006; 1997, 14).

In this chapter, I look at transnational cultures of exchange in feminist theories by focusing on the circulation and reception of feminist ideas among second wave feminists and Kurdish activists in Turkey—particularly, their encounter with Western feminisms and confrontation with each other. In doing so, I consider feminist knowledge production, gendered political praxis, and dynamics of transnational feminist activism as interrelated processes in Turkish context. In my analysis, combining intersectionality approach and the insights provided by research on transnational feminism, I focus mainly on two groups of women activists (Kurdish and Turkish female activists) but the analysis can be seen to address broader questions such as: How do transnational political structures affect the existing gendered identities and how do they interact with the existing gendered hierarchy and difference structures? What are the effects of transnational exchange on feminist knowledge production processes in Turkey? How do different feminisms and movements interact with local feminisms and women's activism and what kinds of transformations take place in this interaction process? While these questions set a context for this piece, they are within the more specific focus of the relationship between Turkish and Kurdish feminisms and how an intersectional analysis can illuminate the power dynamics of transnational and national feminisms.

In the first part of this chapter I consider how the combination of transnational advocacy networks and the analyses of transnational feminisms offer the most relevant framework to understand transnational knowledge production in different women's groups in Turkey. In the second part, I look at the organizational, financial, and ideological exchange as well as solidarity of women's movements in Turkey with other women's nongovernmental organizations (NGOs) beyond the national borders. In the third part I focus on intellectual encounter of Kurdish women with Turkish feminists and Western feminism and their critique on both of these feminisms. In the fourth part of the chapter, drawing on the interviews that I conducted with the Kurdish women's NGO activists, I highlight the intersection of ethnic and gender identities and their mutual interaction in the formation of Kurdish women's political subjectivity.

Transnational Networks and Transnational Cultures of Exchange among Feminisms

Recognizing that the term "transnational" has been employed for over 15 years now in social sciences literature, Inderpal Grewal draws attention to the multiple ways of understanding it (Grewal, 2008, 189). She differentiates mainly between three approaches with respect to their subject matter and discipline within which the term is being employed: (1) migration studies, (2) examination of social movements, and (3) transnationality as signifying cultural praxis and meanings in late capitalism (Grewal, 2008, 189). The significance of the transnational approach for the feminist activists lies, according to Grewal, in the fact that it enables the activists to recognize the diversity of feminisms and practices (Grewal, 2008, 190) and to understand the power relations between them:

> [The activists] can understand that power relations and inequalities reside in all feminisms. In particular, these power differences may be based on class, race, sexuality, nationality, religion, and geopolitics. Local politics are also altered by their situatedness within the transnational since nation-state boundaries cannot be seen as

anything but porous; on the contrary, local and global are not separate and opposite but are linked and altered by their relation to the transnational. (Grewal, 2008, 191)

In this sense, it is especially important to stress that the reception, appropriation, production, interpretation, and the distribution of Western feminism and ideas of first world feminism do not take place in a social vacuum. These should be considered as embedded in unequal power relations.[4]

Transnationalism can both serve as an explanatory frame for the emergence of transnational networks within the borders of nation-state, as well as for to be able to grasp the new emergent forms of gendered political subjectivities and positioning. The main field in which transnational advocacy networks are likely to emerge are, according to Keck and Sikkink, women's activism, human rights, and environmental activism (Keck and Sikkink, 1998, 2). Because the transnational networks are mediated through domestic political structures, these play an important role in the emergence of transnational networks (Ibid., 2). Transnationalism as a research perspective enables the tracing of the changes in the self-perception of actors related to the changes in the construction of their identities and interests (Ibid., 17).[5] Through encounter, exchange, and cooperation with other NGOs in transnational space, the women's NGO activists (Turkish, Kurdish, and Islamic) have access to new techniques, strategies, discursive positioning, and possibilities of political identification, which might enable the transformation of existing gender roles and praxis as well as the emergence of new gender orders, and even the acceleration of this process. Transnationalization approach offers at the same time a relevant research framework in order to capture knowledge transfer, cultural diffusion, and the appropriation of Western feminist ideas and works by different women's groups in Turkey.

One of the most striking features of women's movements and women's NGOs is the existence of their contact and exchange with other women's movements and international NGOs and supranational organizations. This manifests itself not only in the existence of the ideological, intellectual, and organizational solidarity networks with other women NGOs and movements across borders but also in the availability of financial support of the international organizations. In what follows, I will treat these relations first with respect to the ideological and organizational exchange and knowledge transfer. Then I will focus on the financial aspect of this exchange.

TRANSNATIONAL NETWORKING OF WOMEN'S MOVEMENTS IN TURKEY

Two important aspects characterize the dynamic and nature of women's activism in Turkey. The first aspect relates to the extensive NGOization of the sphere of civil society in general and in particular the NGOization of women's movements since 1990s and the further acceleration of this process in 2000s during the Process of Turkey's Accession to European Union. The second aspect, very much related to this first one, is the striking transnational character of women's movements in Turkey, which means that the political engagement of women activists in NGOs in Turkish civil society takes place in an environment of extensive organizational, ideological, and financial exchange with other international NGOs and supranational organizations such as EU and United Nations Organization.

Although the involvement of the women's NGOs in transnational women's networks is considered to have started at the middle of 1990s (Ertürk, 2006, 89) and in this sense, is seen as linked to rise of transnational women's human rights regime at global level and, in Turkish context, to the institutionalization and NGOization of women's movements, it should be noted that the second wave feminist movement has had a transnational character from its very beginning. Nevertheless it should be noted also that though the feminist movement constitutes one of the best documented social movements compared to other movements in Turkey, the transnational networking of movements has been barely addressed, if it is noticed at all, in the literature.[6] This applies to the feminist movement of 1980s as well as the women's movements of after 1990s.

While feminist consciousness raising groups appeared in the public sphere in the 1980s, the emergence of second wave feminism in Turkey can be traced back to the mid-1970s. Tekeli underlines the participation of Turkish female academicians in the first UN World Conference on Women in 1975 in Mexico as one of the decisive factors that played an important role in the emergence of the feminist movement in Turkey (Tekeli, 1989). In this sense, the publication of Tekeli's pioneer article in 1977, which is titled *Siyasal Iktidar Karsisinda Kadin* [The Women Facing the Political Power] in one of the serious social science periodical *Toplum ve Bilim* [Society and Science], influenced the framework for the future development of women's studies and academic feminism in Turkey. In this article Tekeli refers to, among others, the works of French, English, and American feminist writers such as Betty Friedan, Kate Millet, Juliette Mitchell, Shelia Rowbotham, and Simone de Beauvoir (Tekeli, 1977). After 1980, one of the first activities of the feminist women was to organize a symposium on "women's question" in 1982 in Istanbul to which the French feminist Giselle Halimi was also invited (Tekeli, 1989). As one of its first activities, *Kadin Cevresi* [The Women's Circle Co.], founded at the end of 1983, translated feminist classics such as "Conversations between Alice Schwarzer and Simone de Beauvoir" into Turkish (Ibid.). The influence of the second wave feminist movement, and the emergent academic feminism, led to the establishment of women's studies centers in the 1990s. Young Turkish female academics who have completed their PhDs in Western countries and learned about first world feminism played a significant role in the spreading and establishment of feminist ideas in Turkish public sphere. These very well-educated, middle- and upper-class women with professional background returned with their intellectual luggage of Western feminist concepts and categories such as "gender," "patriarchy" (Arat, 1993, 126), "women's liberation," "emancipation," and "womanhood," establishing these as the common denominator uniting women from different social groups on the essentialized basis of their subordination experience.

International networking of women's movements cannot be confined to the scope of ideological-intellectual-organizational exchange and solidarity. Many of women's NGOs were founded and continued to be funded by support of international NGOs and donations of supranational organizations. For example, the publication of the monthly feminist magazine *Pazartesi* (1995–2005), which has played a very influential role on the discussions in feminist public in Turkey, was made possible due to 5 million German mark donation provided by Women's Foundation (FAS) of Heinrich Böll Stiftung (Kocali, 2005, 140).[7] In a similar fashion, the Kurdish Women's Centre (Ka-Mer) could conduct its project "The Development of Permanent Methods in the Struggle against

Killings Committed in the Name of 'Honour' in the Southeast and East Anatolian Regions" because of the financial support of Swedish Istanbul Consulate General, Swiss Embassy, and Open Society Institute in Istanbul (Ka-Mer reports from 2003; 2004; 2005). Similarly feminist NGO projects such as *Amargi* (Women's Academy, Istanbul) and *Gökkusagi* (Kurdish Women's NGO Rainbow, Istanbul) were realized through the financial support of *KAGIDER—Kadin Girisimciler Dernegi* (Women's Fund by Women's Entrepreneurs Association, Istanbul), which was financed by Istanbul Dependance of Georg Soros Open Society Institute (Open Society Institute Report, 2006, 117).

Furthermore the knowledge exchange and transnational networks cannot be confined just to the Turkish feminist scene. Kurdish feminists (i.e., through migrant organizations in Europe) and Islamic women's movements have their own institutional/intellectuals contacts and knowledge networks. An evaluation of the international networking of Kurdish women with other women's NGOs in Europe and America demonstrate that they have many connections and contacts. But the Kurdish women's NGOs enjoy additionally the solidarity and political/organizational support of the migration organizations that are founded in industrialized societies and liberal democracies of West Europe (regarding high presence of Kurdish migrant population particularly in countries such as Germany, France, Sweden, Netherlands, Belgium, and Denmark) and in the United States (Kayhan, 2000).

There are multiple examples of this intellectual and ideological exchange between women's movements and NGOs in Europe and in the United States. What is of interest here is the way in which such international networking led to the significant impact of the second wave women's movement on knowledge production processes and, particularly, on the political processes in Turkey. The above-mentioned pluralization of women's groups and ideological diversification occurring in the beginning of 1990s can be seen as the democratization of landscape of women's activism in Turkey. On the other hand, parallel to the NGOization and transnationalization of women's groups, a fragmentation of the feminist movement occurred. Thus different women's organizations (Islamic, Turkish, or Kurdish) promote their own gender norms, competing with each other (Ertürk, 2006, 82; Kardam, 2005, 165). Kurdish, Islamic, feminist, and kemalist women's NGOs, each propagate their own development and modernization models (Esim and Cindoglu, 1999, 186). There are considerable differences among these three groups of female activists (Kurdish, Turkish, and Islamic) with respect to their politicization processes and strategies of transnational networking and their positioning toward the Turkish state. These three women groups have undergone different processes of integration/ nonintegration into the hegemonic nation-building and modernization project of Turkish state. In other words, the Islamic and Kurdish women have been exposed to other mobilization, politicization structures, and technologies of governmentality compared to Turkish women. Therefore, they have developed different forms of political agency and gendered subjectivity in transnational space and these are products of multiple axes of subordination to which they are exposed to at national, local, and international level.

Knowledge Production and Exchange with the Western Feminism: The Case of Kurdish Activists

The central issues and agendas of the feminist struggle in the 1980s and 1990s can be summarized under the rubric of "body politics." Together with the critique on violence against women, sexual harassment, honor killing, exploitation of female body, feminists have deconstructed the hegemonic images of appropriate womanhood and manhood in the society, pushing against the patriarchal character of family and the institution of marriage. Parallel to their critique on masculinist sociocultural practices and patriarchal values dominating microcosms of daily life, they have addressed the patriarchal character of Turkish state. They emphasized the importance of individuation and liberation process together with equal citizenship rights for the women.[8] Despite considerable success of second wave feminist politics, a new phase began around the millennium with a new political focus. The kind of feminist language and style developed by second wave feminists in the last two decades of the twentieth century was understood as no longer adequate. The *category of women, the notion of emancipation,* and *the process of individuation* as desirable projects for one's life did not and do not mean the same thing for a lower-class Kurdish woman in East Anatolia as it did for a middle-class Turkish woman with a profession and living in West Anatolia. Kurdish women are familiar with the experience of subordination based on their ethnocultural identity. They know already what it means being the "other"; they were exposed to a "double otherization" as Kurdish women. So the intellectual encounter of Kurdish women with Turkish feminists and Western feminism offers an interesting intersection to examine the role of transnational feminism.

Employing the work of Margaret Keck and Kathyrin Sikkink, three political contexts can be identified within which transnational networks would probably emerge: (1) when "channels between domestic groups and their governments are blocked," (2) when activists and political actors believe that transnational networks will support their mission and political agenda, and (3) in the case that the conferences and contacts help in creation and strengthening of the networks (Keck and Sikkink, 1998, 12). A combination of the first and the second context provides the fitting analytical framework for the investigation of women's movements and their transnational networks in Turkey. Yet for a proper understanding of the specific conditions within which the Kurdish women are active politically, it is necessary to consider their sociopolitically marginal position in the Turkish society. I think the availability of their transnational networks can be understood well in the light of analogy to the reflections on the Latin American women's groups by Sonia Alvarez. She emphasizes, in Latin American context, that one of the reasons why the women are engaged in transnational networks beyond the national borders is because they want to reaffirm and reconstruct their marginalized political position and subaltern status in their own societies through the solidarities with other stigmatized groups (Alvarez, 2000, 4). This reasoning can be seen in the situation of Kurdish women in Turkey.

The Kurdish women stand on the intersecting point of various axes of power and political discourses and are exposed to different forms of subordination (gendered, ethnic, and socioeconomic oppression), which is reflected in the formation of her subjectivity and in the issues and problems articulated by Kurdish women's politics.[9] Through their articulation of the sexism of Kurdish community, through the articulation of nationalism and racism of Turkish state, and through their critique of ethnocentrism and epistemic violence of Turkish and Western feminisms, Kurdish women transform their status from being suppressed objects to that of being a privileged subject of a certain political discourse (Kurdish feminist discourse) and of a certain reservoir of knowledge (being a Kurdish woman in Turkish society).

In this context, the Kurdish women do not confine themselves exclusively to gender question, they advocate the necessity of another feminism that should take into consideration national, ethnical, class identities, and differences among women. Therefore the Kurdish women stress constantly that they have two identities and struggle against this double suppression of both: on the one hand they struggle for the liberation of their Kurdish identity, on the other for the liberation as woman (Ayten, 2000, 23).

The critique on Turkish feminist movement in its initial phase by Kurdish activists is threefold.[10] First the Turkish feminist have failed to recognize Kurdish feminism and failed to show solidarity with Kurdish feminists. Second, even when Kurdish women are heard, Turkish feminists display a condescending attitude, an attitude of endurance, toward Kurdish women. Finally, Turkish feminists are criticized for having a narrow understanding of feminism, which disregards other forms of subordination and knowledge (Kayhan, 2000). For example, it is significant that Turkish feminists have translated only the works of white women's movement from America and from Europe into Turkish, and overlooked the works of black feminism and other feminisms (Ibid.).

In order to call into question the racist and discriminating practices of Turkish women, Kurdish feminists refer to the works of black feminism from United States, especially the works of Angela Davis and bell hooks. Unsurprisingly given the history, second wave feminism is publicly understood to represent all of feminists in Turkey. For Kurdish feminists, drawing on black feminism facilitates the articulation of their specific concerns and differentiates their ideological position within a feminist movement and in broader Turkish public sphere (Canan and Halide, 2005, 229, 235). For them, there are clear parallels between the experiences of black women in United States and their own situation in Turkey (Berivan, 1999).

The Kurdish feminists critique the knowledge hierarchies of Turkish feminists as well as Western feminism. Their critique of the pejorative attitude of Western feminists is even harsher than their critique of Turkish feminists. The behavior of Western feminists toward Kurdish women is described by Fatma Kayhan as "the situation of an ape in cage as the object of scientific investigation" and seen as a "typical example of eurocentristic approach of white western feminism" (Kayhan, 2000). Kayhan writes that at first she enjoyed being perceived as a Kurdish feminist and the extensive attention of female researchers from Europe and United States who conducted interviews with her. Yet, she came to recognize the homogenizing and eurocentristic attitude of the researchers and the discrepancies between what she said in interviews and how she was represented (Kayhan, 2000).

Intersection of Gender and Ethnicity in the Political Positioning of Kurdish Women's NGO Activists

The dual character of Kurdish women's identity is emphasized in the literature by Kurdish women as noted above. Being Kurdish and being a woman—and the contradictory interaction pattern between these two—were the dominating themes in interviews that I conducted with the Kurdish NGOs activists.[11] The following selected interview passages demonstrate the dynamics pertaining to (1) awakening of consciousness about being a gendered subject as a source of political identification, (2) political positioning within the discursive and organizational field, and (3) redefinition/intervention in the conventional understanding of feminism and feminist politics.

Before developing an understanding of their political identity as Kurdish feminists, my interviewees were engaged in human rights organizations, leftist ideological activities, and/or organizations within which Kurdish ethnic identity was defined as the political focus. They had become aware of themselves as gendered political subjects, but this process of awareness varied from woman to woman and was not free from contradictions. One of my interview partners, a well-known female activist and a respected person in Kurdish political circles, recalled this emerging consciousness and connected it to a very specific experience of violence toward Kurdish women:

> I had already a consciousness about women's question. When I look back to the '80s, I can remember for instance that many women waited in front of the prison in order to visit their husbands who were also the same persons who exercised violence on their wives.

Violence belongs to the daily life of women. I must have also learned that the women have to experience violence mostly within in the family, which became a normality and which has been even glorified (i.e., holy). When a man is not authoritarian enough towards his wife, it will be joked about him as a henpecked husband. It will be said that he cannot even control his wife. (Interview with Necla)

The development of a consciousness of being a woman and experience of subordination stemming from gender identity is connected to the experiences of exclusion, othering, and isolation that these women had associated with ideology or ethnicity while engaged in other social movements and political organizations. These experiences framed their politicization process and their positioning as a "Kurdish feminist." The women emphasized that either being of Kurdish or being a woman was undermined in each organization:

> I have noticed the following: Each time as I involved in an organization, a part of mine has been made to other. I tried to enter in a leftist organization. In this group I was told: "place your being Kurdish in background a little bit." I was a Kurdish woman. As I talked about Kurdish movement, they told me that I was nationalist. As I mentioned Kurdish question, they said that the revolution should be realized first, and then the *Kurdish Question* will be solved. That happened to me not only in the leftist organizations but also in Kurdish groups too; as I said for instance that I am oppressed as a woman, they claimed that I pursue separatism. (Interview with Belgin)

The problematic relationship between women and other social movements is underlined in these narratives and draws attention to the underlying essentialism:

> I consider being a woman as an ideological fact; it is not just something natural. The emancipation of woman is an ideological question. If you fail to recognize this, you look for spontaneous solutions, which generally ended up in the kitchen: That is how the other movements deal with the *Women's Question*. The women were always actively involved in many liberation movements, but at the end they found themselves in the kitchen. That is because these movements do not offer any specific method of resolution. (Interview with Ayla)

The experiences of other political organizations and the awareness as a gendered subject combined with previous intellectual/ideological questionings led to feminist consciousness and a search for a feminist politics. After the reflection of situation of Kurdish women as the "oppressed of the oppressed" and after engagement with women's movements, these interviewees concluded that an emancipatory women's politic is one of the few political fields within which they can live out their dual identity:

> In theory it is talked about the oppressed of the oppressed. You find this in Marxist theories as well. It is told that the woman is subordinated and exploited. But when you express this as a woman, it means you pursue separatism and gender discrimination. Regarding this point, I could articulate neither my Kurdish identity nor my gender identity in these political circles under these conditions. As I begun to read on women's movement I discovered that is one of the seldom areas in which a woman can realize her gender identity as well as her ethnic identity and make her own politics based on these identities. (Interview with Belgin)

Working in a Kurdish women's organization, or in a women's organization where women of different ethnic and cultural origins come together, seemed to suit their desire to be active politically. Nevertheless, Kurdish women struggle against monolithic understanding of identities and emphasize instead multilayered character of them. Democracies, one interviewee argues, should be redefined with regard to their capacity to account for this multidimensional nature of identities:

> You can be politically active in women's organizations as a woman, but this time it is paid no attention to the identities other than gender. But I want to be able to express my Kurdish identity too. Why should I hide my Kurdish identity? Or why should I not be engaged politically in Kurdish question? Kurdish Question matters to me too. I would like to be engaged in Kurdish movement as well...If we talk about democracy and freedom, we had better not confine ourselves to only one identity. (Interview with Ayla)

Kurdish female activists articulate a multilayered understanding of identities, a multidimensional notion of feminism and feminist politics. The Kurdish women's movement offers a critique of the conventional perception of feminist politics and expands the boundaries of feminist politics in Turkey:

> In Turkey you have this widespread perception that the feminists are not concerned with anything other than women's question. That is not true. We are confronted with such a huge problematic that no women's organization can overcome alone. We talk about a huge problem here. Why do we organize ourselves politically? We want to define the problem; we want to bring it to the public sphere in order to talk about the ways of solutions. Basically we want to make politics. Therefore the women's question should be understood in its many aspects and in its multidimensionality. Poverty belongs also to women's question. Both *Kurdish Question* and democratization process concern the women equally in Turkey. (Interview with Necla)

Necla develops her own understanding of how a feminist politics should look:

> I think there are many definitions of feminism. The definitions can vary. Inspired by bell hooks, we have decided in Ka-Mer[12] that each can define feminism in the way she likes. I do not have an idea of revolution in my understanding of feminism. But we aim at the transformation of the state. As enlightened citizens we would like to have a social welfare state. Thus our aim is transformation. (Interview with Necla)

The oppositional politics and the transformative practice is defined by Kurdish female activists as a "politics of difference," which has the potential to tackle different problems, experiences, and life conditions of different women:

> I think it is desirable to make politics together with human beings from different circles with differences. It is painful to hear their experiences, but this makes you also strong. Pain makes you stronger. When I see this, I want to struggle more. It should be this kind of struggle. Otherwise what we do here, our opposition would not move a lot. The feminism is nice, it is a good device; but as long as I cannot adopt this in my life, as long as I do not confront and exchange my experiences with experiences of the *"other,"* feminism would not mean a lot to me. (Interview with Belgin)

Belgin offers another example of expectations about what a women's politics should aim for:

> The majority of the feminist movements in Turkey tackles the problem of women stemming from their gender identity and pursues a feminist politics on gender question. But we think, feminism cannot just limit itself to body politics. Feminism is more than this. Women's Politics should also carry out politics of resistance against the suppression of the people, against the assimilation, against violence, against militarism and heterosexism. The patriarchy cannot be considered as independently neither from nationalism and nor from militarism. They support each other mutually, and by these means they get institutionalized and established. (Interview with Belgin)

Belgin identifies herself as member of the third wave feminism in Turkey and believes this new understanding addresses a wider spectrum of issues in Turkey than second wave feminism:

> The more the feminists have questioned power relations and relations of domination among women themselves, the more mature it became, and therefore it can offer answers to the many problems of the majority of people. Thus "third wave" has a wider base and perspective. That is why it could expand. (Interview with Belgin)

Given their experience of exclusion from Turkish feminism, it is unsurprising that Kurdish feminist see parallels between their experience and that of black feminists caused excluded by white feminism in the United States and Europe. In a search for an *other* feminism, Kurdish women have directed their attention on the intellectual production of black feminism in the United States:

> The more I learned about black women's movement, the more commonalities I have discovered between them and Kurdish women's movement. Though black women's movement builds part of European and American women's movement, the women's movements in these countries are very much "white"; they make the black women's movement to other. First after the independent organization of black women, they started to criticize the whiteness of women's movement which could bring changes among the white feminist movement. The Kurdish women have undergone a similar process in Turkey. During the 80s the Kurdish women could not even cheer slogans in Kurdish language. Even the articles about

woman's question had not been translated into Kurdish, the problems specific to Kurdish women have found no reaction/response among women's movement. (Interview with Belgin)

Conclusion

As noted in the interview passages above, the Kurdish women emphasize the mutually constitutive character of two axes of differences (gender and ethnicity) as the sources of their identity, and they resist being reduced to one identity that is, being seen as either "woman" by Turkish feminists or as "Kurdish" by Kurdish nationalist liberation movements. In the words of Yuval-Davis, this exemplifies the irreducibility of social divisions (2006, 200). Drawing attention to the debate between *additive* or *constitutive* intersectionality, Yuval-Davis underlines the importance of contextual analysis:

> The point of intersectional analysis is not to find "several identities under one"...This would reinscribe the fragmented, additive model of oppression and essentialize specific social identities. Instead, the point is to analyze the differential ways in which different social divisions are concretely enmeshed and constructed by each other and how they relate to political and subjective construction of identities. (Ibid., 205, 195)

Multiple intersecting sources of subordination operating on the construction of identity cannot be reduced to one source because they are embedded in complex and variable hegemonic power relations. Intersectionality enables an understanding beyond the simple cataloging and measuring of multiple social inequalities (Erel et al., 2007). Intersectionality highlights the complex ways in which social differences and inequalities are embedded in the existing hegemonic power relations and how their meanings become fixed through discursive and institutional power operations and praxes. In this sense, it is crucial to understand social divisions and difference as marked by value-laden judgments, different access to power, and by asymmetrical allocation of resources (Erel et al., 2007, 246):

> In this way the interlinking grids of differential positioning in terms of class, race, and ethnicity, gender and sexuality, ability,

stage in the life cycle and other social divisions, tend to create, in specific historical situations, hierarchies of differential access to a variety o resources- economic, political and cultural. (Yuval-Davis, 2006, 199)

As interviewees here indicate, Kurdish female activists, different practices of power and oppression such as sexism, militarism, capitalism, nationalism, and patriarchate are interwoven and cannot be considered independently. In other words, the identity construction of Kurdish includes aspects such as educational attainment, class positioning, and cultural affiliation as well as other structural factors such as being Alevi, speaking the Kurdish language, and so on. In turn, these factors can be only understood with reference to the hegemonic power of the Turkish nation-state and transnational organizations. Moreover, this multilayered complex and mutually constitutive character of subordination relations sits at odds with second wave (Turkish) feminists' emphasis on individualism and the emancipation process. In facilitating access to, and employing politically, white Western feminism, Turkish feminist groups have recreated a hierarchy of power that prioritized an essentialist model of women and of feminism.[13]

Employing an analytical frame of intersectionality facilitates a demonstration of the interaction and mobilization of the different identities as resources for the realization of political subjectivity as in the case of Kurdish female activists. In this sense, the intersecting axes of differences might have productive and constitutive power. My extensive interviews, only briefly noted here, give voice to critical reflection regarding multiple subordination and offer a valuable opportunity for political action for the relocation and reinterpretation of the production of emancipatory knowledge. As such, intersectionality enables the emergence of new political subjectivities.

Returning to more general points noted in the introduction, it is important to think of transnational feminist exchange and activism alongside intersectionality. Undoubtedly the reception of first world feminism by Turkish female academicians and activists have helped the struggle against the dominance of leftist and nationalist discourses in Turkish public sphere and enabled Turkish feminist to carve out some autonomous space (Acar-Savran, 2005, 123). However, the essentialism of the movement prevented it from developing a sensitivity for the specific problems and life conditions of other groups of women with different affiliations and belongings.[14] Drawing on their knowledge and experience of being a Kurdish woman in their daily life and within the political organizations in which they or their male family members and relatives were actively involved, the Kurdish women challenged one-dimensional understanding of womanhood and universalistic claims of feminist ideology/movement in Turkey. In their attempt to define an *other/different* feminism that is attentive to the specific concerns of Kurdish women, they made use of *other/different* transnational feminist networks. This included the deployment of black feminist texts. Still we cannot assume that, as in the case of Kurdish and Turkish feminist activists, transnational feminism is a space that is more democratic and free from oppressive relations in contrast to the national level. On the contrary, we need to be aware of, and map, how multiple intersecting inequalities and social differences articulate hierarchies of differences and power relations operative at local, national, and global arenas of feminist politics and the consequences for the production of feminist knowledge. As Kaplan reminds us, "the relation between experience and knowledge is now seen to be not of correspondence but one fraught with history, contingency, and struggle" (1997, 149). Feminist knowledge production and reception of feminist ideas in transnational space can neither be thought of independently from hegemonic relations that determine the social locations of women in the countries within which they live nor from power relations and differences among women working transnationally.

NOTES

1. This is a very short overview of the historical development of second wave feminism and the emergence of women's movements in Turkey. For a more detailed discussion see Al-Rebholz (2012).
2. For a more detailed discussion on the feminist analyses of the de/construction of *modern Turkish woman* by nationalist discourses please see Al-Rebholz (2010).
3. The concept "different knowledge projects" as proposed by Sandra Harding is discussed in Yuval-Davis (2006).
4. For more on the importance of considering the embeddedness, temporal and spatial, of feminisms and feminist practices see Grewal and Kaplan (1997) and Kaplan (1997).

5. Keck and Sikkink emphasize the structure and actor-centered character of their approach (1998, 5). Drawing on the new social movements' research and research on NGOs, they stress the actor-centered direction of their analysis through the concepts like shared worldview, common discourses, shared norms and values, framing, storytelling, and symbolic politics (Keck and Sikkink, 1998, 17).
6. One exception is Ertürk (2006). In the context of the second wave feminism in Germany, Regina Dackweiler and Reinhild Schäfer notice that the internationality of the women's movement gets little attention in the literature and so they emphasize the importance of international theoretical exchange "to grasp as a resource which is available to the women's movement and which influenced its development positively" (Dackweiler and Schäfer, 1999, 201).
7. The financial support was stopped by the foundation in 2000 and the publishing of the magazine continued for 18 months due to the financial support of another American foundation.
8. For a more detailed account of the themes dominant in the two initial decades of second wave feminist movement in Turkey see Al-Rebholz (2007).
9. For a detailed analysis and account of sociopolitical context enabling and restricting conditions for a political mobilization of Kurdish women in Turkish public sphere in the aftermath of 1980 coup D'etat and the background, for example, family history, political experiences, motivations, and reasons of the formation of different types of gendered political subjectivity among Kurdish women, see Caglayan (2007, 165–223).
10. This is now changing as some feminists begin to see the essentialism in employing "womanhood" as the only relevant category of analyzing subordination relations. Regarding the honor killings and the official state politics and public discourse that try to label honor killings as an ethnic phenomenon specific to Kurdish population, (rather than as a product of patriarchal gender relations in Turkey), one can observe the increasing emergence of solidarity and cooperation networks between Turkish and Kurdish feminists. In another context, feminist anthropologist Aksu Bora offers a critical examination of Turkish nationalism and Kemalist modernization as the prerequisite of proper feminist politics in Turkey. She states that "regarding the relationship between Kurdish women and feminism, it is not only a question of recognition of difference, but also it must be considered as a chance for a critical self-reflection on the side of feminists" (Bora, 2004, 109).
11. These interviews are drawn from a larger project, entitled "Competing Conceptions of Civil Society and the Formation of Different Intellectuality Modes in 1990s Turkey: Liberal, Radical Feminist

and Kurdish Feminist Discursivities in Comparison." The interview passages used in this chapter have been translated into English by the author and serve as an example of the intersection of ethnic and gender identity based on the case of Kurdish women activists.
12. Kurdish Women's Centre, Diyarbakir.
13. Similarly, Kathy Davis criticizes global feminism noting that the power relations—hegemonic relations within which the women are embedded, living in different areas of world—are often neglected (Davis, 2009, 197). She adds that the meaning of family, community, and social bonds were not taken into consideration by the notion of global sisterhood.
14. Upon reflection, one socialist feminist confesses, they feared that feminist politics would be rather divided if one expresses other subordination axes beyond gender identity. For instance, Turkish feminists could not understand why the emphasis on Kurdish as mother language by Kurdish feminists in the public sphere should play such an important role in women's politics (Acar-Savran, 2005, 124).

REFERENCES

Acar-Savran, Gülnur. 2005. "Kaktüs Dergisi Deneyimi." In *Özgürlügü Ararken*, edited by S. Amargi, 119–135. Istanbul: Amargi Kadin Bilimsel ve Kültürel Arastirmalar Yayincilik ve Dayanisma Kooperatifi.
Al-Rebholz, Anıl. 2012. *Das Ringen um Die Zivilgesellschaft. Intellektuelle Diskurse, oppositionelle Gruppen und soziale Bewegungen seit 1980*. Bielefed: Trancript.
———. 2010. "Regieren der Geschlechterverhältnisse im Wandel: Transnationale Strategien der Frauenbewegungen in der Türkei." *Femina Politica* 2: 74–87.
———, Anıl. 2007. "Feminist Production of Knowledge and Redefinition of Politics in Turkey." In *Wissenschaf(f)t Geschlecht*, edited by Lena Behmenburg, Mareike Berweger, Jessica Gevers et al., 217–234. Königstein: Ulrike Helmer Verlag.
Alvarez, Sonia E. 2000. "Translating the Global: Effects of Transnational Organizing on Local Feminist Discourses and Practises in Latin America." http://www.antenna.nl/~waterman/alvarez.html (accessed on May 8, 2010).
Anthias, Floya, and Nira Yuval-Davis. 1983. "Contextualizing Feminism—Gender, Ethnic and Class Divisions." *Feminist Review* 15: 62–75.
Arat, Yesim. 1993. "Women's Studies in Turkey: From Kemalism to Feminism." *New Perspectives on Turkey* 9: 119–135.
Ayten. 2000. Letter to the Editor. *Roza* 17: 23.
Berivan. 1999. Irkciligi farketmek. *Roza* 16: 9–11.

Bora, Aksu. 2004. "Feminizm: Sinirlar ve Ihlal Imkani." *Birikim* (August/September): 106–112.
Caglayan, Handan. 2007. *Analar, Yoldaslar, Tanricalar*, 125–163. Iletisim: Istanbul.
Canan and Halide. 2005. "Feminist Kürt Kadin Olusumlari." In *Özgürlügü Ararken* edited by S. Amargi, 221–238. Istanbul: Amargi Kadin Bilimsel ve Kültürel Arastirmalar Yayincilik ve Dayanisma Kooperatifi.
Dackweiler, Regina, and Reinhild Schäfer. 1999. "Lokal—national—international. Frauenbewegungspolitik im Rück—und Ausblick." In *Neue Soziale Bewegungen*, edited by Ansgar Klein et al., 199–224. Opladen: Westdt. Verlag.
Davis, Kathy. 2009. "Globale Lokalisierung des feministischen Wissens: Die Übersetzungen von *Our Bodies, Ourselves*." In *Gender Mobil?*, edited by Helma Lutz, 194–214. Münster: Westfälisches Dampfboot Verlag.
Durakbasa, Ayse. 1998. "Cumhuriyet Döneminde Modern Kadin ve Erkek Kimliklerinin Olusumu." In *75 Yilda Kadin ve Erkekler*, edited by Tarih Vakfi, 29–50. Istanbul: Tarih Vakfi Press.
Erel, Umut, Jinthana Haritaworn, Ercarnacion Gutierrez Rodriguez, and Christian Klesse. 2007. "Intersektionalität oder Simultaneität?!—Zur Verschränkung und Gleichzeitigkeit mehrfacher Machtverhältnisse— Eine Einführung." In *Heteronormativität*, edited by Jutta Hartmann et al., 239–250, Wiesbaden: VS Verlag.
Ertürk, Yakin. 2006. "Turkey's Modern Paradoxes: Identity Politics, Women's Agency, and Universal Rights." In *Global Feminism: Transnational Women's Activism, Organizing, and Human Rights*, edited by Myra Marx Ferree et al., 79–109. New York: New York University Press.
Esim, Simel, and Dilek Cindoglu. 1999. "Women's Organizations in 1990s Turkey: Predicaments and Prospects." *Middle Eastern Studies* 35(1): 178–188.
Grewal, Inderpal. 2008. "The Transnational in Feminist Research: Concept and Approaches." In *Mehrheit am Rand?: Geschlechterverhältnisse, globale Ungleichheit und transnationale Handlungsansätze*, edited by Heike Brabandt et al., 189–199. Wiesbaden: VS Verlag.
Grewal, Inderpal, and Caren Kaplan. 1997. "Introduction: Transnational Feminist Practises and Questions of Postmodernity." In *Scattered Hegemonies: Postmodernity and Transnational Feminist Practises*, edited by Inderpal Grewal and Caren Kaplan, 1–33. Minneapolis: University of Minnesota Press.
Kandiyoti, Deniz. 1994. "Identity and Its Discontents: Women and Nation." In *Colonial Discourse and Post-Colonial Theory*, edited by Patrick Williams et al., 376–391. New York: Harvester Wheatsheaf.

Kaplan, Caren. 1997. "The Politics of Location as Transnational Feminist Critical Practice." In *Scattered Hegemonies: Postmodernity and Transnational Feminist Practises*, edited by Inderpal Grewal and Caren Kaplan, 137–152. Minneapolis: University of Minnesota Press.
Kardam, Nüket. 2005. *Turkey's Engagement with Global Women's Human Rights*. Aldershot: Ashgate Publishing.
Kayhan, Fatma. 2000. "Roza dört yasinda. Ne istedik, ne yaptik, ne oldu?." *Roza* 17: 7–17.
Keck, Margaret E., and Kathyrin Sikkink. 1998. "Introduction: Transnational Advocacy Networks in International Politics." In *Activists Beyond Borders*, edited by Margaret E. Keck and Kathyrin Sikkink, 1–38. Ithaca, NY: Cornell University Press.
Kerestecioglu, Inci Özkan. 2004. "Women's Movement in the 1990s: Demand for Democracy and Equality." In *The Position of Women in Turkey and in the European Union: Achievements, Problems, Prospects*, edited by Ka-Der Press, 75–97. Istanbul: Ka-Der Press.
Kocali, Filiz. 2005. "Pazartesi Dergi Deneyimi (1995–2000 Dönemi)." In *Özgürlügü Ararken*, edited by Amargi, 137–151. Istanbul: Amargi Kadin Bilimsel ve Kültürel Arastirmalar Yayincilik.
Tekeli, Sirin. 1989. "80`lerde Türkiye'de Kadinlarin Kurtulusu Hareketinin Gelismesi." *Birikim* (July): 34–41.
———. 1977. "Siyasal Iktidar Karsisinda Kadin." *Toplum ve Bilim* (Winter): 69–107.
Yuval-Davis, Nira. 2006. "Intersectionality and Feminist Politics." *European Journal of Women's Studies* 13(3): 193–209.
———. 1997. *Gender & Nation*. London: Sage Publication.

Reports by NGOs

Ka-Mer. 2005. "Who's to Blame?." By Ka-Mer Woman's Centre, Diyarbakir.
———. 2004. "No More 'If Only' S'." By Ka-Mer Woman's Centre, Diyarbakir.
———. 2003. "Killings in the Name of 'Honour'." By Ka-Mer Woman's Centre, Diyarbakir.
Open Society Institute Report. 2006. Acik Toplum 2001–2006. By Open Society Institute Assistant Foundation, Istanbul.

6

Gender Variance: The Intersection of Understandings Held in the Medical and Social Sciences

Ryan Combs

When examining the medical and social position of gender variant people, it is important to consider the divergent understandings of sex, gender, gender identity, and, to some extent, sexuality, and the ways in which these beliefs influence health practice. Doctors and policy makers rely upon evolving, ambiguous notions of gender to make decisions about who to treat when approached by gender variant people. This chapter discusses how gender variant experiences, such as those of trans and intersex people, are conceptualized differently in social science and medical literature.[1] In addition, it explores how social, biological, medical, and discursive constructions of gender affect treatment. I do not attempt to give definitive definitions of sex, gender, gender identity, or gender dysphoria; instead, I highlight the etiological and definitional ambiguity found in the literature and the problems posed by this inconsistency.[2]

This research engages in intersectional analysis in the fields of politics and health policy studies. Earlier in this book, contributor Wendy Smooth discusses several characteristics of intersectional analysis. Among those aspects of particular interest here are the rejection of essentialism; the insistence upon variation within categories of social identity; the recognition that social identity categories and power systems shift across time and location; and the idea that power and oppression are not mutually exclusive. Working across disciplinary boundaries using an intersectional analysis can help us begin to understand the complex picture in this area of health practice. Inconsistent understandings of sex, gender, and gender identity across specialties give rise to ambiguity that, in turn, complicates the policy and politics of health. An intersectional framework helps us better understand the complexity found in this area of health-care decision making.

Ambiguous definitions of gender, sex, and gender identity are problematic in two ways. First, they raise questions about authenticity and individual agency. Who is setting the discourse about gender variant people? Who is able to make decisions about what constitutes an authentic gender identity? Which states of being require treatment and which do not? Second, they bring to the surface structural concerns about rationing and service delivery. If there is ambiguity about gender identity as a concept, who is qualified to make treatment decisions about it? How should practitioners construct treatment plans and allocate resources to an issue that is so difficult to categorize? I argue that these problems stem in part from the different and sometimes incongruent definitions used. I begin by tracing a history of gender variant experiences in medicine, which conceptualizes gender difference through a pathological framework. Then, I consider contemporary contributions from the field of social sciences, which problematize binary constructions of gender.[3] I conclude by discussing how intersectional analyses help us understand gender variance and responses to it.

Gender Identity in Psychiatry and Medicine: Pioneers in Sexology

The treatment of trans people, where one's conception of their innermost gender does not match their physical sex, is heavily influenced by the practitioner's viewpoint about the origin of the individual's dilemma. Through the medical lens, gender variance is usually considered pathological (Ekins and King, 1996; Kessler and McKenna, 2000). Locating the treatment of gender dysphoria in these fields has created a very strong association between gender variant identities and mental disorder. A psychomedical perspective informs public, as well as healthcare, discourse about transsexualism. Hines (2007) notes:

> Over the last century, medical perspectives have occupied a dominant position that has significantly affected how transgender is viewed and experienced in Western society. Although contemporary medical approaches represent a more complex understanding of transgender practices than previously offered, I have argued that there remain serious problems in the correlation of transgender and biological and/or psychological pathology. (Hines, 2007, 183)

Likewise, Hird (2002) says that psychiatric and medical perspectives have been the main theoretical avenue by which transsexualism has been analyzed. Below, I consider a few of the key players in medicine and discuss what they say about gender and gender dysphoria.

In the historical narratives, the modern medicalized concept of gender variant identities finds one of its earliest and most meaningful roots in the work of Prussian-born physician Dr. Magnus Hirschfeld. Historian Susan Stryker describes Hirschfeld, who was active in medicine from the late 1890s to the early 1930s, as a "pivotal figure in the political history of sexuality and gender" (2008, 38) and a "pioneering advocate" for trans people (2008, 39). In 1897, Hirschfeld founded the Scientific Humanitarian Committee, the world's first social movement organization for homosexual people and, in 1919, he opened the Institute for Sexual Science in Berlin (Stryker and Whittle, 2006; Stryker, 2008). According to Meyerowitz (2002), Hirschfeld campaigned for homosexual rights and published widely on the topic.

While early sexologists considered people with cross-gender identities homosexual, Hirschfeld was among the first to conceptualize them separately, as "transvestites" (See also Hirschfeld, 2006, 28–39). Hirschfeld and his team used this term to describe people with cross-gender identities that included both those who cross-dressed and those who underwent "sex transformation" (Meyerowitz, 2002, 15). Meyerowitz adds that Hirschfeld believed that "hermaphrodites, androgynes, homosexuals, and transvestites constituted distinct types of sexual 'intermediaries,' natural variations that all probably had an inborn organic basis" (2002, 19). Hirschfeld arranged the first documented male-to-female (MTF) genital transformation surgery for a trans woman named Lili Elbi in 1931 (Meyerowitz, 2002; Stryker, 2008).[4]

In 1947, as the study of sex and sexuality was becoming topical in the United States, Dr. Alfred Kinsey became the director of the newly founded Institute for Sex Research at Indiana University. Kinsey played an important role in changing the way sex was studied and the way human sexuality was understood. Rather than placing moral value on some sexual practices over others, Kinsey, a professor of zoology, approached human sexuality as a taxonomist (Bullough, 1998). He created a 0–7 scale for sexual orientation, which ranged from exclusively heterosexual to exclusively homosexual. He was among the first to argue that homosexuality was along a spectrum of "normal" sexual behavior (Kinsey, Pomeroy, and Martin, 1948). His books *Sexual Behaviour in the Human Male* in 1948 and *Sexual Behaviour in the Human Female* in 1953 were controversial because of their explicit discussions about the taboo subject of sex. Kinsey's pioneering work contributed to a liberalization of attitudes about sexuality both in the academy and in popular culture (Bullough, 1998).

Kinsey became interested in transgender and cross-dressing people in the late 1940s and early 1950s (Meyerowitz, 2001). Although gender identity was not a focal point of Kinsey's research, he came across and interviewed transgender people while collecting sexual histories. It was around that time that Kinsey met Louise Lawrence, a person assigned male at birth but began living full time as a woman in 1942. Lawrence provided Kinsey with resources about trans issues and had influenced some of his ideas about gender and sexuality (Meyerowitz, 2006). Kinsey's work was influential in developing biological sex and gender as different concepts; his writing on the subject of gender variance helped to solidify his theories on sexual difference (Meyerowitz, 2001). However, while Kinsey accepted cross-dressing and cross-gender identity, he hit the "limits of his sexual liberalism" when considering the idea of genital surgery (Meyerowitz, 2001, 89).

Harry Benjamin

The work of endocrinologist Dr. Harry Benjamin—a man who had connections with both Magnus Hirschfeld and Alfred Kinsey—would prove the most significant in creating a space within medicine for transsexual people (Stryker and Whittle, 2006). Although he originally specialized in tuberculosis, Benjamin became interested in trans people after Dr. Alfred Kinsey contacted him about a patient in 1948. Benjamin, who popularized the term "transsexual," appeared to feel sincere empathy for trans people and has been described as "compassionate though paternalistic" (Stryker and Whittle, 2006, 45). He believed in a mixed etiology for gender variance, which he considered psychopathological, and argued that trans identities (along with homosexual identities) are immutable. Benjamin's work focused almost exclusively on those along the male-to-female spectrum, presumably because he rarely came across female-to-male trans people.

In Benjamin's 1954 article entitled *Transsexualism and Transvestism as Psycho-Somatic and Somato-Psychic Syndromes*, Benjamin states that transvestites are heterosexual (meaning people who were born male—assigned and attracted to females), while transsexual people are homosexual (meaning people who were born male—assigned and attracted to males). He believed this so strongly that he commented that "for (transsexual people) to be attracted to 'other females' appears to be a perversion" and "homosexual inclinations always exist in a transsexualist whether they result in actual physical contact or not" (Benjamin, 2006, 47). These beliefs seem odd and heterosexist by today's standards. In addition, Benjamin believed that physical and facial characteristics should be considered in determining suitability for treatment, presumably to ensure that trans women's transition would produce a passable outcome.

In 1966, Benjamin published an influential book entitled *The Transsexual Phenomenon*, in which he defined transsexualism as a medical condition, charted possible treatments, and discussed his views on their efficacy. Benjamin's approach was motivated by a belief that trans people are often unable to function in their original gender and were at risk of suicide (Denny, 2006). For example, he writes the following in the conclusion of *The Transsexual Phenomenon*:

> From the therapeutic end, it cannot be doubted or denied that surgery and hormone treatment can change a miserable and maladjusted person of one sex into a happier and more adequate, although by no means neurosis-free, personality of the opposite sex. (1966, 92)

Significant in Benjamin's work was the idea that transsexual people's gender identity cannot be changed; therefore efforts to adapt to their birth sex are fruitless. He proposed instead that the individual's physical body should be matched up to their identity. Although Benjamin was an endocrinologist, he believed that psychiatrists should "have the last word" about whether or not someone can transition between genders (2006, 50).

Harry Benjamin's model became very prominent after *The Transsexual Phenomenon*'s publication and heralded medical and psychiatric treatment for gender variant conditions on a wider scale. This was not without drawbacks. Both doctors and patients tended to narrate the trans experience "almost entirely in terms of misery and anguish" (Denny, 2006, 175). Benjamin's model resulted in a quite narrow view of who was considered legitimately transsexual:

> To qualify for treatment, it was important that applicants report that their Gender Dysphoria manifested at an early age; that they have a history of playing with dolls as a child, if born male, or trucks and guns, if born female; that their sexual attractions were exclusively to the same biological sex; that they have a history of failure at endeavours undertaken while in the original gender role; and that they pass or had potential to pass successfully as a member of the desired sex. (Denny, 1992, as cited in Denny 2006, 177)

This, according to Denny, led to patients being denied treatment for reasons such as their sexual orientation, relationship status, attractiveness, success in their original gender role, and knowledge about transsexualism. Following their hormone and surgery treatments, trans people were encouraged to reenter society and blend in as "normal" men and women.

An examination of Benjamin's work offers not only a history of trans as a term and concept, but also a story about the premise of diagnosis and treatment that holds authority to the present day. The importance of Benjamin's influence cannot be understated as it signaled an important shift underpinning contemporary medical and popular discourse. The "true transsexual" narrative proposed by Benjamin influenced the approaches taken at the onset of wide-scale treatment of gender variant conditions through gender clinics in the mid-1960s (Rudacille, 2005). Its significance was to provide trans people with space in existing male/female gender categories through clinical assessment and access by providing a medically supported transition. In this system, surgery became synonymous with gender change. Trans people's gender identities were legitimated through medical assessment and treatment processes.

John Money

Among those influenced by Benjamin in the 1960s was Dr. John Money at Johns Hopkins University in Baltimore, home to the first gender identity clinic.[5] Sexologist John Money explored the topic of gender by paying special attention to intersex and transsexual individuals. After receiving his PhD from Harvard University in 1952, Money took a job at the Psychohormonal Research Unit at Johns Hopkins. There he conducted research into the psychological development of gender for over 50 years. Money's work had a great impact on modern understandings of sex and gender. Concurrent with the start of the second wave feminist movement, Money can be credited with conceptualizing a person's gender as a separate entity from their physical sex—coining terms like gender role and gender identity to describe one's inner sense of their gender (Colapinto, 2001). Also among his major contributions to this area of medicine were the pioneering of transsexualism as a diagnostic category and the academic legitimization of hormones and surgery as treatments for transsexual people (Bullough, 2003).

By 1965, the first transsexual surgery in the United States was completed at Johns Hopkins Hospital, creating a media storm (Colapinto, 2001). In 1969, Money coauthored a textbook with Dr. Richard Green called *Transsexualism and Sex Reassignment*, which established a protocol for treating transsexual people (Denny, 2006). He then coauthored a book with Anke Ehrhardt entitled *Man and Woman, Boy and Girl*, where they put forward the view that gender was malleable for a certain period after birth (Money and Ehrhardt, 1972). Money quickly became famous for his gender malleability hypothesis, which held that gender identity could be assigned during a window in the early years of life. During this time, according to Money, nurture overrules nature. An experiment with his theory of malleability would determine Money's lasting legacy.

John/Joan Case

John Money's reputation was ultimately tarnished when his methods failed with regard to case of John/Joan, aka David Reimer (Fausto-Sterling, 2000b; Colapinto, 2001; Butler, 2001). David Reimer was a non-intersex male child whose penis was severed during a botched circumcision in the mid-1960s. Reimer's parents, who were understandably distraught by the event, came across Dr. Money's work with transsexual and intersex people when he presented it on a television show. David's parents met with Money and decided to raise David as a girl. David and his identical twin brother made annual visits to Baltimore to see Money's team. Money used David's story (then called Brenda) as evidence to promote his theories about gender. However, the picture Money presented about a happy and well-adjusted girl did not match up with David's reality or the observations of his parents, particularly as he grew older. So although David's parents and doctors raised him as a girl and painstakingly socialized him as female during his childhood, his male gender identity became apparent in his teenage years. After he found out the truth about his history, he immediately transitioned from a female gender role to living as male (Colapinto, 2001). Although some intersex people who have been gender assigned are reported to be happy and content with their gender, David's innate sense of his gender could not be overruled by socialization (Gearhart, 1989). The outcome of David Reimer's failed gender assignment prompts interesting questions about the nature of gender.

In 1997, a follow up to David Reimer's case was published. Diamond and Sigmundson (1997) found that although David was consistently admonished for displaying masculine behaviors and preferences, his resistance to female identity and reluctance to pursue further surgery to obtain female genitalia persisted throughout his childhood. Using the new lens of Reimer's "true" male gender, the authors concluded that "no support exists for the postulates that individuals are psychosexually neutral at birth or that healthy psychosexual development is dependent upon the appearance of the genitals" (Diamond and Sigmundson, 1997, 303).

This finding has significant implications for trans people. It raises questions about whether people have an innate sense of their gender cemented before birth. It also acknowledges that gender identity is not determined by genitals. Diamond succinctly expands his thoughts about the difference between sex and gender in a later piece: "It can be said that one is a sex and one does gender; that sex typically, but not always, represents what is between one's legs, whereas gender represents what is between one's ears" (Diamond, 2002).

While Money advocated surgery for some trans people, his insistence that "appropriate" gender identity could be taught in the early years revealed a tension. As Diamond points out, attempts to map gender onto the body through socialization have been unsuccessful as demonstrated acutely in the case of David Reimer. Therefore, socialization therapies are not a viable option. This suggests that the best route for clinicians is to listen to patients' understandings of their gender (i.e., what is between their ears) and respond to these realities by providing a range of possibilities about mapping gender onto their bodies through medical (physical) means.

A Social Science Critique of the John/Joan Case

Perhaps the most important intervention into contemporary debates regarding the evolution of gender theories has been from Judith Butler. In maintaining that gender is discursively constructed, Butler offers critiques of gender discourse. She has recently turned her attention to intersex and trans subjects by looking at binary gender systems and the psychomedical model.

Butler (2001) explores the John/Joan case from an altogether different perspective than the medical specialists. She argues that this case neither confirms nor denies social construction or essentialist theses; rather we should read it another way. Drawing upon Foucault's "politics of truth," Butler suggests that David Reimer was treated as less than human because his gender was unintelligible. She asks questions about the ways in which existing outside of the gender norm affects how one is recognized as human. Butler writes:

> The very criterion by which we judge a person to be a gendered being, a criterion that posits coherent gender as a presupposition of humanness, is not only one that, justly or unjustly, governs the recognizability of the human but one that informs the ways we

do or do not recognize ourselves, at the level of feeling, desire, and the body, in the moments before the mirror, in the moments before the window, in the times that one turns to psychologists, to psychiatrists, to medical and legal professionals to negotiate what may well feel like the unrecognizability of one's gender and, hence, of one's personhood. (2001, 622).

Butler makes the case that doctors exert their power to determine truths for those who exist outside of the gender norm. While doctors search for the "true" gender of intersex children and look for ways to create, through surgery and socialization, the corresponding sex, Butler suggests that what gets lost is the ability for people to exist as themselves, whatever that looks like. She draws attention to the fact that intersex people and trans people increasingly seek spaces to exist outside of sexual and gender dimorphism.

What is important to Butler is how the central subject in the John/Joan case, David Reimer, experiences his own truth. In his words, Reimer rejects the proposal by doctors that without a penis he will be, essentially, unlovable. When interrogated, scrutinized, and ultimately coerced into an ill-fitting norm, he begins to resist. The discourse Reimer employs retrospectively critiques the norm, rejects the intrusions of medicine, and defines his own worth. From Butler, we learn that the way in which gender is conceptualized, described, and discussed is important. Her work suggests that allowing doctors to adjudicate gender is problematic and unjust.[6]

Ambiguous Ideas about Gender

Medicine has predicated its understanding of gender on theories that have continuously evolved over time. This has produced ambiguity in the literature about gender and gender variance. Gender does not have a universal definition, neither has medicine agreed upon a test to determine the "truth" about someone's gender. The current medical model's approach to gender variance sits between, and is a bad marriage of, the psychiatric, the medical, and the social. As we have seen with Kinsey and Money, doctors have research, political, and medical agendas that feed into their decision making. In addition, they are restricted by, or at least influenced by, the social constraints of the time and place in which they work.

The contemporary gender discourse utilized by medical specialists reflects understandings that lie at the intersection between internalized norms and the external realities of the medical model. Kinsey, Money, and Benjamin each hit limits in their own tolerance. Although Kinsey was accepting of cross-dressing and cross-gender identities, he was unwilling to accept surgery as an appropriate treatment—partly because he was unconvinced of its efficacy, but also because of the conflicts such surgeries pose to his belief about the central importance of human sexual function (Meyerowitz, 2001). Money hit the limits of his own authority as, despite his best efforts, he refused to accept that his aggressive methods were unable to reassign Reimer's gender (Butler, 2001). Benjamin hit his limit as he was unable to accept lesbian, gay, or bisexual-identified trans people as "true transsexuals" (Benjamin, 1966). Many consider these beliefs outdated; they provide evidence of the complexity of understandings about gender, sex, and gender identity and their evolution over time. Considering the constraints of ambiguity about these three concepts, the most logical approach when providing care for gender variant people seems to be for doctors to listen to a patient's understanding of their gender (i.e., what is happening between their ears) and make determinations that are not only informed by medical knowledge, but also patient-led.

This section has summarized some of the main threads of thought in the medical sciences about gender variant people; the next turns to social science in earnest. It discusses the work of several social scientists and theorists and, in doing so, returns to understandings of social construction and binary gender.

Social Construction

From the 1970s onward, the literature on gender develops the idea that gender is more than simply an expression of a biological characteristic, that is, what one's body dictates through chromosomes, hormones, gonads, and genitalia. For example, some have argued that gender is a socially constructed phenomenon. An early seminal work looking at the social construction of gender was the content analysis in Erving Goffman's *Gender Advertisements*, which examined gender displays in over five hundred photographs found mostly in ads printed in newspapers and magazines. He analyzed the ways in which gestures and postures reflect learned gender behaviors. He found that men were more likely to adopt dominant positions while women more frequently took subordinate ones (Goffman, 1976). Through a process that Goffman calls "hyper-ritualization," he demonstrated that advertisers ritualized gender stereotypes in their work, resulting in consistent portrayals of women as subordinate to men.

Kessler and McKenna began to lay further foundation for theories about gender's social construction in their 1978 book *Gender: An Ethnomethodological Approach* (Kessler and McKenna, 1978). They argued that just as gender is socially constructed, so too is biology (Hines, 2007). Kessler and McKenna listened closely to the experiences of trans people in their work. Drawing upon interview data, they discussed how transsexual people demonstrate that gender can be and is constructed. For example, transsexual people illustrate that gender is not necessarily fixed to sex assignment at birth, in contrast to Western ideas about binary gender. Nevertheless, they stated that, as opposed to breaking the rules about gender,

> the existence of transsexualism, itself, as a valid diagnostic category underscores the rules we have for constructing gender, and shows how these rules are reinforced by scientific conceptions of transsexualism. (Kessler and McKenna, 2000, 11—abridged reprint of the original 1978 chapter)

Kessler and McKenna contended that of transsexual people's concerns with "passing" in a new gender and medical as well as the legal profession's treatment of the issue, "natural" versions of gender are reproduced as a result.

Fellow ethnomethodologists West and Zimmerman (1987) reviewed existing perspectives on gender and sex in the literature to produce a theoretical reconceptualization of the terms. They rejected biological determinants of gender in favor of a social model and argued that gender is a social process embedded in day-to-day interaction. To them, gender is not something that exists outside of the practices that create it. It is, in their words, not an attribute of an individual but, rather, an "emergent feature of social situations: both as an outcome of and a rationale for various social arrangements and as a means of legitimating one of the most fundamental divisions in our society" (1987, 126). They argued that a true understanding of the issue requires three categories: sex, gender, and sex category. Sex is understood to be socially agreed biological classifications. Sex category is the group we assign to people based on the assumptions we make from social cues. Gender is the activity that "emerge(s) from and bolster(s) claims to membership in a sex category" (1987, 127). "Doing" gender is unavoidable in their view, "because of the social consequences of sex category membership: the allocation of power and resources not only in the domestic, economic, and political domains but also in the broad arena of interpersonal relations" (1987, 145).

Social constructionist Judith Lorber discussed gender as something that is "done." Her work explored how gender is signaled to others, beginning at birth and continuing throughout one's life. She described how gender is constructed and reinforced through the repetition of these processes (Lorber, 2000). According to Lorber, every aspect of our lives is infused with gender:

> Gender is so pervasive that in our society we assume it is bred into our genes. Most people find it hard to believe that gender is constantly created and recreated out of human interaction, out of social life, and is the texture and order of that social life. Yet gender, like culture, is a human production that depends on everyone constantly *doing gender*. (Lorber, 2000, 106)

Lorber believed that gendering serves a social function; it divides labor and ascribes particular sets of aspirations, motivations, and personal characteristics.[7] She argued that disruptions to gender norms such as that of transvestites and transsexual people, allow us to reflect on how gender is produced. Like nontrans people, trans people's gender status is constructed by dressing and behaving in ways associated with men or women. Lorber also discussed the ways in which the processes of gender are policed through social sanction. Sexist hierarchies are inherent in the division of labor, where men's work is more valued and women's work is held in less esteem. The construction of gender, in her opinion, has served to make women submit to men. Feminists such as Lorber are unequivocal in their rejection of essentialism. They believe that women have been forced to take a submissive role due to social functions and history, rather than the result of any biological, hormonal, or genetic predisposition.[8]

Post-structuralism and Performativity

Post-structuralism is a school of thought that critiques existing social structures and rejects essentialism. Post-structuralists such as Michel Foucault, Judith Butler, and others have engaged with the topics of gender and sexuality and demonstrated how gender is produced independently of biological sex. Foucault, for example, has made valuable contributions that inform feminist and queer theory in relation to medicine; in particular his theories about how and by whom power is employed, as well as about the body and sexuality. Foucault believed that power is not necessarily tied to any particular identity category; rather, power is available to certain people in certain situations. Foucault's ideas of biopower and the medical gaze (also called the clinical gaze) are relevant to this discussion.

Biopower refers to the ability of the state to exert power to regulate the human body (Foucault, 1984). Foucault sees the regulation of human bodies as instruments of capitalism's economic management, to "ensure not only their subjection but the constant increase of their utility" (1984, 279). In other words, it serves the capitalist state's interest to produce normatively gendered, heterosexual people. In addition, Foucault's notion of biopower highlights the power relationship between the medical profession and the patient. The medical gaze, arising out of Foucault's work in *The Birth of the Clinic: An Archaeology of Medical Perception* (Foucault 1973), refers to metanarratives that have been created about medicine in modernity. In this particular metanarrative, doctors are thought to have the power to see through illness and determine truth using the lens of medical science. The concepts of biopower and medical gaze are important because of the light they shed on the power relationship between the clinician, the patient, and the state.

Earlier, Judith Butler's analysis of the John/Joan case was discussed. We now turn to her most influential work, *Gender Trouble*, which builds upon the work of Foucault. She contended that gender identity is not fixed; it is created and recreated through practices that reinforce the binary norm. Butler proposed the concept of performativity to show how gender is repeatedly produced:

> The parodic repetition of gender exposes as well the illusion of gender identity as an intractable depth and inner substance. As the

effects of a subtle and politically enforced performativity, gender is an "act," as it were, that is open to splittings, self-parody, self-criticism, and those hyperbolic exhibitions of "the natural" that, in their very exaggeration, reveal its fundamentally phantasmatic status. (Butler, 1990, 200)

Butler's *Gender Trouble* represented a turning point in feminism. She questioned the categorical foundation upon which feminist assertions have been made, stating that "the internal paradox of this foundationalism is that it presumes, fixes, and constrains the very 'subjects' that it hopes to represent and liberate" (1990, 203). This calls into question gender as a binary category, opening up possibilities for a range of articulations of gender.

Although *Gender Trouble* is Butler's most influential work thus far, it is also her most controversial. Over the years, she revisited the topics covered in light of criticisms and updated her theoretical standpoint. In her 1993 book *Bodies that Matter*, Butler "revise(d) the performance-related terms she used in *Gender Trouble*" and "explained the strained categories of materiality and corporeality" (Roden, 2001, 26). In addition, in *Undoing Gender* (2004), Butler acknowledged the lack of attention paid to trans activism in *Gender Trouble* and looked at the burgeoning trans movement as the basis for a new gender politics.

Despite the unquestionable influence of Butler's work, she has also been widely criticized, particularly by other feminists. For example, Nussbaum (1999) presents a number of critiques of Butler in an article for *The New Republic*. According to Nussbaum, Butler neglects to engage thoroughly with important literature; there is a lack of acknowledgment of and discussion about the contradictions between theorists from which she draws her arguments. Nussbaum was also displeased with the ways in which Butler's work steps back from the activism and real-world applicability that permeates through so much other feminist theoretical work. From Nussbaum's perspective, Butler's work too often remains noncommittal and abstract. As structures of power are framed as ubiquitous, Butler's work does not properly acknowledge or contribute to the feminist movement's concern with women's material conditions (Nussbaum, 1999).

Academics engaged with transgender topics have something to say about *Gender Trouble* as well. Namaste (2000) argues that Butler's work remains too abstract and is divorced from trans people's lived experience. She believes that *Gender Trouble* fails to take into account the context in which certain types of gender performances take place and the limitations that these contexts pose. For example, she argues that although claims for radical gender expressions are important, but such theorizations downplay real risks attached to gender transgression in everyday life, such as the threat of transphobic violence. Also, Prosser (2006) argues that queer theorists such as Butler have celebrated (and relied upon) transgender subjectivities that comfortably support the performativity argument, while disfavoring or even dismissing transsexual narratives as essentialist. He argues that transgressive gender expressions are celebrated in Butler's work at the expense of those expressions that fall on either side of the binary. As Butler seeks to break down conventional (binary) expressions of gender, Prosser believes that her work ultimately enforces a hierarchy in its own right with regard to trans subjectivities.

Intersectionality and Transgender Studies

As demonstrated in this review of the literature, academic disciplines such as sexology, biology, psychology, and feminist theory have conceptualized gender variance in unique and sometimes contradictory ways. Despite headway made by second wave feminists to loosen the boundaries of gender, in the view of Whittle, feminist theory has "consistently failed to afford transgender people a voice" (2002, 81). Emerging from a discursive turn in feminist and postmodern theories, queer theory has begun to provide a space for trans voices to converge. Influenced by the work of Foucault, queer theory set out to disrupt and undermine the binary foundations of modernist thought (Whittle, 2002). It is interested in expanding the scope of inquiry from looking at gay men and lesbians (as representative of sexuality) and women (as representative of gender), to include other sexualities and genders falling outside of the norm.

In addition, transgender subjectivity and relevant sociopolitical issues began to gain academic credence in the early 1990s. This took place because of a combination of activism, postmodern/queer theories, challenges to traditional ideas about gender and sexuality, tabloid interest, and popular culture (Hines, 2007).

Recently, transgender studies has emerged as a field that takes a multidisciplinary approach to the subject. Under its remit, Stryker explains:

> Transgender studies, as we understand it, is the academic field that claims as its purview transsexuality and cross-dressing, some aspects of intersexuality and homosexuality, cross-cultural and historical investigations of human gender diversity, myriad specific sub-cultural expressions of "gender atypicality," theories of sexed embodiment and subjective gender identity development, law and public policy related to the regulation of gender expression, and many similar issues. (2006, 3)

The discipline of transgender studies expands the remit of study beyond the traditional models and allows for more accurate and pointedly respectful work on the topic of gender variance.[9]

Nonbinary Understandings

The field of medicine has appeared particularly tied to binary thinking. Hird (2002) argues that hegemonic psychomedical discourse relies upon a strictly two-gender paradigm. Some contemporary social science theorists and researchers, however, challenge binary distinctions, believing them inadequate to explain the panoply of gender identities and expressions. Halberstam (2005) asserts that the ways in which nonnormative gender expressions shifted in medical discourse from homosexuality to transsexuality, along with the present-day descriptions of same-sex relationships, serve to reinforce binary understandings of gender. Hines (2007) argues that approaches to transgender people have also tended to rely upon heteronormative frameworks. Hird (2002) sees a shift in understandings of transsexualism from authenticity to performativity. Noting that gender authenticity is consistently the subject of medical research focus, Hird posits that "psychological analyses of transsexualism focus on the issue of authenticity because the discipline remains wedded to sex and gender as coherent, stable and 'real' concepts" (2002, 578).

Kate Bornstein's *Gender Outlaw* is one of the most widely quoted manifestos for breaking down the boundaries of gender. Like Lorber (2000) and Tausig, Michello, and Subedi (1999), Bornstein considers binary gender to be the structure through which power dynamics produce sexist (and transphobic) oppression. She proposes that gender

> could be seen as a class system. By having gender around, there are these two classes—male and female. As in any binary, one side will always have more power than the other. One will always oppress the other. The value of the two gender system is nothing more than the value of keeping the power imbalance, and all that depends on that, intact. (1994, 113)

Bornstein's work in *Gender Outlaw* comments on binary gender categories from a transgender subjective space. She argues for a third option and encourages us to envisage "a society free from the constraints of non-consensual gender" (1994, 111).

Bodies

Gender complexity is not the only phenomenon under consideration; physical complexity is important as well. In the literature, medicine has tended to view gender in terms of its relationship to the physical body. When the concept of gender is used, it has implied a split into two discrete binary categories that parallel male/female sex classifications. As the work of Bornstein shows us that gender exists on a spectrum, the work of Fausto-Sterling (2000b) and others demonstrates that physical sex falls across a range as well. Although the two-sex idea is embedded deeply in Western social and legal culture, there are in fact a number of gradations between male and female. Intersex people can have several different chromosomal, hormonal, or gonadal configurations. Thus, Fausto-Sterling argues that a two-sex system denies the complexity that exists in nature.

Even where sexual diversity extends beyond male and female, as is the case when people have intersex reproductive or sexual anatomy, treatment options are framed in ways that reflect and reinforce binary divisions. Rather than making room for difference, though, doctors have been compelling intersex people to "choose an established gender role and stick with it" since the Middle Ages (Fausto-Sterling, 2000a, 115). She argues that 1960s medical discourse about intersex people painted their lives as miserable, lonely, and freakish—claims that were without empirical basis. Intersex people have been expected to conform to heterosexual and binary existences. At the behest of doctors, many parents chose surgery for intersex babies to move their bodies into either male or female categories.

Fausto-Sterling rejects the quest for uniformity; she contends that this desire fulfills a cultural need rather than a natural one. Surgical treatment should be offered at the age where the patient is able to understand and consent to procedures, and should be planned cooperatively with the physician, the patient, and other specialists in gender diversity. So, in Bornstein, we hear a call to open up our understanding of gender and in Fausto-Sterling, we equally hear a call to open up our understanding of physical sex. Social scientists often see gender very differently. Binary gender, upon which most medical discourses are predicated, has been challenged by social scientists as being insufficient in articulating the range of experiences that humans have with gender. Rather, social scientists have often focused their attention upon the ways in which gender is discussed, developed, and conceptualized in the social world. Arising from this work is a school of thought that argues that gender is fluid and/or socially constructed.

Conclusion

This chapter has highlighted the various ways in which sex, gender, gender identity, and gender variance have been conceptualized in the medical and social sciences. These concepts have ambiguous, contested meanings that have shifted rapidly in response to the emergence of new and interesting scholarship. Medical science has attributed gender variance to hormonal, chromosomal, social, and/or behavioral causes. Social science has interpreted gender as a tool of the state, a class, a process, and a performance. Gender has been conceptualized as binary or existing along a spectrum.

Evidence from the literature suggests that gender variant people engaged with health services have contended with intersectional oppression. Sexism, homophobia, and transphobia have influenced the interpretation of what it means to be a man, woman, or someone who identifies in between. At times, the medical model has responded inadequately to the complex realities of gender variant people's lives. Doctors have presented a host of erroneous or inaccurate expectations to those who experience their gender differently to the labels assigned to them at birth. Despite this, many gender variant people are invested heavily in accessing services using the medical model and consider such treatments essential in articulating themselves to the outside world. A social constructionist approach presents a different picture of gender variance, but concerns remain about its adequacy as a full explanation of gender variant subjectivities, particularly transsexual ones. Poststructuralism puts forward the important critiques of gender, but it does not provide adequate spaces for people who feel comfortable adhering to the gender binary.

Although there is uncertainty in the literature about how theories of social construction and performativity intersect with the medical model, we can see through this review that understandings of sex, gender, and gender identity—namely social/discursive construction and biological theories—have interacted and informed each other in treatment locations. The disconnection between the understandings posited by various disciplines complicates our understanding of gender and of medicine's response to sex/gender difference. The medical model currently sets the frame in which gender variant people negotiate physical transition, but a post-structural analysis of gender can be useful in informing more respectful and appropriate treatment.

This chapter has focused on a health-care policy gap caused by ambiguous understandings of gender in medicine. In this case, an intersectional analysis has been used to consider what lessons we can learn from stakeholder disciplines. The range of views posited in different disciplines allows us to see the full picture of health care for gender variant people more clearly and, I would argue, respond more effectively. It also highlights that ambiguity makes policy making difficult. One-size-fits-all policies—especially those developed in social, cultural, or professional isolation—cannot adequately address the challenges posed by complex or ambiguous circumstances. Intersectional approaches allow a more full understanding of a social phenomenon. Thus, they should be considered as a policy development tool for reconciling cases of ambiguity.

Notes

1. "Trans" is used here as an umbrella term to refer to people whose gender identities do not match with the gender they were assigned at birth. Intersex describes people whose reproductive or sexual

anatomy does not fit into male or female categories. For the purpose of this chapter, I discuss both groups under the heading "gender variant" but, admittedly, this phrase inadequately describes the nuances of each category.
2. In brief, gender dysphoria is a medical term for the state of discomfort with one's gender.
3. Binary gender is the idea that gender is a dichotomy of men and women, with no variability or gray area between the two categories.
4. By 1933, fascism had overwhelmed the German state. The Nazis destroyed Hirschfeld's institute, its files and books that year. Hirschfeld—a gay Jewish man—died in exile in France two years later.
5. The gender clinic model of treating gender dysphoria and intersex conditions spread across the United States and the United Kingdom in the 1960s–1970s.
6. Along the same vein, post-structuralist sociologist Viviane Namaste (2000) warns that limiting discourse about trans lives to psychiatric and medical sites results in the erasure of trans people from many other segments of social life. Ghettoizing trans people to these spaces, will "reinforce a more general obliteration of TS/TG people from the social world" (Namaste, 2000, 265).
7. Tausig, Michello, and Subedi (1999) would agree. They see gender as describing cultural obligations and believe gender is used as a system of stratification.
8. While offering insight into the social processes that define the parameters of gender, the concept of social construction as the sole source of gender production has proven problematic in certain ways. There is a danger of justifying the harmful project of gender/sexuality resocialization through reparative therapy (also called conversion therapy), which has been employed by psychiatrists and religious organizations to reorient LGBT people toward heterosexual, cisgender identities (Exodus International, 2010; Haldeman, 1994). These treatments are considered risky and ineffective by the major professional medical associations (American Medical Association, 2010; American Psychiatric Association, 2000; American Psychological Association, 2009; Cohen, "British Medical Association," 2010). In relation to trans people, it was argued by Benjamin (1966) that psychotherapeutic approaches taken to change transsexual people's gender identities are unsuccessful. The lack of success in resocializing trans people's gender would seem to indicate, at the very least, that social construction arguments do not capture the complete picture. Thus, a takeaway point from the contribution of social constructionist positions is that they further complicate our understanding of gender and compound the ambiguity around the subject.

9. Namaste reminds us to avoid distilling gender variant peoples' lives and experiences into merely a condition that they embody. She writes, "research and theory in psychiatry, the social sciences, and humanities are preoccupied with issues of origin, etiology, cause, identity, performance, and gender norms. These questions are not unwarranted, but our lives and our bodies are made up of more than gender and identity, more than the theory that justifies our very existence, more than mere performance, more than an interesting remark that we expose how gender works. Our lives and our bodies are much more complicated, and much less glamorous, than all that" (Namaste, 2000, 1).

References

American Medical Association. 2010. *AMA Policy Regarding Sexual Orientation*. Available from http://www.ama-assn.org//ama/pub/about-ama/our-people/member-groups-sections/glbt-advisory-committee/ama-policy-regarding-sexual-orientation.page (accessed on October 5, 2012).

———. 2000. *Therapies Focused on Attempts to Change Sexual Orientation (Reparative or Conversion Therapies): Position Statement*. Available from: http://www.psych.org/Departments/EDU/Library/APAOfficialDocumentsandrelated/PositionStatements/200001.aspx (accessed on October 5, 2012).

American Psychological Association. 2009. *Insufficient Evidence that Sexual Orientation Change Efforts Work, Says APA*. Press Release, 5 August. Available from http://www.apa.org/news/press/releases/2009/08/therapeutic.aspx (accessed on October 5, 2012).

Benjamin, H. 2006. "Transsexual and Transvestism as Psycho-Somatic and Somato-Psychic Syndromes." In *The Transgender Studies Reader*, edited by Susan Stryker and Stephen Whittle. New York: Routledge.

———. 1966. *The Transsexual Phenomenon*. New York: The Julian Press, Inc.

Bornstein, K. 1994. *Gender Outlaw: On Men, Women and the Rest of Us*. New York: Routledge.

Bullough, V. 2003. "The Contributions of John Money: A Personal View." *The Journal of Sex Research* 40(3): 230–236.

———. 1998. "Alfred Kinsey and the Kinsey Report: Historical Overview and Lasting Contributions." *The Journal of Sex Research* 35(2): 127–131.

Butler, J. 2001. "Doing Justice to Someone: Sex Reassignment and Allegories of Transsexuality." *GLQ: A Journal of Lesbian and Gay Studies* 7(4): 621–636.

———. 1990. *Gender Trouble: Feminism and the Subversion of Identity.* New York: Routledge.
Cohen, D. 2010. "BMA Meeting: Conversion Therapy for Homosexuals Should Not Be Funded by the NHS." *BMJ* 341: c3553.
Colapinto, J. 2001. *As Nature Made Him: The Boy Who Was Raised as a Girl.* New York: Harper Collins.
Denny, D. 2006. "Transgender Communities." In *Transgender Rights*, edited by Paisley Currah, Richard M. Juang, and Shannon Price Minter. Minneapolis: University of Minnesota Press.
———. 1992. "The Politics of Diagnosis and a Diagnosis of Politics: The University-Affiliated Gender Clinics, and How They Failed to Meet the Needs of Transsexual People." *Chrysalis Quarterly* 1(3): 9–20.
Diamond, M. 2002. "Sex and Gender are Different: Sexual Identity and Gender Identity are Different." *Clinical Child Psychology and Psychiatry* 7(3): 320–344.
Diamond, M., and K. Sigmundson. 1997. "Sex Reassignment at Birth: Long-term Review and Clinical Implications." *Archives of Pediatric and Adolescent Medicine* 151(3): 298–304.
Ekins, R., and D. King. 1996. *Blending Genders: Social Aspects of Cross-Dressing and Sex-Changing.* London: Routledge.
Exodus International. 2010. *Mission & Doctrinal Statement*, Available from http://www.exodusinternational.org/content/view/33/61/ (accessed on October 5, 2012).
Fausto-Sterling, A. 2000a. "The Five Sexes: Why Male and Female Are Not Enough." In *The Social Construction of Difference and Inequality: Race, Class, Gender and Sexuality*, edited by Tracy E. Ore. Mountain View: Mayfield.
Fausto-Sterling, A. 2000b. *Sexing the Body.* New York: Basic Books.
Foucault, M. 1984. *The Foucault Reader*, edited by Paul Rabinow. London: Penguin.
———. 1973. *The Birth of a Clinic: An Archaeology of Medical Perception.* London: Tavistock Publications, Ltd.
Garfinkel, H. 1967. *Studies in Ethnomethodology.* Englewood Cliffs: Prentice Hall.
Gearhart, J. P. 1989. "Total Ablation of the Penis after Circumcision with Electrocautery: A Method of Management and Long-Term Follow Up" *Journal of Urology* 142: 799–801.
Goffman, E. 1976. *Gender Advertisements.* London: Macmillan.
Halberstam, J. 2005. *Transgressing Gender: Two is Not Enough for Gender Equality: The Conference Collection.* Zagreb: CESI.
Haldeman, D. 1994. "The Practice and Ethics of Sexual Orientation Conversion Therapy." *Journal of Consulting and Clinical Psychology* 62(2): 221–227.

Hines, S. 2007. *TransForming Gender.* Bristol: Policy Press.
Hird, M. J. 2002. "For a Sociology of Transsexualism." *Sociology* 36(3): 577–595.
Hirschfeld, M. 2006. "Selections from the Transvestites: The Erotic Drive to Cross-Dress." In *The Transgender Studies Reader*, edited by Susan Stryker and Stephen Whittle. New York: Routledge.
Kessler, S., and W. Mckenna. 2000. "Gender Construction in Everyday Life: Transsexualism." *Feminism & Psychology* 10(1): 11–29.
———. 1978. *Gender: An Ethnomethodological Approach.* Chicago: University of Chicago Press.
Kinsey, A., W. Pomeroy, and C. Martin. 1948. *Sexual Behavior in the Human Male.* Bloomington: Indiana University Press.
Lorber, J. 2000. "The Social Construction of Gender." In *The Social Construction of Difference and Inequality: Race, Class, Gender, and Sexuality*, edited by Tracy E. Ore. Mountain View: Mayfield.
Meyerowitz, J. 2006. "A Fierce and Demanding Drive." In *The Transgender Studies Reader*, edited by Susan Stryker and Stephen Whittle. New York: Routledge.
———. 2002. *How Sex Changed: A History of Transsexuality in the United States.* Cambridge: Harvard University Press.
———. 2001. "Sex Research at the Borders of Gender: Transvestites, Transsexuals, and Alfred C. Kinsey." *Bulletin of the History of Medicine* 75(1): 72–90.
Money, J., and A. Ehrhardt. 1972. *Man & Woman, Boy & Girl: Gender Identity from Conception to Maturity.* Baltimore: Johns Hopkins University Press.
Namaste, V. 2000. *Invisible Lives: The Erasure of Transsexual and Transgender People.* Chicago: University of Chicago Press.
Nussbaum, M. 1999. "The Professor of Parody." *The New Republic,* February 22.
Prosser, J. 1998. *Second Skins: The Body Narratives of Transsexuality.* New York: Columbia University Press.
Roden, F. 2001. "Becoming Butlerian: On the Discursive Limits (and Potentials) of Gender Trouble at Ten Years of Age." *International Journal of Sexuality and Gender Studies* 6(1/2): 25–33.
Rudacille, D. 2005. *The Riddle of Gender: Science, Activism, and Transgender Rights.* New York: Random House.
Stryker, S. 2008. *Transgender History.* Berkeley: Seal Press.
———. 2006. "(De)subjugated Knowledges." In *The Transgender Studies Reader*, edited by Susan Stryker and Stephen Whittle. New York: Routledge.
Stryker, S., and S. Whittle, eds. 2006. *The Transgender Studies Reader*, New York: Routledge.

Tausig, M., J. Michello, and S. Subedi. 1999. *A Sociology of Mental Illness*. Upper Saddle River: Pearson Education.
West C., and D. Zimmerman. 1987. "Doing Gender." *Gender & Society* 1(2): 125–151.
Whittle, S. 2002. *Respect and Equality: Transsexual and Transgender Rights*. London: Cavendish.

7

Intersectional Analysis at the Medico-Legal Borderland: HIV Testing Innovations and the Criminalization of HIV Non-Disclosure

Daniel Grace[1]

HIV testing technologies are evolving, and HIV-related criminal prosecutions are increasing. A new generation of HIV tests allows for much earlier detection of infection following the transmission event. HIV has an increased risk of transmission during the first eight weeks following infection due to greater infectivity in this very recent or acute phase (Brenner et al., 2007; Hayes and White, 2005; Hollingsworth, Anderson, and Fraser, 2008; Pao et al., 2005). As the Health Initiative for Men (HIM) puts it, HIV is "hottest at the start" (HIM, 2011). From a public health perspective, the importance of timely diagnosis during the acute phase is suggested from various data showing behavior change following an HIV-positive diagnosis (Marks et al., 2005). As such, the use of "early" HIV tests has important public health implications for the detection of HIV and the prevention of onward transmission. This has been the rationale for using these tests in pilot programs to help address the high rates of HIV among gay, bisexual, and other men who have sex with men (MSM)[2] in British Columbia (BC), Canada, as well as in other settings globally (Gilbert et al., 2011). What has not been thoroughly examined, however, is the possible relationship between these innovations in laboratory technologies and related

HIV testing initiatives and the increasing use of the criminal law to prosecute alleged cases of HIV non-disclosure in Canada.

Exposing or transmitting HIV to another person can increasingly be subject to criminal prosecution in many areas of the world (Grace, 2012; Pearshouse, 2008). In the Canadian context, researchers have noted the intensification of HIV non-disclosure criminal cases since 2004 (Mykhalovskiy and Betteridge, 2012; Mykhalovskiy, Betteridge, and McLay, 2010). A growing body of diverse policy actors argue that criminal approaches to disease control within and beyond Canada are highly problematic because they undermine public health efforts while creating a stigmatized viral underclass (Burris and Cameron, 2008; Eba, 2008; Elliott, 2002; Grace, 2012; Grace and McCaskell, in press; International Community of Women Living with HIV/AIDS, 2009; Jürgens et al., 2009; UNAIDS Reference Group, 2009; UNDP, 2012).[3]

Medical technologies have significant implications for policy, sexuality, and the law. As such, it is important to bring into conversation these different, and at times conflictual, approaches to HIV prevention and governance (e.g., targeted HIV testing technologies and the application of criminal law powers), which have remained largely discrete research and policy discussions to date, in order to elucidate how populations are impacted by such approaches to public health. I argue that both targeted HIV testing initiatives and the prosecution of alleged HIV non-disclosure cases ignore the structural drivers of the epidemic and problematically frame the "problem" that must be addressed. While testing is an important albeit insufficient aspect of HIV-prevention efforts, the increasing trend toward criminalizing HIV non-disclosure cases in Canada poses significant challenges in scaling up an effective national and provincial HIV response. This exploratory chapter, which focuses upon HIV/AIDS responses in British Columbia, is informed by the Descriptive and Transformative Questions of an Intersectionality-Based Policy Analysis (IBPA) and considers policy issues and intersectional subject positions at the "medico-legal borderland"—a field of inquiry that "suggests multiple possibilities for analysis including investigation of new forms of social control, the intersection of criminal law and health care governance and the emergence of hybrid health/crime subjects" (Mykhalovskiy, 2011, 674; Timmermans and Gabe, 2003).

In the first section of this chapter, I review the concept of intersectionality and argue that this paradigm offers an important critical perspective that can help researchers and policy actors understand complex health issues for diverse populations, including gay, bisexual, and other MSM. Next, I explore two discrete though conceptually related public health issues by explicating the work of researchers and civil society who are addressing *the need to consider the science of Acute HIV Infection (AHI), HIV transmission patterns and new testing technologies,* and *the danger in shifting to "law and order" approaches that criminalize HIV non-disclosure cases in Canada.* I examine three major descriptive policy factors while reviewing the research evidence and public health work being conducted in these areas: (1) *What HIV-related "problems" are being addressed*; (2) *The factors contributing to these representations;* and (3) *The effects produced by these approaches* (Hankivsky et al., 2012, IBPA Section 1). With this review presented, I focus on two additional considerations with a decidedly transformative thrust: (1) *Ways to improve these approaches to the problem and/or mitigate some of the possible harms caused by these approaches,* and (2) *Different approaches to thinking about addressing HIV/AIDS in and beyond the population of gay, bisexual, and other MSM* (Hankivsky et al., 2012, IBPA Section 2).

By considering complex public health issues together using an IBPA Framework, key tensions can be identified *within* and *across* different approaches to HIV/AIDS prevention and governance. This analysis supports calls for the need to expand access to new HIV testing technologies in British Columbia in order to increase awareness of HIV-positive status and detect cases of AHI so as to support prevention programs and enrollment into treatment programs; adapt existing prosecutorial guidelines to help eliminate or reduce the application of the criminal law to cases of alleged HIV non-disclosure in British Columbia; and meaningfully invest in HIV-prevention efforts that address the structural drivers of the epidemic.

Method

In this chapter, I use components of an Intersectionality-Based Policy Analysis (IBPA) Framework to better understand the complex interplay between medical technologies and legal problems (Hankivsky et al., 2012). An IBPA Framework draws on the principles of intersectionality to enable researchers and policy actors to gain a better understanding of who is benefiting from (and who is excluded from) health policy goals, priorities, and related resource allocation. Differing from more traditional sex- and gender-based analysis and health equity impact assessment techniques, this intersectionality-based approach requires concurrent consideration of the complex relationships between mutually constituting factors of social location and structural disadvantage at multiple levels so as to conceptualize determinants of inequity in and beyond health. The IBPA Framework has two core components: (1) a set of guiding principles (*intersecting categories, multi-level analysis, power, reflexivity, time and space, diverse knowledges, social justice, and equity*) and (2) a list of 12 overarching questions (divided into *descriptive* and *transformative* subsets) to help guide, frame, and shape respective policy analyses. The IBPA guiding principles are intended to ground the 12 key questions, including their supporting subquestions, in order to ensure that each is asked and answered in a way that is consistent with an intersectionality-informed analysis. While some users of The IBPA Framework will explore all questions and subquestions to help guide their analysis, in my chapter I focus on certain questions, tailoring them to fit the specific policy contexts under investigation. My use and modification of a subset of these sensitizing questions are traced in the sections to follow and enable an elucidation of the problem under investigation and an exploration of the ways that policy responses may be more intersectional. This represents a first step in applying intersectionality to a complex policy field that I locate at the "medico-legal borderland" (Mykhalovskiy, 2011; Timmermans and Gabe, 2003).

Throughout this analysis I make use of diverse data sources including various awareness campaign activities committed to supporting the health and human rights of people infected with and affected by HIV and AIDS in Canada in order to articulate the work activities and arguments of this group of heterogeneous social actors. In doing so, I seek to make explicit the space from which this intersectionality-based inquiry begins: the commitment of this paradigm to supporting a social justice agenda (Dhamoon and Hankivsky, 2011; Hankivsky et al., 2012). In this chapter I also draw upon qualitative research and policy analysis in this field with focused attention on the work of two Canadian studies: (1) Mykhalovskiy, Betteridge, and McLay (2010), who interviewed key informants in Ontario (n = 53)[4]; and (2) Grace and MacIntosh (2010; MacIntosh and Grace, 2010), whose analysis brings the science and law of HIV transmission into conversation vis-à-vis insights from HIV-positive and -HIV-negative gay men in British Columbia (n = 55).

This analysis is informed by my collaborative research experience with the Canadian Institutes of Health Research (CIHR) team in the study of acute HIV infection in gay men (2009–present). The research team is investigating the use of new HIV testing technologies, including nucleic-acid amplification testing (NAAT), for early HIV detection and response.[5] As part of a much larger research study, work with this interdisciplinary team has uncovered some of the ways in which the criminalization of HIV non-disclosure poses many challenges for people living with HIV/AIDS, public health practitioners, and HIV researchers in British Columbia. For example, the experience of our team working with community partners reveals the ways in which conducting HIV research under the specter of criminalization poses many challenges and ethical concerns for researchers and community-based organizations (CBOs). Previous work and ongoing transnational research has informed my thinking in this field and allowed access to key texts and empirical data used in this analysis (Grace 2012; Grace and Hankivsky, 2011; Grace and MacIntosh, 2010; MacIntosh and Grace, 2010).

INTERSECTIONALITY AND SEXUALITY

To begin, I define intersectionality as a theoretical approach and mode of inquiry that can help to illuminate and interpret complex systems of power, penalty, and privilege (Crenshaw, 1991, 1997; Grace, 2010; Hankivsky and Christoffersen, 2008; McCall, 2005; Weber, 2001). Theories of intersectionality offer important challenges for HIV/AIDS researchers, social theorists, activists, and policy actors when they seek to conceptualize categories and examine systems of inequity. In short, categories must not be reified, and intersectionality is a sensitizing paradigm that allows one to make sense of complexity and difference in the everyday world.

Researchers of intersectionality work to critically explore the intersections of multiple axes and levels of oppression and privilege so as to elucidate aspects of identity, social difference, and structural inequity (Winker and Degele, 2011). The simultaneous, interdependent interactions of factors such as gender (expression), sex, sexuality, ethnicity, class, indigeneity, HIV status, age, and (dis)ability must be considered within the context of broader structures and systems of oppression, including, but not limited to, racism, sexism, colonialism, and heterosexism.

This approach can expand critically upon social determinants of health research paradigms by focusing attention to questions of power, history, complexity, and relationality (Grace and Hankivsky, 2011). While subjective lived experiences of inequity must be accounted for, one must not lose sight of the complex structural conditions and power asymmetries that help to produce health disparities. The pathways to health inequity are not always straightforward, and a lens of intersectionality helps to foreground the urgency of attending to the messiness and complexity of the social world in order to provide richer and more accurate accounts that can inform evidence-based policy responses.

Intersectionality can help make visible the kinds of mutually constituting intersections that must be considered in complex policy fields. Theoretically expanding upon the oppression-focused "matrix of domination" (Collins, 2000), an IBPA demands that policy actors consider the complex, dialectical nature between systems of penalty and privilege and the individuals and groups who have intersectional standpoints along various social identities and lived actualities (e.g., racialized gay men). The concept of an "intersectional standpoint" (or intersectional subject positions) that I advance here builds upon the heritage of standpoint feminism and critical race theory in the work of Collins (Collins, 1998, 2000; Smith, 2004). I argue that rather than focus on the centrality of one unitary category to understand lived experience (e.g., women's standpoint; see Smith, 2004) intersectional standpoint brings into focus that multiple systems and social identities (e.g., gay men who are differentially raced and classed) simultaneously inform the place from which subjects view and experience the world—including their experiences of health policy.

Thinking about how we use categories of most-at-risk population (MARPs) in policy strategies—e.g., what groups like "gay,"

"MSM," or "Black MSM" may reveal and/or erase—is important in this field of inquiry. The policy effects of so-called behavior or epidemiological categories, such as MSM and WSW (women who have sex with women), must also be considered. Young and Meyer (2005) discuss how the use of categories can lead to the erasure of sexual minorities, arguing that the "purportedly neutral terms" of MSM and WSW are highly problematic insofar as "they obscure social dimensions of sexuality; undermine the self-labeling of lesbian, gay, and bisexual people; and do not sufficiently describe variations in sexual behavior" (1144). Furthermore, I agree with Hindman (2011), who argues that we must not fractionalize social groups by "treating formerly broad descriptive categories such as 'woman' or 'African-American' as smaller, internally-coherent empirical units" (190). This is consistent with an IBPA approach, as IBPAs emphasize heterogeneity and context-specific analysis.

A limited amount of scholarship in this interdisciplinary field of intersectionality has addressed explicitly issues of sexuality and HIV status among gay and bisexual men (Meyer et al., 2011; Taylor, Hines, and Casey, 2011). For example, in a recent critical review of intersectional theorizing, Hindman (2011) notes the conceptual complexity of dealing with questions of intersectionality:

> Within LGBTQ political mobilization, in-group marginalization does not fall neatly along lines of race, ethnicity, or gender, though intersectionality has undertaken the important and significant task of shedding light on these imbalances. Beyond descriptive traits lie complex issues of desire, self-affirmation, in-group contestation, and individual and collective expectations, all of which coalesce to determine not only which people, but also which practices and which political interests comprise the group. The tortuous history of signification offers a powerful testament to the agonism, compromise, and complexity that characterize the discourse on LGBTQ sexuality. (205)

IBPA has the potential to take intersectionality work on sexuality and HIV further because it requires that the discourse of policy *problems* be critically analyzed; that groups who are adversely affected by dominant policy frameworks be identified; and that policy interventions that come from affected stakeholders be integrated meaningfully.

IBPA Part 1 (Descriptive): The "Problem" Being Addressed, the Reason for this and the Effects of this Approach

In offering a discussion of two approaches to HIV prevention and governance, first, I review the use of new HIV testing technologies in British Columbia to detect AHI. This approach to HIV constructs the HIV-related problem to be both high viral loads during early stage of infection (which leads to a significant proportion of new HIV infections), and high rates of HIV among MSM, with many being unaware of HIV-positive status. Second, I discuss the context in which these tests are taking place: a climate of increased criminalization of alleged HIV non-disclosure. I argue that this criminalization approach to public health constructs the HIV-related problem to be the people living with HIV who do not disclose their HIV status to sexual partners, which puts these partners at risk of HIV infection. Table 7.1 acts as a summary of some of the key descriptive questions adapted from the IBPA sensitizing framework: *(1) What is the "problem" being addressed?; (2) How has this representation of the "problem" come about?;* and *(3) What effects are produced by this approach to the "problem?"*

Acute HIV infection and HIV Testing: "Hottest at the Start"

Growing evidence strongly suggests that a significant proportion of all new HIV infections arise from individuals with AHI, who have very recently acquired the virus. During this stage of infection, persons with AHI may be up to 26 times more infectious compared to those in later stages of infection (Hollingsworth, Anderson, and Fraser, 2008). Research explicates that depending on the stage of the epidemic, partner concurrency, and the rate of partner change, between 11 and 49 percent of new HIV infections may occur during this approximately eight-week period of "hyper-infection" (Brenner et al., 2007; Hayes and White, 2005; Pao et al., 2005). This knowledge, coupled with an awareness of the high concentration of HIV among gay, bisexual, and other MSM in British Columbia has led for calls to raise awareness of AHI among this heterogeneous group of men.

Table 7.1 Descriptive IBPA Questions

Modified IBPA Questions, Section 1	Targeted Testing for Acute HIV Infection	Criminalization of HIV non-disclosure
What is the "problem" being addressed?	• High viral loads during early stage of infection leads to significant proportion of new HIV infections • High rates of HIV among MSM (with many being unaware of HIV-positive status)	• People living with HIV who do not disclose their HIV status to sexual partners and put them at significant risk of HIV infection
How has this representation of the "problem" come about?	• Scientific advances in testing technologies that shorten the "window period" between HIV transmission and being able to detect the infection • Body of research on the significance of AHI to HIV transmission rates • Provincial, national, and international focus on biomedical solutions to HIV prevention	• Sensational media stories construct ideas of many "evil" and "reckless" perpetrators who intend to transmit HIV • NO research demonstrating efficacy of criminalizing non-disclosure in preventing HIV transmission • Provincial, national, and international trends demonstrate increasing criminalization of HIV non-disclosure
What effects are produced by this approach to the "problem"?	• Many positive effects from the viewpoint of detecting HIV infections earlier; demonstrated efficacy in detecting cases of HIV that would have been missed by other testing technologies[6] • Limited access to new tests along lines of geography (only available in urban settings in Vancouver) and sexual behavior (to gay, bisexual, and other MSM) • Need to secure funding to ensure continued access to tests at the end of the CIHR research project	• NO positive effects from a equity and public health perspective • Stigmatizes people living with HIV and leads to the social construction of criminals and victims along intersecting categories of "race," immigration status, gender, and HIV status • High rates of prosecution among racialized heterosexual men; trend indicating an increase in the prosecutions of gay men

Continued

Table 7.1 Continued

Modified IBPA Questions, *Section 1*	Targeted Testing for Acute HIV Infection	Criminalization of HIV non-disclosure
	• Increased community-based awareness campaigns of AHI and testing options for some key populations (must assess if knowledge is lower among some groups than others) • Supports a biomedical-focused approach to HIV prevention in a climate of "treatment as prevention" logic • Criminalization of HIV non-disclosure stigmatizes people living with HIV and may serve as a deterrent to getting tested for HIV • Increased HIV testing and AHI detection could lead to increased HIV non-disclosure cases among specific populations, including gay, bisexual, and other MSM • Both of these approaches to HIV prevention and governance ignore the structural drivers of the epidemic.	• Creates a barrier for researchers and health service providers • Confusion among people living with HIV of legal obligations to disclose HIV status and about the meaning of "significant risk"

The HIM has developed a useful summary of salient health information that gay, bisexual, and other MSM in British Columbia should know about AHI and HIV testing. The key points they highlight help to elucidate the work of community organizations trying to translate complex health messages to publics in accessible ways.[7] The accompanying public health campaign—featuring advertisements on free condom packs, magazines, bathroom stalls, bus shelters, and online—explains that HIV is "hottest at the start" and a "powerhouse in the sack" in the early stages of infection.

This campaign has been informed partially by qualitative research conducted with gay men in Vancouver and Victoria (Grace and MacIntosh, 2010; MacIntosh and Grace, 2010). Among other factors, the intersections of age, geography (living in urban or rural parts of the province), and HIV status were important categories. For example, MacIntosh and Grace point to different knowledge levels of HIV prevention and testing access according to these intersectional factors. This qualitative research highlights the confusion for many gay men in the meaning of different HIV testing terminology (e.g., "rapid" HIV tests versus "early" HIV tests) and window periods (e.g., how long one has to wait after a risk event to get tested for HIV) (Grace and MacIntosh, 2010; MacIntosh and Grace, 2010). MacIntosh and Grace (2010) argue that many gay men appear to be "waiting out the window": waiting 3–6 months after a risk event based on outdated information about HIV testing windows.[8] Knowledge translation and exchange (KTE), along with a commitment to developing feasible short-, medium-, and long-term solutions, is central to the transformative commitments of an IBPA. This is a small example of the collective efforts of researchers to work in ways consistent with the paradigm of intersectionality through ongoing collaborations with CBOs to help have best available evidence inform HIV testing and prevention activities in the region.

It is important to recognize the many positive effects of new testing campaigns from the viewpoint of detecting HIV infections earlier. For example, researchers have demonstrated efficacy in detecting cases of HIV that would have been missed by other testing technologies (Gilbert et al., 2011). However, limited access to new tests along lines of geography (only being available in urban settings in Vancouver) and sexual behavior (only to gay, bisexual, and other MSM) must be further considered through the lens of intersectionality. Securing funding to ensure the continued availability of tests is also required. Finally, as already discussed, it is important to acknowledge the extent to which this testing initiative supports a biomedical-focused approach to HIV prevention in a climate of "treatment as prevention" logic in and beyond British Columbia.

THE CRIMINALIZATION OF HIV NON-DISCLOSURE: "THE CREEP OF CRIMINALIZATION"

In 1998 the Supreme Court of Canada found that a man from British Columbia was guilty of assault (including sexual assault or aggravated sexual assault) for not disclosing his HIV-positive status before having sex where a significant risk of transmission existed. The *Cuerrier* decision created precedence for other HIV non-disclosure cases across Canada, as the Criminal Code is federal law (Betteridge, 2009; Canadian HIV/AIDS Legal Network, 2011). In Canada one does not need to transmit HIV to be charged; only the "significant risk" of transmission through exposure to the virus must be determined. Much has been written about the confusion in the current legal landscape in Canada, including under which circumstances a person must disclose one's HIV-positive status (Betteridge, 2009; Symington, 2009). For example, while vaginal and anal intercourse without a condom seems to meet the significant risk of transmission test set out in *Cuerrier*, many ambiguities exist regarding disclosure obligations when condoms are used, viral loads are low, and/or the sexual behavior has a low risk for transmission (e.g., oral sex).[9] At present, British Columbia's attorney general has a four-page policy manual related to HIV transmission with its section on aggravated sexual assault citing the *Cuerrier* decision.[10]

A significant intensification of HIV non-disclosure criminal cases in Canada has been observed since 2004 (Mykhalovskiy and Betteridge, 2012; Mykhalovskiy, Betteridge, and McLay, 2010). From 1989 to 2009, 98 individuals in Canada were charged with criminal offenses (resulting in 104 charges) related to HIV non-disclosure (Mykhalovskiy, Betteridge, and McLay, 2010; see Grace and Macintosh, 2010). By September 2011 this number had risen to more than 120 people living with HIV being

INTERSECTIONAL ANALYSIS   169

charged.[11] An escalation in the severity of charges laid, media attention to criminal HIV cases, and overall anxiety and debate within the "HIV community" has also been observed in Canada (Larcher and Symington, 2010, 3; Grace and McCaskell, in press). British Columbia has the third highest number of people being charged in HIV non-disclosure cases after Ontario and Quebec (Mykhalovskiy, Betteridge, and McLay, 2010, 10; Mykhalovskiy and Betteridge, 2012). When disaggregating HIV non-disclosure cases in British Columbia by sex, it is clear that the majority of persons accused are men (12 men; 2 women; 1989–2010). Further disaggregating by sex and ethnicity revels, three Caucasian men being charged, three Black men, and six men of unknown ethnicity. In cases of women, one was Aboriginal and the other of unknown ethnicity.[12] While some of the data on ethnicity is missing or unavailable, this previously unpublished information on British Columbia charges may point to a disproportionally high number of black men being charged in non-disclosure cases, echoing trends in the rest of the country. For example, Mykhalovskiy, Betteridge, and McLay (2010) discuss the large number of charges against black heterosexual defendants in Ontario and argue:

> Understanding the large number of recent cases involving Black male defendants requires careful consideration of the sexual cultures in which they participate and the organization of HIV non-disclosure therein. It also requires a deeper understanding of how police and Crown prosecutors respond to Black male defendants. (13; see Larcher and Symington, 2010)

Current advocacy work related to HIV non-disclosure is focusing on how racialized men are being constructed as "criminals" in Canada (Larcher and Symington, 2010; see Davis, 2007) and why the criminalization of HIV non-disclosure may be particularly dangerous for women in the context of sub-Saharan Africa (Armien, 2008; Open Society Institute, 2008; Grace, 2012).

The majority of defendants in British Columbia have been cases where men have been charged with not disclosing their status to women (n = 11). To date there has only been one known case of a man not disclosing his status to a same-sex sexual partner (n = 1; 2 cases unknown) (Betteridge and Mykhalovskiy, 2011). However, analysis of recent demographic patterns reveals an overall increase in Canada with respects to the number of criminal cases involving gay or bisexual men being accused of HIV non-disclosure (Mykhalovskiy, Betteridge, and McLay, 2010, 13).

Drawing on research with people living with HIV and service providers in Ontario, Mykhalovskiy (2011) has contributed to the scant empirical data in this field finding:

(1) the concept of significant risk poses serious problems to risk communication in HIV counseling and contributes to contradictory advice about disclosure obligations;
(2) criminalization discourages PHAs' [people living with HIV] openness about HIV non-disclosure in counseling relationships; and
(3) the recontextualization of public health interpretations of significant risk in criminal proceedings can intensify criminalization. (668)

This research makes explicit the unintended consequences of discursive vagueness and relates to proceedings currently before the Supreme Court of Canada (cases from Manitoba and Quebec) where the issue of significant risk is central.[13] Further, the above points build upon the descriptive statistics presented earlier (Betteridge and Mykhalovskiy, 2011) and the work calling for a review of policy options in Ontario (Mykhalovskiy, Betteridge, and McLay, 2010; Grace and McCaskell, in press).

Research by Grace and MacIntosh (2010) focused on the knowledge and concerns of HIV-positive and HIV-negative gay men related to AHI and the criminalization of HIV non-disclosure. The qualitative component of this research project involved 55 face-to-face interviews conducted during the spring and summer of 2009 in British Columbia. A portion of these informants (n = 23) specifically discussed concerns about the criminalization of HIV exposure and/or transmission in the Canadian context. Few men were aware of the increased risk of HIV transmission during the early phase following infection, or of innovations in HIV testing technology that can shorten the "window" between HIV infection and detection. As respondents discussed issues related to the criminalization of HIV non-disclosure in Canada, themes of responsibility and intersectional stigmas, and questions regarding the meaning of significant risk and legal repercussions of non-disclosure to sexual partners dominated the men's narratives. Men articulated both why disclosure of one's HIV status is important and how it can be highly problematic to disclose. Just as men sought to have the science of AHI explained, many men discussed knowledge gaps and ambiguities related to HIV legal issues and AHI.

When specifically discussing legal issues and practices of HIV disclosure, three main themes emerged from the qualitative interviews regarding why the disclosure of one's HIV-positive status to (potential) sexual partners is problematic. First, many men do not know their HIV status, or they may be in denial of their HIV-positive status. Second, practices of disclosure—such as the language used between men when discussing their HIV status, or the meaning of using or not using condoms—can be unclear or misunderstood. For example, men highlighted how the language used between potential sexual partners can be confusing. One man explained that a lot of men say—online or in person—that "I'm safe" or "I'm clean." This man questioned what such utterances may camouflage: "'I'm clean'—what does that mean? . . . and a lot of guys will go with that word" (47 year old, HIV negative). Work by the HIV/AIDS Legal Clinic Ontario (HALCO) supports how disclosure of HIV status may be confusing or misread by sexual partners (2008, 22). Betteridge (2009) puts it this way: "If you are going to disclose your HIV status to your sex partner, make it count. Avoid code words or hints like 'poz' and 'positive'" (para. 5). Third, the appropriate method by which to record how and when someone discloses their status to sexual partners was seen as unclear or unrealistic by many men (Betteridge, 2009; HALCO, 2008). An IBPA demands that this kind of knowledge is included within the policy process in order to better understand how that which may be conceived of as simple in a policy (e.g., disclosure of HIV status) is rendered complicated by the contingencies of everyday life.

Finally, the extent to which "intersectional stigmas" may be produced due to mutually informing epidemics—*or syndemics*—of HIV, criminalization, and heterosexism is worth interrogating. The concept of intersectional stigmas can allow researchers and policy actors to understand unintended policy effects and unpack the ways in which HIV stigma intersects and coconstitutes other kinds of socially constructed (criminalization-related) stigmas and related structural opportunities for political participation. For example, Berger (2004) explicates how stigmas intersect within social structure among HIV-positive and HIV-negative female sex workers and drug users: "Their experience of stigma that incorporates sexuality, race, class, and gender helps us to ascertain their unique responses to their struggle en route to political participation" (30). Early HIV research noted the relative privilege of white, middle-class gay men, who had more economic and cultural capital than other infected groups, including those within other gay and lesbian, bisexual, and transgendered networks (Epstein, 1991). Current intersectionality research addressing funding regimes of gay men's health calls into question the extent to which researchers, CBOs, and AIDS service organizations (ASOs) have been able to gain the material and economic resources to effectively mobilize a proportional response to the state of the HIV epidemic in British Columbia for gay, bisexual, and other MSM (Ferlatte, 2012; see Aguinaldo, 2008). Policy actors must consider the extent to which policy approaches can meaningfully address intersectional stigmas and inequities, promote social justice, and not reinforce stereotypes, biases, or produce further inequities.

IBPA Part 2 (Transformative): Possible Improvements to Current Approaches and Other Ways of Addressing the Public Health Issue

Emerging research, primarily based in the United States, the United Kingdom, and Canada, is clarifying the many problems with trying to prevent the spread of HIV within a culture of increased criminalization (Adam et al., 2008; Burris et al., 2007; Dodds, Bourne, and Weait, 2009; Galletly, DiFranceisco, and Pinkerton, 2009; National Aids Trust, 2011). Building on the analysis above, and employing the lens of IBPA, I offer an overview of some possible ways to improve these existing approaches to the problem, as well as potential ways to think about this public health issue differently, including the need to address structural drivers of the epidemic and understand the relationships across medical and legal state apparatuses. Table 7.2 addresses two additional IBPA questions in order to synthesize some of the key transformative tensions within and across the two public health

Table 7.2 Transformative IBPA Questions

Modified IBPA Questions, *Section 2*	Targeted Testing for Acute HIV Infection	Criminalization of HIV non-disclosure
What needs to be done to improve this approach to the problem?	• Wider and continued availability of tests to detect AHI (ensure all people who could benefit have access to the test by removing barriers such as geographic availability) • Continued partnerships and support of community-based organizations (CBOs) and AIDS service organizations (ASOs) • Continued medical and psychosocial support of newly infected persons (this includes giving clear information about the state of the science and the law, including the disclosure responsibilities of people living with HIV)	• Greatly reduce the application of the criminal law to cases of HIV non-disclosure, recognizing that only in exceptional cases does the law have a role to play (e.g., where intentional and successful HIV transmission actually occurs); follow key international policy guidelines (UNAIDS/UNDP, 2008; UNDP, 2012) • Support calls to develop prosecutorial guidelines (Crown Council Policy Manual) at the provincial level to define the scope of the law and clarify the meaning of "significant risk" based on best available scientific evidence; engage with civil society groups and people living with HIV in this process • Responsible reporting by police and media outlets that does not stigmatize people in alleged HIV non-disclosure cases

Continued

Table 7.2 Continued

Modified IBPA Questions, Section 2	Targeted Testing for Acute HIV Infection	Criminalization of HIV non-disclosure
Can the problem be thought about differently?		• Understanding HIV transmission requires attending to the broader social and structural conditions which produce differential vulnerabilities for infection • This way of approaching the problem is compatible with a critical social determinants of health perspective and places emphasis on equity, social justice, complex power relations, and the context-specific nature of HIV risk and resilience
What are the structural and political challenges of doing so?		• Canadian and international public health funding largely focused on biomedical approaches to HIV prevention • Narrow policy focus on the risk behaviors of individuals and groups • Stigma around HIV and other intersections of vulnerability (e.g., sexual orientation, gender expression, sex work, drug use) • Financial constraints and competition for limited resources • The need to both fund and make use of research in policy making (including qualitative, mixed-methods and community-based research) to better understand the unique needs of populations along diverse intersections of vulnerability.

approaches reviewed: (1) *What needs to be done to improve this approach to the "problem?"* and (2) *Can the "problem" be thought about differently and what are the structural and political challenges in doing so?* I build upon material presented in Table 7.2 in the discussion that follows, by paying focused attention to calls for prosecutorial guidelines that would reduce or eliminate the use of the criminal law in alleged cases of HIV non-disclosure.

Intersectionality adds necessary complexity when considering issues of sexuality, science, HIV/AIDS, public health, and the law. Policy actors must address questions of relationality and complexity so as to account for the broader conditions in which health differences are organized. The IBPA Framework used in this preliminary analysis may help to spark such critical policy thinking. In addition, it should facilitate finding ways to safeguard all people from the potential social and legal ramifications of an acute HIV diagnosis, including those with heightened vulnerability due to their intersectional subject positions. On a related front, it highlights how the use of intersections and the social determinants of health language could become mainstreamed in global HIV/AIDS texts such as a recent UNAIDS report in which the authors emphasize the need to address a confluence of intersecting factors related to HIV vulnerability:

> The intersection between social exclusion, inequality and HIV risk underscores the need to address the epidemic's social dimensions. Without courageous action to alleviate the social roots of HIV risk and vulnerability, it will be impossible to reach global HIV goals. (UNAIDS, 2011, 38)

More research is needed to examine the relationship between new HIV testing technologies and the criminalization of HIV non-disclosure, and intersectionality-informed analysis may be helpful in this work. For example, while the gay men interviewed in Grace and MacIntosh's (2010) analysis had much expert knowledge to share, many expressed a lack of knowledge regarding AHI, new HIV testing technologies, and the specifics of how criminal law is being applied to cases of HIV non-disclosure in Canada. These knowledge gaps point to areas were increasing the health and legal literacy of gay, bisexual, and other MSM could support community and public health goals. The relationship between criminalization and access to treatment, care, and support must also be further examined. As Mykhalovskiy (2011) has argued:

> In a perverse fashion, rather than promoting openness, criminalization has made it more difficult to provide meaningful HIV prevention counseling and support about HIV non-disclosure. While the use of the criminal law may be warranted in some circumstances, the expansive use of a vague legal concept of significant risk does little good either for preventing HIV transmission or for the credibility of the criminal justice system. (675)

In addition, further research is required to explore other related issues of criminalization and HIV testing technologies, including the complex field of phylogenetic analysis, which considers how two or more HIV strains are related (NAT, 2011).

The work of organizations such as HIM, among others, must continue to be supported, as they are working to raise awareness of HIV and AHI in British Columbia alongside efforts to support sex-positive messaging that targets determinants of health, such as heterosexism. For example, HIM has spearheaded campaigns that address broader determinants of gay men's health and recognize the role of the law as one distal determinant. HIM launched the "Vancouver/*Fabulous since 1969*" campaign during the 2010 Olympics, which included posters reading: "*Gay love has been legal in Canada since 1969, protected by the Constitution since 1992 and celebrated with marriage since 2005.*"[14] Focusing only on biomedical solutions to HIV can risk framing the problem of HIV transmission as one that exists only at the individual level of risk, rather than focusing on the structural conditions that produce differential risks along complex intersections of social identity and location. While the law can support health equity, it can play a highly problematic role in criminalizing people living with HIV, creating stigma, and negatively impacting population health (see Aguinaldo, 2008; Burris, 2011; UNDP, 2012).

In the context of large-scale efforts to increase HIV testing in Canada, a growing number of groups have worked to articulate why the criminalization of HIV non-disclosure is a problem in Canada. For example, *AIDS ACTION NOW!* along with more than a dozen ASOs has supported the call of the *Ontario Working Group on Criminal Law and HIV Exposure* (CLHE) to ask for prosecutorial guidelines for cases of HIV non-disclosure, believing that

> guidelines are needed to ensure that HIV-related criminal complaints are handled in a fair and non-discriminatory manner. The guidelines must ensure that decisions to investigate and prosecute such cases are informed by a complete and accurate understanding of current medical and scientific research about HIV and take into account the social contexts of living with HIV. (CLHE, 2011, 1)

Like HIM's aforementioned work on AHI, this campaign has endeavored to translate key issues in accessible and actionable ways while making use of the best available, albeit limited, criminalization-related scientific evidence in the Canadian context (Grace and McCaskell, in press).[15] This awareness campaign is part of the work of a growing community of transnational actors focusing on issues of justice and equity in order to raise attention to why the criminalization of HIV non-disclosure is problematic (Larcher and Symington, 2010; Grace, 2012).

ASOs and advocacy groups are working to consider how the blunt force of the criminal law is both ineffective and may be increasingly dangerous for some subsets of the population, within and beyond the Canada context. I argue that applying the lens of intersectionality is a natural extension of the kind of thinking and advocacy that many ASOs and community groups are conducting as part of their efforts to problematize the application of the criminal law to cases of alleged HIV non-disclosure. To date, the initiatives I cite have not explicitly invoked the language or paradigm of intersectionality, and more research is required in this field to better understand how systems of penalty and privilege may result in differential impacts and applications of the criminal law and experiences of intersectional stigma.

Echoing calls in Ontario for prosecutorial guidelines, Positive Living BC chair Glyn Townson recently explained the need for such a text in British Columbia: "The bottom line is we want everyone to have an enjoyable, full sex life, and making criminals out of people for natural human behaviour is a little bit problematic" (quoted in Christopher, 2011, para. 2). Thinking about this issue from an intersectional perspective, policy actors could question the extent to which some intersectional subjects may be more likely to be criminalized and stigmatized by increasing targeted testing practices, prosecutions, and media spectacle. The shortened window period between a risk event and positive test result makes it increasingly likely that people have a better idea of how they were infected with HIV and who may have infected them. The extent to which this may lead to increased charges within the gay community is unknown. While biomedical solutions to HIV prevention and treatment are important, the current (dominant) logic of *treatment as prevention* does little (if anything) to address the social and structural determinants of heath for sexual minorities, including gay, bisexual, and other MSM. In fact, structural factors, including the criminalization of HIV non-disclosure, support systems of oppression, marginalization, and health disparity. Rather than simply posit gay, bisexual, and other MSM as homogeneous MARPs, policy actors could consider both the heterogeneity of this population and the role of distal systems of privilege and penalty in Canada. Such work requires that complex, historically situated factors, including, but not limited to, colonialism, heterosexism, capitalism, and patriarchy be meaningfully considered as part of the HIV response, and IBPA promises a rich resource to address these specificities and complexities.

Conclusion

Policy analysis, argues Fischer (1987), "lies squarely (if uncomfortably) between science and ethics" (cited in Kenny and Giacomini, 2005, 257). It is at these coconstituting, sometimes uncomfortable intersections, that an IBPA is conducted: analyzing the social constructions of policy problems and the empirical actualities of inequity through a critical paradigm that remains committed to a set of ethics of equity, social justice, and rigorous empirical inquiry. These normative ethics—"what ought to be done in specific circumstances" (Kenny and Giacomini, 2005, 253)—demand that policy actors foreground their commitments and values in order to realize the transformative potential of an IBPA. Currently in its nascent stages of application to this complex health field, more work is needed to consider the extent to which the research paradigm of intersectionality, and an IBPA Framework specifically, can be used effectively to address the specific health needs of heterogeneous groups who have disproportionally high rates of HIV infection, including gay, bisexual, and other MSM. For example, recent conference and meeting presentations in British Columbia have begun a dialogue with civil society, researchers, and policy actors about the limits and possibilities of intersectionality in the field of gay men's health (Hankivsky, 2010; Grace and Hankivsky, 2011). However, it is important to acknowledge that this paradigm of analysis is but one way to understand the complex policy field under investigation and should be complemented by other critical social science literature including that which attends to the public health implications of shifting sexual landscapes and "technologies of risk" for gay men (Race, 2001). For example, Kane Race's scholarship in this field is consistent with the focus within an IBPA on questions of power, politics, and problem definition:

> If, as Foucault argued, political technologies advance by reframing what is essentially a political problem in the neutral language of science (Dreyfus and Rabinow, 1982: 196), then we must attend to the power effects of the seemingly neutral—but undeniably useful—technologies of medicine, if we are to respond effectively to HIV/AIDS. (2001, 168–169)

Calls have been made to recognize the value and urgency of integrating intersectionality, along with other theories, such as the minority stress model, life course perspective, and social ecology perspective, into research and policy approaches that address the needs of lesbian, gay, bisexual, transgender, and queer (LGBTQ) communities (Institute of Medicine, 2011). While this attention to questions of intersectionality and sexuality represents an exciting development reflective of critical thinking within this field, I caution that the operationalization of intersectionality by the Institute of Medicine as a perspective that examines "an individual's multiple identities and the ways in which they interact" risks obfuscating important discussions of power, history, and social structure central to this mode of inquiry and recasting the discussion of LGBTQ health as one of identity politics removed from sustained considerations of structural disadvantage (Institute of Medicine, 2011, 2). The mainstreaming of intersectionality in policy and research discussions is exciting, but principles of equity, power, social justice, and the multileveled nature of the issues being addressed must not be lost along the way (Hankivsky et al., 2012). As Dhamoon (2011) urges, "in the process of mainstreaming intersectionality, it is crucial to frame it as a form of social critique so as to foreground its radical capacity to attend to and disrupt oppressive vehicles of power" (230).

Rather than predetermine all of the social determinants of HIV transmission, intersectionality demands that researchers remain open to the process of discovery when considering complex, intersecting, proximal, and distal factors. The same is true for policy actors as they critically engage in the process of an IBPA and work to consider equity-focused solutions to the problem of HIV transmission. While much focus has been placed on the public health implications of low viral load in a so-called post-AIDS era (Dowsett and McInnes, 1996), this analysis signals the need for further reflection on the implications of utilizing new testing technologies that detect HIV infection when viral loads are at their highest. The wide availability of new HIV testing technologies that can detect AHI must be welcomed alongside an increased focus on the structural drivers of the epidemic that produce differential vulnerabilities depending on one's intersectional standpoint and a sustained consideration of the social context in which technologies are being implemented including the state's legal climate. No evidence exists that the use of the criminal law will prevent HIV transmission in Canada. Instead, the criminalization of HIV non-disclosure poses a range of public health challenges and may even serve as a deterrent to people coming forward for HIV testing, including for new testing technologies capable of detecting AHI. Current efforts to support the creation of prosecutorial guidelines as a harm reduction strategy to limit the application of the criminal law in Ontario underscore the need for such guidelines to be revised in British Columbia in order to clarify disclosure obligations for people living with HIV and mitigate the stigmatizing, dangerous, and overly broad use of existing criminal law powers.

Notes

1. I am thankful for the feedback provided by Olena Hankivsky, Olivier Ferlatte, and Ilan Meyer and acknowledge the resources provided by Cecile Kazatchkine, Josephine MacIntosh, Glen Betteridge, and Eric Mykhalovskiy. I am grateful for the comments of three anonymous peer reviewers on a previous iteration of their chapter and wish to note the important contributions of many members of the CIHR Team in the Study of Acute HIV infection in Gay Men.

2. While I use the category of MSM in the chapter due to its common application in the public health and epidemiological literature, I position it as highly problematic (Young and Meyer, 2005). My limited use of this behavioral category—used in HIV research since at least the early 1990s—is to capture men who do not identify as gay or bisexual (e.g., may identify as straight or heterosexual) but who have sex with men. It is important to consider the related conceptual challenge of nonidentity categories, such as MSM, and what I call "identity-behavior" intersections, such as Black MSM. Further, I argue that recent meta-analyses of HIV infection risk disparities among Black MSM (relative to other MSM) in Canada, the United States, and the United Kingdom (Millett et al., 2012) offer much promise for understanding HIV transmission patterns but would benefit from intersectional thinking in order to more robustly account for the complex social and structural factors that produce differential vulnerability.
3. The Oslo Declaration on HIV Criminalization, prepared by international civil society in Oslo, Norway, on February 13, 2012, has compiled relevant international resources in this field as part of their transnational advocacy, retrieved from http://www.hivjustice.net/wp-content/uploads/2012/02/Oslo_declaration.pdf. Also see information on a recent Canadian documentary addressing the issue of criminalization and HIV-positive women, retrieved from http://www.positivewomenthemovie.org/.
4. This included lawyers, medical health professionals, medical and mental health professionals, and AIDS Service Organization (ASO) staff (n = 25) and people living with HIV/AIDS in Ontario (n = 28).
5. The website for the CIHR Team in the Study of Acute HIV Infection in Gay Men, which includes published research and background information on AHI, is http://www.acutehivstudy.com/.
6. Gilbert et al. (2011).
7. For more information on this campaign, including HIM's key messages on AHI, visit http://checkhimout.ca/hottest/.
8. This research has also informed other public health outreach activities, including working with AIDS Vancouver Island (AVI) and HIM in 2010 to conduct awareness campaigns in gay bars in Victoria, British Columbia.
9. Betteridge (2009) explains that people may even have a duty, under existing interpretations of *Cuerrier*, to disclose their possible HIV-positive status if "the person knows there is a real possibility that he or she has HIV, but has not received an actual HIV-positive test result" (para. 4).
10. A recent article in the gay and lesbian newspaper *Xtra!* reviews why key policy actors believe new HIV guidelines are needed for BC

prosecutors (Christopher, 2011). See Grace and McCaskell (in press) for further information on HIV activism in this field.
11. For updated information on Canadian non-disclosure charges and material on HIV/AIDS and the law, see www.aidslaw.ca.
12. Data provided by Betteridge and Mykhalovskiy (2011).
13. Supreme Court of Canada. Court File Nos. 33976/34094. Her Majesty the Queen and Clato Lual Mabior, and Her Majesty the Queen and DC.
14. For more information about this and other HIM campaigns, visit: http://checkhimout.ca/. It is also worth noting that employees and volunteers of HIM have been a part of discussions about intersectionality (e.g., reading group meetings, special guest lectures) hosted by the Institute for Intersectionality Research and Policy (IIRP) at Simon Fraser University.
15. For more information on this campaign, visit: http://www.aidsactionnow.org/?p=349.

References

Adam, B., R. Elliot, W. Husbands, J. Murrary, and J. Maxwell. 2008. "Effects of the Criminalization of HIV Transmission in Cuerrier on Men Reporting Unprotected Sex with Men." *Canadian Journal of Law & Society* 23(1–2): 143–159.

Aguinaldo, J. P. 2008. "The Social Construction of Gay Oppression as a Determinant of Gay Men's Health: 'Homophobia Is Killing Us.'" *Critical Public Health* 18(1): 87–96.

Armien, J. 2008. "Invisibility of Gender Violence Augmented…: Implications of HIV Criminalization." *ALQ* (September/November 2008): 30–33. Retrieved from http://www.icw.org/files/ALQ_Double_Edition_08_-_Criminalisation.pdf

Berger, M. T. 2004. *Workable Sisterhood: The Political Journey of Stigmatized Women with HIV/AIDS.* Princeton: Princeton University Press.

Betteridge, G. 2009. "Law and Discloure." *The Positive Side* (Spring/Summer). Retrieved from http://www.catie.ca/en/positiveside/springsummer-2009/law-disclosure

Betteridge, G., and E. Mykhalovskiy. 2011. Unpublished data on BC HIV non-disclosure cases.

Brenner, B. G., M. Roger, J. P. Routy, D. Moisi, M. Ntemgwa, C. Matte, and Quebec Primary HIV Infection Study Group. 2007. "High Rates of Forward Transmission Events after Acute/Early HIV-1 Infection." *Journal of Infectious Diseases* 195(7): 951–959.

Burris, S. 2011. "Law in a Social Determinants Strategy: A Public Health Law Research Perspective." *Public Health Reports* 126(3): 22–27.

Burris S., L. Beletsky, J. Burleson, P. Case, and Z Lazzarini. 2007. "Do Criminal Laws Influence HIV Risk Behavior? An Empirical Trial." *Arizona State Law Journal* 39: 467–517.
Burris, S., and E. Cameron. 2008. "The Case against Criminalization of HIV Transmission." *JAMA* 300(5): 578–581.
Canadian HIV/AIDS Legal Network. 2011. *Criminal Law and HIV Non-Disclosure in Canada: Questions and Answers.* Retrieved from http://www.aidslaw.ca/publications/publicationsdocEN.php?ref=1222.
Christopher, N. 2011. "New HIV Guidelines Needed for BC Prosecutors." *Xtra!* (Wednesday, May 25). Retrieved from http://www.xtra.ca/public/Vancouver/New_HIV_guidelines_needed_for_BC_prosecutors-10217.aspx
Collins, P. H. 2000. *Black Feminist Thought: Knowledge, Consciousness, and the Politics of Empowerment.* 2nd ed. New York: Routledge.
———. 1998. "'Its All in the Family': Intersections of Gender, Race, and Nation." *Hypatia* 13(3): 62–82.
Crenshaw, K. 1997. "Beyond Racism and Misogyny: Black Feminism and 2 Live Crew." In *Women Transforming Politics: An Alternative Reader,* edited by C. J. Cohen, K. B. Jones, and J. C. Tronto, 549–568. New York: NY Univ. Press.
———. 1991. "Demarginalizing the Intersection of Race and Sex: A Black Feminist Critique of Antidiscrimination Doctrine, Feminist Theory, and Antiracist Politics." In *Feminist Legal Theory,* edited by K. Bartlett and R. Kennedy, 57–80. Boulder: Westview.
Davis, A. 2007. "Race and Criminalization: Black Americans and the Punishment Industry." In *Race, Ethnicity, and Gender,* 2nd ed., edited by J. F. Healey and E. O'Brien. Pine Forge Press, Thousand Oaks.
Dhamoon, R. K. 2011. "Considerations on Mainstreaming Intersectionality." *Political Research Quarterly* 64(1): 230–243.
Dhamoon, R. K., and O. Hankivsky. 2011. "Why the Theory and Practice of Intersectionality Matter to Health Research and Policy." In *Health Inequities in Canada: Intersectional Frameworks and Practices,* edited O. Hankivsky, 16–50. Vancouver, BC: UBC Press.
Dodds, C., A. Bourne, and M. Weait. 2009. "Responses to Criminal Prosecutions for HIV Transmission among Gay Men with HIV in England and Wales." *Reproductive Health Matters* 17(34): 135–145.
Dowsett, G., and D. McInnes. 1996. "Gay Community, AIDS Agencies and the HIV Epidemic in Adelaide: Theorizing 'Post AIDS'." *Social Alternatives* 15(4): 29–32.
Eba, P. 2008. "One Size Punishes All...A Critical Appraisal of the Criminalization of HIV Transmission." *ALQ* (September/November 2008): 1–10. Retrieved from http://www.icw.org/files/ALQ_Double_Edition_08_-_Criminalisation.pdf

Elliott, R. 2002. *Criminal Law, Public Health and HIV Transmission: A Policy Options Paper.* Geneva: UNAIDS.

Epstein, S. 1991. "Democratic Science? AIDS Activism and the Contested Construction of Knowledge." *Socialist Review* 21(2): 33–50.

Ferlatte, O. 2012. "Are There Enough Gay Dollars? An Intersectionality-Based Policy Analysis of HIV Prevention Funding for Gay Men in British Columbia, Canada." In *An Intersectionality-Based Policy Analysis Framework*, Simon Fraser University. Available at http://www.sfu.ca/iirp/ibpa_downloads.html.

Galletly, C., W. DiFranceisco, and S. Pinkerton. 2009. "HIV-Positive Person's Awareness and Understanding of Their State's Criminal HIV Disclosure Law." *AIDS and Behavior* 13(6): 1262–1269.

Gilbert, M., M. Kwag, M. Steinberg, D. Grace, and M. Rekart. 2011. "Sustaining an Effective Response to Acute HIV Infection Among Gay Men." Paper presented at the Gay Men's Health Summit: Health and Sexual Rights, Vancouver, November 3–4, 2011.

Grace, D. 2012. "This Is Not a Law: The Transnational Politics and Protest of Legislating an Epidemic." Dissertation. University of Victoria, Canada. Retrieved from http://hdl.handle.net/1828/3944

———. 2010. "When Oppressions and Privileges Collide: A Review of Research in Health, Gender and Intersectionality in Late (Post) Modernity." *Canadian Journal of Humanities and Social Sciences* 1(1): 20–24.

Grace, D., and O. Hankivsky. 2011. "Praxis, Power and Possibility: Intersectionality as a Critical Research Paradigm for International HIV/AIDS Researchers." Paper presented at Locating the Social: 1st International Social Science and Humanities Conference on HIV, Durban, South Africa, June 11–13, 2011.

Grace, D., and J. MacIntosh. 2010. "Responsibilities, Significant Risks and Legal Repercussions: Interviews with Gay Men as Complex Knowledge-Exchange Sites of Scientific and Legal HIV Information." Paper presented at the XVIII International AIDS Conference, Vienna, July, 18–23 2010.

Grace, D., and T. McCaskell. 2013, in press. "'We Are Not Criminals': Activists Working to Address the Criminalization of HIV Non-Disclosure." In *HIV Politics, Policy, and Activism*, edited by D. Ray. New York: Praeger.

Hankivsky, O. 2010. "Exploring the Promise of Intersectionality for Gay Men's Health." Paper presented at the Gay Men's Health Summit, British Columbia, Canada, November 23, 2010.

Hankivsky, O., and A. Christoffersen. 2008. "Intersectionality and the Determinants of Health: A Canadian Perspective." *Critical Public Health* 18(3): 271–283.

Hankivsky, O., D. Grace, G. Hunting, O. Ferlatte, N. Clark, A. Fridkin, and T. Laviolette. 2012. "Intersectionality-Based Policy Analysis." In *An Intersectionality-Based Policy Analysis Framework*, Simon Fraser University. Retrieved from http://www.sfu.ca/iirp/ibpa_downloads.html.

Hayes, R. J., and White R. G. 2005. "Amplified HIV Transmission during Early-Stage Infection." *Journal of Infectious Diseases* 193(4): 604–605.

Health Initiative for Men [HIM]. 2011. "HIV: Its Hottest at the Start." Retrieved from http://checkhimout.ca/hottest/

Hindman, M. D. 2011. "Rethinking Intersectionality: Towards an Understanding of Discursive Marginalization." *New Political Science* 33(2): 189–210.

HIV/AIDS Legal Clinic Ontario [HALCO]. 2008. "HIV Disclosure: A Legal Guide for Gay Men in Ontario." Retrieved from http://www.halco.org/wpcontent/uploads/2011/06/HIV_Disclosure-legal_guide_for_gay_men_in_Ontario_2008_Dec-English.pdf

Hollingsworth, T. D., R. M. Anderson, and C. Fraser. 2008. "HIV-1 Transmission, by Stage of Infection." *Journal of Infectious Diseases* 198(5): 687–693.

Institute of Medicine. 2011. *The Health of Lesbian, Gay, Bisexual, and Transgender People: Building a Foundation for Better Understanding.* Report Brief. March 31, 2011.

International Community of Women Living with HIV/AIDS. 2009. ICW Concerned Over Trend to Criminalize HIV Transmission. Retrieved from www.icw.org/node/354.

Jürgens, R., J. Cohen, E. Cameron, S. Burris, M. Clayton, R. Elliot, and D. Cupido. 2009. "Ten Reasons to Oppose the Criminalization of HIV Exposure or Transmission." *Reproductive Health Matters* 17(34): 163–172.

Kenny, N., and M. Giacomini. 2005. "Wanted: A New Ethics Field for Health Policy Analysis." *Health Care Analysis* 13(4): 247–260.

Larcher, A. A., and A. Symington. 2010. "Criminal and Victims? The Impact of the Criminalization of HIV Non-Disclosure on African, Caribbean and Black Communities in Ontario." November 2010. Toronto, ON: African & Caribbean Council on HIV/AIDS in Ontario.

MacIntosh, J., and D. Grace. 2010. "Waiting out the Window: Missed Opportunities for Early Testing and Detection of Acute HIV Infection among Gay Men in British Columbia." Paper presented at the XVIII International AIDS Conference, Vienna, July 18–23, 2010.

Marks, G., N. Crepaz, J. W. Senterfitt, and R. S. Janssen. 2005. "Meta-Analysis of High-Risk Sexual Behavior in Persons Aware and Unaware

They Are Infected with HIV in the United States." *Journal of Acquired Immune Deficiency Syndromes* 39(4): 446–453.
McCall, L. 2005. "The Complexity of Intersectionality." *Signs* 30(3): 1771–1800.
Meyer, I. H., S. C. Ouellette, R. Haile, and T. A. McFarlane. 2011. "'We'd Be Free': Narratives of Life without Homophobia, Racism, or Sexism." *Sexuality Research & Social Policy* 8(3): 204–214.
Millett, G. A. et al. 2012. "Comparisons of Disparities and Risks of HIV Infection in Black and Other Men Who Have Sex with Men in Canada, UK and USA: A Meta-Analysis." *Lancet* (July 2012): 11–18.
Mykhalovskiy, E. 2011. "The Problem of 'Significant Risk': Exploring the Public Health Impact of Criminalizing HIV Non-Disclosure." *Social Science & Medicine* 73(5): 668–675.
Mykhalovskiy, E., and G. Betteridge. 2012. "Who? What? Where? When? and with What Consequences? An Analysis of Criminal Cases of HIV Non-Disclosure in Canada." *Canadian Journal of Law and Society* 27(1): 31–53.
Mykhalovskiy, E., G. Betteridge, and D. McLay. 2010. *HIV Non-Disclosure and the Criminal Law: Establishing Policy Options for Ontario*. Toronto: Ontario HIV Treatment Network.
National Aids Trust [NAT]. 2011. "Estimating the Likelihood of Recent HIV Infection—Implications for Criminal Prosecution." HIV Forensics II. Report. Retrieved from http://www.nat.org.uk/media/Files/Policy/2011/RITA%20Testing%20Report.pdf
Ontario Working Group on Criminal Law and HIV Exposure [CLHE]. 2011. "Prosecutorial Guidelines Petition. Ontario Working Group on Criminal Law and HIV Exposure." Retrieved from http://ontarioaidsnetwork.on.ca/clhe/
Open Society Institute. 2008. "10 Reasons to Oppose the Criminalization of HIV Exposure or Transmission." Retrieved from http://www.soros.org/sites/default/files/10reasons_20081201.pdf
Pao, D., M. Fisher, S. Hue, G. Dean, G. Murphy, P. A Cane, and D. Pillay. 2005. "Transmission of HIV-1 during Primary Infection: Relationship to Sexual Risk and Sexually Transmitted Infections." *AIDS* 19(1): 85–90.
Pearshouse, R. 2008. "Legislation Contagion: Building Resistance." *HIV AIDS Policy Law Rev.* 13(2/3): 1–11.
Race, K. 2001. "The Undetectable Crisis: Changing Technologies of Risk." *Sexualities* 4(2): 167–189.
Smith, D. E. 2004. "Women's Perspective as a Radical Critique of Sociology." In *The Feminist Standpoint Theory Reader*, edited by S. Harding, 21–34. New York: Routledge (Orig. pub. 1974).

Symington, A. 2009. "Criminalization Confusion and Concern: The Decade since the Cuerrier Decision." *HIV/AIDS Policy & Law Review* 14(1): 5–10.
Taylor, Y., S. Hines, and M. E. Casey. 2011. *Theorizing Intersectionality and Sexuality.* New York: Palgrave Macmillan.
Timmermans, S., and J. Gabe. 2003. *Partners in Health, Partners in Crime.* Oxford: Blackwell.
UNAIDS. 2011. *AIDS at 30: Nations at the Crossroads.* Retrieved from http://www.unaids.org/unaids_resources/aidsat30/aids-at-30.pdf
UNAIDS Reference Group. 2009. *Statement on Criminalization of HIV Transmission or Exposure.* Retrieved from http://data.unaids.org/pub/Report/2009/20090303_hrrefgroupcrimexposure_en.pdf
UNAIDS/UNDP. 2008. *Criminalization of HIV Transmission.* Policy Brief. Geneva, Switzerland. Retrieved from http://data.unaids.org/pub/basedocument/2008/20080731_jc1513_policy_criminalization_en.pdf
UNDP. 2012. *HIV and the Law: Risks, Rights and Health.* The Global Commission on HIV and the Law. Retrieved from www.hivlawcommission.org
Weber, L. 2001. *Understanding Race, Class, Gender, and Sexuality: A Conceptual Framework.* Boston: McGraw-Hill.
Winker, G., and N. Degele. 2011. "Intersectionality as Multi-Level Analysis: Dealing with Social Inequality." *European Journal of Women's Studies* 18(1): 51–66.
Young, R. M., and I. H. Meyer. 2005. "The Trouble with 'MSM' and 'WSW': Erasure of the Sexual-Minority Person in Public Health Discourse." *American Journal of Public Health* 95(7): 1144–1149.

8

Crossroads or Categories? Intersectionality Theory and the Case of Lesbian, Gay, and Bisexual Equalities Initiatives in UK Local Government

Surya Monro and Diane Richardson

> It is not at all clear whether intersectionality should be limited to understanding individual experiences, to theorizing identity, or whether it should be taken as a property of social structures and cultural discourses.
>
> (Davis, 2008, 68).

The last 40 years have seen major transformations in the theorization of sexuality, with wide-ranging implications for the fields of social theory and policy. Intersectionality theory has emerged during this period, as a means of addressing the complex ways in which social characteristics are routed through each other. The origins and development of intersectionality theory has been well documented by authors such as Brah and Pheonix (2004), Walby (2007), Nash (2008), Shields (2008), and Grabham et al. (2009). Intersectionality theory contributes to our understandings of sexuality in that it can be used to bridge two seemingly disparate approaches to understanding of sexuality: those that take a foundational approach, framing sexuality and gender—or other forces, such as the material—as fundamental to the ways in which individual and social identities are shaped, and those that seek to deconstruct foundational categories (Davis, 2008). Intersectionality studies have focused primarily on gender, class, and race; where included, sexuality is often placed in a marginal position (see Crenshaw, 1997; Shields, 2008; Hurtado and Sinha, 2008). There have been some exceptions, including Beckett's (2004) study of the operation of heterosexuality in the lives of lesbian and disabled women, and Fish's (2008) research on lesbian, gay, bisexual, and transgender (LGBT) identities and health care. Many chapters in this edited collection, including this chapter, contribute to the intersectional scholarship concerning sexualities.

The concept of intersectionality has been the subject of confusion (Davis, 2008), and there have been controversies around whether intersectionality should be seen as a crossroads (Crenshaw, 1991), as axis of difference (Yuval-Davis, 2006), or as a dynamic process (Staunaes 2003, cited in Davis, 2008, 68). There are tensions within the field of intersectionality studies, relating to broader debates within sexuality studies and feminisms, concerning whether to pursue category-based analysis or to develop analysis along a range of foundational axis (see Walby, 2007 and Weldon, 2008). Concerns have also been raised that intersectionality analysis has led to a problematic focus on the individual, identity, and representation (Conaghan, 2009). As Valentine states, "the contemporary focus within the social sciences on the fluidity of identity categories and the complexity of intersections risks losing sight of the fact that within particular spaces there are dominant spatial orderings that produce moments of exclusion for particular groups" (2007, 19).

Following Crenshaw (1991), conventional approaches to intersectionality focus on the place where more than one force of inequality is operating. However, subsequent authors have developed other interpretations, for instance, McCall's (2005) intracategorical, anticategorical, and intercategorical forms of intersectional analysis, and Walby's (2007) separation of multiple inequalities into different approaches, which tend to fall into either systems-oriented approaches or postmodernist, deconstructive, and identity-focused ones. This chapter was suggested by the work of these authors, building in particular on McCall's intercategorical approach, which interrogates relations of inequality between whole groups, and manages the complexity of this by reducing analysis to one or two intergroup relations at a time (McCall, 2005, 61).

This chapter discusses the conceptualization and application of the term "intersectionality." It explores questions concerning the remit of intersectionality theory, specifically debates between the conventional approaches that focus on the interstices, or crossroads, between different social forces and categories, and those who argue instead for attention to specific social categories and forces that may be seen as foundational. In order to explore this debate, the chapter examines the operation of two structuring forces within the context of LGB equalities initiatives in UK local government: sexuality and spatiality. The category of sexuality is shown to be important in shaping the lives of LGB people and the work of the local authorities that interface with them. The category of the spatial was selected because empirical findings indicate that the spatial dimension is key to the structuring of sexualities at a local level; the level at which local authorities interface with the population. The chapter draws on scholarship in the field of geographies of sexuality[1], the trajectory of which is well rehearsed by authors such as Collins (2004), and Brown, Browne, and Lim (2007). The focus of the chapter is narrowed in that it looks at LGB equalities, and transgender (T) is not included[2]; transgender is discussed elsewhere (see for example Monro, 2005; Hines, 2007; and Monro and Richardson, 2010).

The chapter begins by providing an overview of the literature and the contemporary situation regarding local government sexualities equalities initiatives, noting the major recent policy changes, and then summarizing the types of work that are taking place and the ways in which local authorities do—or do not—deal with intersectionality. In doing so it develops understanding of sexuality as a foundational category, and addresses the intersectional nature of sexuality, within the context of UK local government. The chapter then brings in a second category via an exploration of spatiality, focusing on the lives of the LGB people whom local authorities represent and the spatialized interventions that local authority actors develop concerning LGB equalities. We conclude by arguing for an intersectionality studies that interrogates social categories as well as their interstices, as illustrated by our use of data regarding LGB equalities work in local government, where spatiality forms one aspect of the complex and situated structuring of sexualities.

The empirical content of the chapter is based on anonymized findings from a large Economic and Social Research Council funded study of local authorities in Northern Ireland, Wales, and Northern and Southern England.[3] We utilized a participative action research approach (McNiff, 1998), specifically Action Learning Sets, which met 4 times in each region (a total of 16 meetings, with members representing different local authorities, community organizations, and partner agencies from across the regions). We also tracked the development and implementation of sexualities equalities policies in four local authorities that were purposively sampled to represent authorities of different types, levels of performance, political colors, activity concerning equalities, and levels of deprivation. We did fieldwork with strategic level and frontline local authority workers (focusing on two different service areas for each authority), and their partners in statutory sector and voluntary/community sector agencies (a total of 37 interviews). A further strand of the methodology consisted of interviews with key national stakeholders across the 3 countries (15 interviews), and a final strand comprised of 5 interviews with local authority members (councillors). This chapter is based on data from North East England and Wales, including 2 Action Learning Sets, 18 interviews in case study localities, and interviews with 10 national stakeholder representatives.[4] The data is used primarily as evidence for the argument that category-based, as well as interstice-based, approaches to intersectional analysis are necessary.[5]

LGB Equalities Initiatives in Local Government

There is a small but growing body of work concerning sexuality and equality and diversity initiatives in local government. A number of writers, including Carabine (1995, 1996a, 1996b), Cooper (1994, 1997), and Tobin (1990), focus on developments in the 1980s and early 1990s. This era saw the development of lesbian and gay equalities work amongst some left-wing local authorities, and a subsequent right-wing backlash that led to the introduction of Section 28,[6] and the collapse of most sexuality equalities initiatives. The next phase of sexuality equalities work, which was brought in by a politically more heterogeneous tranche of local authorities in the 1990s, was quite different in many ways, with a shift taking place toward programs addressing homophobic violence, and a decline in overtly political affirmations of gay identity, as well as some areas of work such as AIDS initiatives (Cooper and Monro, 2003; Carabine and Monro, 2004; Monro, 2006, 2007). The most recent body of work is just emerging (Monro and Richardson, 2010; and Richardson and Monro, 2012).

Fieldwork was conducted at a time when the field of UK LGB equalities work was undergoing a period of rapid change, fueled by the introduction of a range of new legislation, including the Adoption and Children Act 2002, the Civil Partnerships Act 2004, and the Equality Regulations (Sexual Orientation) 2007.[7] A tranche of policy directives and implementation mechanisms were being developed in tandem with statutory drivers. LGB equalities initiatives were further affected by the recently introduced Commission for Equality and Human Rights, as well as the Single Equality Act (2010).[8]

Overall, the research findings indicated that LGB equalities work has become a normalized aspect of the local authority service provision remit to a degree, alongside other strands of equalities (race, gender, disability, age, faith, and Welsh language in Wales), partially as a result of the legislative drivers. However, although LGB equalities work is established in some authorities, provision is patchy, and sexualities equalities initiatives remain marginalized in relation to other equalities strands. The larger metropolitan, unitary, and borough councils are generally more active concerning LGB equalities work, but some of the rural councils are proactive in this field.

The research findings showed that there are debates amongst local authority actors about the extent to which LGB service users have sexualities-specific interests or needs, as opposed to interests/ needs that are shared with the rest of the population. This issue is of importance to discussions about intersectionality, in explorations of the extent to which sexuality is examined as a category within the local authority context. Areas of local authority provision that are of key importance to LGB people revolve around hate crime and bullying, especially homophobic and biphobic bullying of children and staff in schools. Health and social care are areas of concern, including, for example, awareness of the needs of older people in same-sex relationships. Housing is another key area, including same-sex partner provision, and provision for people made homeless due to homophobic abuse. Culture and leisure are also of importance, including the licensing of lesbian and gay venues, support for Pride and Mardi Gras events, and library provision. In the UK, a small number of workers are specifically employed by local authorities to ensure that legislative equality duties are adhered to by their organizations, and that diversity in the local communities is supported, and workers in specific service areas also tasked with some equalities work.

An intersectional analysis of sexualities equalities initiatives in local government will be concerned with the discursive and cultural construction of LGB issues in local government. Within local authorities and their statutory partners, sexualities equalities work is associated with the private sphere, and with a lack of visibility as compared to strands associated with people who may have more physically evident characteristics. The research findings indicate that sexualities equalities work is particularly subject to affective issues such as nervousness and embarrassment, as well as normative judgments around notions of choice, legitimacy, and worthiness, so that, for instance, disability related issues are likely to be seen as more worthy of support than sexualities equalities issues. The supposedly private nature of sexuality issues has a number of impacts in the local authority context, including ongoing difficulties with carrying out monitoring concerning employee and service user sexual orientation.

Although the research demonstrated that there are specific attributes associated with local authority LGB equality initiatives, it also revealed the wide variation across local authorities regarding the discursive formation of sexualities equalities work, as well as the ways in which such formations played out in terms of policy and practice. Local authorities differed considerably in terms of institutional norms concerning sexualities equalities; embedded pro-equalities cultures were present in some, whereas others had cultures of homophobic banter and active resistance to sexualities equalities work. Overt homophobia was evidenced in some cases, for instance, a female equalities worker in a Welsh authority described how "I have had red lines through reports, where I've used the terminology 'lesbian, gay, bisexual'"; she was told to replace this with the term "different communities." Homophobia impacted directly in service provision in certain ways, for instance, many local authorities place firewalls on their computers, preventing members of the public (and in some cases, workers) from accessing information regarding LGB services and support groups. Issues were particularly apparent in schools:

> A lot of the schools are still extremely twitchy when it comes to homophobic abuse within schools, both the learners being homophobically abused and equally staff, and then you've almost got that sort of black hole of "Well, if we admit we've got a problem, we've got to deal with it, that would knock our ratings, how do we deal with it?, what can we do to deal with it?, and how far can we go down the line to educate people?," and it's that sort of almost "Let's put it on the too difficult pile." (Police Officer, Southern England)

The particular positioning of local authorities, as accountable to their local electorate, interfaces with LGB concerns in a distinct way as compared to other statutory bodies. Councillors are highly sensitive to pressure from their local communities, who can be actively homophobic and who can exercise homophobic as well as pro-equality views via the mechanisms of local democracy. A substantial number of research participants across the UK referred to the potentially negative impact of councillors who are predominantly from majority communities (white, male, heterosexual); these may be unsympathetic to minority community issues. There was evidence of councillors being deliberately obstructive, unwittingly homophobic or heterosexist, or simply ignorant or disengaged, for instance:

> We've got a real problem, I think, with our councillor's lack of knowledge about equality issues across the board. We've tried to engage them several times, we've got [Councillor] equality champions for every single strand, yet some of them don't even know which strand they're meant to be championing. (Welsh Action Learning Set member)

The importance of party political support for the equalities agenda was evident in the earlier research (Monro, 2006), but there have been some changes in England and Wales, specifically around the shift toward greater cross-party support for the equalities agenda, as well as the impact of the legislation and the related normalization of LGBT equalities work.

To summarize, the field of local authority sexualities equalities work has emerged alongside, although often marginal to, other areas of equalities work such as race and disability. Whilst it has become normalized to a degree, it is patchy across different authorities, with evidence of homophobic cultures within some local authorities, as well as proactive LGB equalities work. Sexuality can be considered to be an important structuring force within the context of local government service provision, because the LGB population that local authorities serve have some sexuality-specific interests and needs; sexuality equalities is constructed as having particular affective and political sensitivities; and homophobia may be institutionalized in some local authorities in ways that other forms of prejudice are not.

Intersectionality at the Local Authority Level

In the 1980s, a small number of local authorities began doing lesbian and gay equalities work, taking what could be seen as an intersectional approach to equalities (Cooper, 1994), although there were significant omissions regarding bisexuality. Historically, the term "intersectionality" was not generally used by local authorities, and this absence has continued. The notion of intersectionality does, however, have currency amongst national players, one of whom said that

> I don't think they [the local authorities] have reached the stage where they are talking about intersectionality much, and I think the strands-specific approach is pretty, still pretty strong—or they jump right up to generic—local authorities that have been doing work in this area for a long time are maybe doing well, but there is little discussion of the particular issues faced by, for example, someone who is gay and Sikh. We use the term multiple disadvantage, not intersectionality. (National stakeholder)

Despite the absence of intersectionality rhetoric in local government, the research findings evidenced a substantial shift toward an intersectional approach to equalities work, with the development of integrated frameworks for conducting work on the different equalities strands in tandem having been introduced over the last few years[9], as well as the establishment of the Commission for Equalities and Human Rights, which takes an intersectional approach at a national level. These integrated frameworks, which deal with the different equalities strands in conjunction, are being used to manage equalities work more strategically, as well as to make it more politically palatable. For instance:

> The more innovative public sector organisations have worked out that it is easier to take a multi-strand to equality than a single-strand approach—it is quicker and politically it plays well, it allows people to be more imaginative in thinking about the links—for example local Pride festivals which incorporate family friendly initiatives." (National stakeholder)

The implementation of intersectional approaches to sexualities equalities work in local government is achieved via impact assessments, as well as briefings to service directorates and professional trainings associated with specific service areas (such as social work). Impact assessments involve examining service plans and policies to ensure that the needs and interests of marginalized social groups are taken into account. Frontline staff work to the service plans and policies, routinely taking approaches that can be seen as intersectional; in other words, they attempt to be aware of the different facets of identity that service users have. The research provided evidence that intersectional approaches to training are being taken, for example, one local authority worker in Wales described the way in which she carries out a generic equalities training with staff in which there is discussion about the social construction of identity, with attention being paid to sexual diversity, and that "we try and get people to understand that we don't just have one label, we are a cocktail of many different things."

The development of integrated approaches to service provision is not a panacea in which LGB people will have their interests respected and recognized alongside those of a host of other service users. There are indications from the research findings that integrated approaches may lose some of the more marginalized interests. The focus of service provision is necessarily on those perceived to be in most need, and whilst this will include some sections of the LGB population, it does not always address the interests of others. The following quote illustrates the ways that intersections between aging, ability, ill health, and sexuality are dealt with by local authority actors, as well as the way in which such approaches can inadvertently construct notions of a universal, possibly heterosexual, citizen, masking the specificities of LGB identities:

> We don't provide services because people are lesbian or gay or bisexual because there is a criteria under the government's social care or community care designations, what we do is we provide all services... all of it is open to people who meet the criteria, if they are LGB and elderly and frail, or if they're LGB and disabled, if they are LGB and learning difficulties then they will get those services. (Local authority worker, North East)

Alternative approaches to service provision combine targeted and integrated approaches, for instance, a local authority worker described the way in which a young person who has been made homeless because they came out to their parents might not then feel comfortable talking to an apparently heterosexual housing worker about being gay, necessitating some LGB-specific provision.

The development of integrated equalities work in local authorities is related to the debates in intersectionality studies about category-based versus interstice-related approaches, demonstrating the way in which local authorities are attempting to deal with multiple social characteristics, as well as potential difficulties with intersectional approaches. Developments concerning the equalities strands also foreground the difficulties associated with applying intersectionality to group levels, both in conceptual terms and in service planning and delivery terms. Analysis of the interstices is relatively easy at the level of individual service user, but harder at the group level, where people have diverse intersectional identities. Grouping people risks erasing difference, but is nevertheless necessary if policies are to be formulated and implemented. The concerns outlined in the literature, about the potentially individualizing nature of intersectionality theory (Grabham et al. 2009), are arguably justified unless group, category-based approaches are also taken; partially foundational approaches are the only way in which analysis at the institutional level can be achieved.

Sexuality in Intersection with the Spatial

The experiences of LGB people living in particular localities are key to understanding local government initiatives, given the commitment to community engagement that is part of local government modernization, following the Local Government Act (2000). The role of space in structuring LGB people's lives, and thus in shaping the policies and practices of the local authorities that service them, was strongly evident in our research. The findings substantiated the assertion that "sexuality—its regulation, norms, institutions, pleasures and desires—cannot be understood without understanding the spaces through which it is constituted, practised, and lived" (Brown, Browne, and Lim, 2007, 4). The importance of space is reflected in the literature, with respect to, for instance, working-class lesbians and spatiality; Taylor (2007), for example, found that a combination of low-income and spatial barriers formed major impediments to some working-class lesbians accessing lesbian-friendly spaces in the UK. This part of the chapter addresses two interrelated aspects of spatiality in relation to LGB equalities initiatives: prejudice and geography.

As we have noted above, the chapter refers to developments in geographies of sexuality, including research concerning rural and small town sexualities (Bell and Valentine, 1995; Little, 2003). As well, the chapter speaks to the "undesirable others" discussed by Casey (2007) in his examination of an urban commercial gay scene; Casey found that processes of exclusion of lesbians and gay men who are older, disabled, female, poor, or supposedly unattractive operate to construct the boundaries of urban gay spaces. Local authorities, in their focus on service provision, include such "unwanted" people squarely within their remit, whilst also having responsibility for planning and licensing for the commercial gay areas within their localities.

Our research reflected the literature on spatiality and LGB people, indicating that visible LGB communities tended to be concentrated in urban areas. Some cities were seen as more hospitable to LGB people than others, with developed gay scenes, and LGB people traveled to get to these areas. Equalities initiatives such as youth service provision for LGB people and health drop-in centers were also largely located in the larger towns and cities, although there were some exceptions, such as a LGB youth group based in a small town in Wales. We found that prejudice against LGB people appeared to be heightened in rural or small town localities, with a number of both Welsh and English contributors making comparisons between these localities and large cities, where there is more diversity generally; this finding reflects the work of queer geographers such as Bell and Valentine (1995) and Binnie (2004). A number of contributors to the research discussed the way in which the geographical dispersal of people, into small, close-knit communities, entails a lack of understanding of diversity. This lack of understanding of sexual diversity structured the work of local authority actors, for example:

> I think it is this fear of, fear of not getting it right, 'cause people do want to do a good job here, that's something that I think is fantastic about [locality] really, em, how dedicated people are in difficult situations really, but people do want to do a good job but I think they're worried if they don't know enough, the community isn't very, there seems to be no infrastructure and it seems to be very hidden, you know, and if those gay members of staff that are working in departments like Children and Young People are afraid of the stigmatisation of being predatory, not appropriate to work with children, all these other stereotypes that are bound, that haven't gone away in Wales, that perhaps if you were working in Manchester, Brighton or elsewhere, you'd know that wasn't sensible way of thinking, those stereotypes would have already been challenged, you know, you'd know that was an antiquated way of thinking, or completely wrong but here, there's no, there's only me I think sometimes who goes around challenging that, em, you know. (Welsh local authority worker)

The Welsh case study and Action Learning Set indicated that the geographical dispersal of the Welsh population and attendant difficulties with communication and travel emerged as a major—in some instances a predominant—factor in the way that LGB people's lives are structured and the local authority work that may (or may not) be taking place concerning LGB equalities within Wales. A number of Welsh contributors from the case study (both workers and community members) talked about the difficulties that LGB people have accessing LGB social spaces, due to geographical barriers. The spatial characteristics of the country also pose a barrier to community organization, with the lesbian Welsh LGB community organization representative discussing the obstacles to conducting community consultations in mid Wales: "it is very difficult because mid Wales is very spread out, and has a lot of mountains in between major towns." These geographical barriers structure local authority equalities work, including community engagement and community-building, which involve people taking part in consultations, workshops, and other events. The barriers even affected our capacity to conduct the Action Learning Sets, which provided space for local authority workers and other stakeholders (including LGB community representatives) to develop strategies for addressing LGB equalities in the statutory sector; we had to postpone Action Learning Set sessions twice due to transport difficulties associated with flooding in rural Wales.

The way in which social forces are routed through each other to forge marginalized subject positions was apparent when examining findings concerning LGB people in Wales. In other words, it is not just barriers concerning space that affect LGB people, it is the effects of space, poverty, and other factors, taken together. Many of the contributors to the research discussed the ways in which Welsh LGB people are socially excluded when they live in rural areas *and* are young, older, economically deprived, cannot drive or do not have access to private transport, or access to the Internet, or are ill or disabled. These issues are dealt with in different ways by local authority actors and local authority strategies. In some cases, exclusion remains hidden and unaddressed. For instance, a lesbian employee who was a youth worker for a local authority described the way in which a rural young man came out to his parents, who stopped him going to the gay venue in his local town, so that "his support network was cut off completely, then he will end up with mental health issues... everybody knew about it but nobody could do anything about it." However, issues such as LGB people's access to public transport, and the need for isolated young LGB people to connect with other young LGB people, were recognized by some of the local authority contributors to the research. There were also a number of examples of local authority actors acting proactively to address marginalizing intersections, as evidenced in the following interview snippet, provided by a Welsh housing worker:

Contributor: "We were looking at housing somebody that was HIV positive, and it was like, 'I don't house people with that.'"
Interviewer: "Who said that?"
Contributor: "Pardon?"
Interviewer: "Who said 'I don't house people with that?'
Contributor: "A colleague, like kicked off."
Interviewer: "Right, OK. So did this person refuse to deal with them?"

Contributor: "No, it's been dealt with now."
Interviewer: "What happened to make that? I mean, did they kick off and then you had to talk them around or did you have to wave policy documents at them or?"
Contributor: [inaudible] [nervously laughs]
Interviewer: "So what actually happened then? When this person kicked off, what happened?"
Contributor: "Em, we were looking at allocating a flat, and the person had a hundred medical points for being, he's got full blown AIDS, and I just overheard a conversation that was going on, and it was like, 'oh,' I interrupted and said, 'why haven't you...isn't so and so on the list?,' 'yeah, we've overlooked him' 'why?,' 'I don't want to house anybody with that,' 'well, you can't do that, you cannot do that."

Overall, our findings demonstrated the importance of the spatial in shaping the cultures of the communities that local authorities represent. Geographical factors played a key role in shaping the lives of LGB people, including the sorts of prejudice they might face, and spatially structured intersectional marginalization was noticeable with respect to the LGB population. The intersection between sexuality and spatiality was dealt with in different ways by local authorities; marginalized identities remained hidden in some cases, whilst in others a pro-equalities agenda was implemented.

Conclusion

This chapter has sought to clarify the remit of intersectionality studies, in particular the debate concerning whether intersectionality studies should focus on the interstices between social categories, or rather focus on interrogating particular social categories. It has done this by demonstrating that attention to the category of space is important in understanding the structuring of sexualities, within the context of UK local authority sexualities equalities work.

The chapter sites its examination of the debate concerning intersections and categories partially at the institutional level, via its exploration of local authority equalities initiatives. Whilst the notion of intersectionality is absent from local authority discourse, strategies have been developed within the realm of sexualities equalities policy making and practice in order to deal with the tensions between category-specific and interstice-oriented approaches to equalities. The strategies that are employed include equality policies that address different equality strands in tandem, recognizing what is often termed "multiple disadvantage," the use of impact assessments that assess intersectional disadvantages amongst service users, and trainings that encourage service providers to analyze identity complexity. These strategies enable large institutions to address complexity at the group level, rather than at the level of the individual subject sited at the intersection of particular social forces. However, it seems that local authorities tend to focus on individual equality strands, and that addressing multiple or intersecting strands takes work to a level of complexity that can be challenging, especially given the resource constraints that authorities face. This tendency illustrates the difficulties associated with intersectionality in the arena of local government policy making and practice. Analysis of the interstices between social characteristics is relatively straightforward at the level of the individual, but once group-level conceptualization is undertaken a category-based approach is required to a degree.

The importance of specific categories in structuring social life does not render a focus on the interstices between them (a focus that has more usually been associated with intersectionality theory) defunct. As Weldon (2008) states, it is possible to think of social characteristics[10] as having some independent effects and some intersectional effects. In this chapter we argue for an approach that combines interstice-based analysis with an examination of particular social categories, in this case sexuality and the spatial. Attention to specific categories, which can in some cases be seen as foundational, is important both as a means of achieving depth of analysis and as a way of developing intersectionality theory into something that can be applied at the institutional level. Attention to the interstices is also crucial, because it enables sensitivity to other social characteristics, such as the material, ability, faith, and age. In this chapter, the marginalizing effects of poverty, youth, and illness were pronounced when viewed in intersection with LGB identities and spatial barriers. The chapter concludes that a focus purely on foundational analysis, without concurrent sensitivity to the ways in which social forces are routed through each other, is insufficient in understanding the social construction of sexuality.

Notes

1. As well as other fields.
2. Except of course where trans people are also LGB.
3. ESRC grant no. RES-062-23-0577 "Organisational Change, Resistance and Democracy: Lesbian, Gay, Bisexual and Transgender Equalities Initiatives in Local Government." We would like to thank the two research associates who worked on the project: Dr Michaela Fay, who conducted the research in the North East, and Dr. Ann McNulty, who undertook the research in the South of England and Northern Ireland as well as data analysis and writing. We wish to extend thanks to the contributors and our advisory group members for their input to the project.
4. The data that was available at the time of writing.
5. Some of the material was published previously in *Sociology* 44(5).
6. Section 28 of the Local Government Act (1998, since repealed), determined that local authorities could not intentionally promote, via published material or teaching, same-sex relationships or homosexuality as a "pretended family relationship."
7. The Adoption and Children Act (2002) allows unmarried couples (including same-sex couples) to apply for joint adoption of children. The Gender Recognition Act (2004) provides improved levels of legal recognition for transsexual people. The Civil Partnerships Act (2004) provides a number of rights for registered same-sex couples. The Equality Regulations (Sexual Orientation) 2007 bans employment discrimination on the grounds of sexual orientation (see www.stonewall.org.uk, www.pfc.org.uk, both accessed on August 18, 2009).
8. The Equality Act was passed in April 2010.
9. These are the Equality Standard in England, which has been replaced by the Equality Framework for Local Government (I&DeA, 2009) and the Equalities Improvement Framework for Wales, see http://www.wlga.gov.uk/english/equality-improvement-framework-for-wales/ (accessed on October 08, 2009).
10. Weldon focuses on gender, race, and class.

References

Beckett, C. 2004. "Crossing the Border: Locating Heterosexuality as a Boundary for Lesbian and Disabled Women." *Journal of International Women's Studies* 5(3): 44–52.

Bell, D., and G. Valentine. 1995. "Queer Country: Rural Lesbian and Gay Lives." *Journal of Rural Studies* 11(2): 113–122.

Binnie, J. 2004. *The Globalization of Sexuality*. London: Sage.

Brah, A., and A. Phoenix. 2004. "Aint I a Woman? Revisiting Intersectionality." *Journal of International Woman's Studies* 5(3): 75–86.

Brown, G., K. Browne, and J. Lim. 2007. "Introduction, or Why Have a Book on Geographies of Sexualities?" In *Geographies of Sexualities*, edited by K. Browne, J. Lim, and G. Brown, 1–18. Aldershot: Ashgate.

Carabine, J. 1996a. "Heterosexuality and Social Policy." In *Theorising Heterosexuality*, edited by D. Richardson, 55–74. Buckingham: Open University Press.

———. 1996b. "A Straight Playing Field of Queering the Pitch? Centring Sexuality in Social Policy." *Feminist Review* 54: 31–64.

———. 1995. "Invisible Sexualities: Sexuality, Politics, and Influencing Policy-Making." In *A Simple Matter of Justice?* edited by A. Wilson, 91–109. London: Cassell.

Carabine, J., and S. Monro. 2004. "Lesbian and Gay Politics and Participation in New Labour's Britain." *Social Politics: International Studies in Gender, State and Society* 11(2): 312–327.

Casey, M. 2007. "The Queer Unwanted and Their Undesirable Otherness." In *Geographies of Sexualities*, edited by K. Browne, J. Lim, and G. Brown, 125–136. Aldershot: Ashgate.

Collins, A. 2004. "Sexuality and Sexual Services in the Urban Economy and Socialscape: An Overview." *Urban Studies* 41(9): 1631–1641.

Conaghan, J. 2009. "Intersectionality and the Feminist Project in Law." In *Intersectionality and Beyond: Law, Power, and the Politics of Location*, edited by E. Grabham, D. Herman, D. Cooper, and J. Krishnadas, 21–48. Oxon: Routledge-Cavendish.

Cooper, D. 1997. "Governing Troubles: Authority, Sexuality and Space." *British Journal of Sociology of Education* 18(4): 501–517.

———. 1994. *Sexing the City: Lesbian and Gay Politics within the Activist State*. London: Rivers Oram.

Cooper, D., and S. Monro. 2003. "Governing from the Margins: Queering the State of Local Government." *Contemporary Politics* 9: 229–255.

Crenshaw, K. W. 1997. "Intersectionality and Identity Politics: Learning from Violence against Women of Colour." In *Restructuring Feminist Political Theory: Feminist Perspectives*, edited by M. Stanley and V. Naryan, 178–193. Cambridge: Polity Press.

———. 1991. "Mapping the Margins: Intersectionality, Identity Politics, and Violence against Women of Colour." *Stanford Law Review* 43(6): 1241–1299.

Davis, K. 2008. "Intersectionality as Buzzword: A Sociology of Science Perspective on What Makes a Feminist Theory Successful." *Feminist Theory* 9(1): 67–85.

Fish, J. 2008. "Navigating Queer Street: Researching the Intersections of Lesbian, Gay, Bisexual and Transgender (LGBT) Identities in Health Research." *Sociological Research Online* 13(1): not paginated.

Grabham, E. with D. Herman, D. Cooper, and J. Khrisnadas. 2009. "Introduction." In *Intersectionality and Beyond: Law, Power, and the Politics of Location*, edited by E. Grabham, D. Herman, D. Cooper, and J. Krishnadas, 1–17. Oxon: Routledge-Cavendish.

Hines, S. 2007. *Transforming Gender: Transgender Practices of Identity, Intimacy and Care*. Bristol: The Policy Press.

Hurtado, A., and M. Sinha. 2008. "More than Men: Latino Feminist Masculinities and Intersectionality." *Sex Roles* 59: 337–349.

I&DeA. 2009. *Equality Framework for Local Government*. London: I&DeA.

Little, J. 2003. "Riding the Rural Love Train: Heterosexuality and the Rural Community." *Sociologica Ruralis* 43(4): 401–417.

McCall, L. 2005. "The Complexity of Intersectionality." *Signs* 30(3): 1771–1800.

McLaughlin, J., Casey, M., and Richardson, D. 2006. "Introduction: At the Intersections of Feminist and Queer Theory." In *Intersections Between Feminist and Queer Theory*, edited by D. Richardson, J. McLaughlin, and M. E. Casey, 1–18. Basingstoke: Palgrave Macmillan.

McNiff, J. 1998. *Action Research: Principles and Practice*. Basingstoke: MacMillan Education.

Monro, S. 2007. "New Institutionalism and Sexuality at Work in Local Government." *Gender, Work and Organisation* 14(1): 1–19.

―――. 2006. "Sexualities Initiatives in Local Government: Measuring Success." *Local Government Studies* 32(1): 19–39.

―――. 2005. *Gender Politics: Activism, Citizenship and Sexual Diversity*. London: Pluto Press.

Monro, S., and D. Richardson. 2010. "Intersectionality and Sexuality: The Case of Sexualities and Transgender Equalities Work in Local Government." In *Theorizing Intersectionality and Sexuality*, edited by Y. Taylor, S. Casey, and S. Hines, 99–118. Basingstoke: Palgrave Macmillan.

Nash, J. C. 2008. "Re-thinking Intersectionality." *Feminist Review* 89: 1–15.

Richardson, D., and S. Monro. 2012. *Sexuality, Equality and Diversity*. Basingstoke: Palgrave Macmillan.

Shields, S. A. 2008. "Gender: An Intersectionality Perspective." *Sex Roles* 59: 301–311.

Taylor, Y. 2007. *Working Class Lesbian Life: Classed Outsiders*. Basingstoke: Palgrave Macmillan.

Tobin, A. 1990. "Lesbianism and the Labour Party: The GLC Experience." *Feminist Review* 34: 56–66.

Valentine, G. 2007. "Theorizing and Researching Intersectionality: A Challenge for Feminist Geography." *The Professional Geographer* 59(1): 10–21.

Walby, S. 2007. "Complexity Theory, Systems Theory, and Multiple Intersecting Social Inequalities." *Philosophy of the Social Sciences* 37(4): 449–470.

Weldon, S. L. 2008. "The Structure of Intersectionality: A Comparative Politics of Gender." *Politics & Gender* 2: 235–248.

Yuval-Davis, N. 2006. "Intersectionality and Feminist Politics." *European Journal of Women's Studies* 13(3): 193–210.

Contributors

Anıl Al-Rebholz is postdoctoral researcher and lecturer at Cornelia Gothe Centre for Women's and Gender Studies at Goethe University, Frankfurt am Main in Germany. Her latest work, published in German, considers the transformation of oppositional politics and discursive practices in Turkey in the last three decades. Her research stems from interviews conducted with the protagonists of Turkish feminist movement, Kurdish women's movement, and liberal and human rights movement. Currently, her research areas include transnationalization, migration, gender as well as political sociology, and knowledge production processes.

Ryan Combs is a qualitative researcher at the University of Manchester's Institute of Population Health. His work focuses on health inequalities, marginalized populations, and public policy. Dr. Combs is currently writing a book about transgender health policy in the UK, which will be published by Manchester University Press.

Daniel Grace is a postdoctoral research fellow at the University of British Columbia, Faculty of Medicine, as part of a Canadian Institutes for Health Research (CIHR) funded multidisciplinary investigation exploring the use of new HIV testing technologies for early detection and response among gay men in British Columbia, Canada. Daniel has a PhD in sociology from the University of Victoria, British Columbia (2012); is a research associate at the Institute for Intersectionality Research and Policy, Simon Fraser University; and a visiting fellow at the London School of Hygiene & Tropical Medicine (2013). His ongoing research interests include global health, HIV/AIDS, transnational legislative reform processes, and social inequality.

Kate Livingston is a doctoral student in the Department of Women's, Gender, and Sexuality Studies at The Ohio State

University in Columbus. Her research considers how public discourses about women's sexual, reproductive, and maternal lives shape adoption law, policy, and practice in the United States. Her current projects focus on the impact of abortion politics on US adoption policy.

Penny Miles conducts research on social care for older LGB (lesbian, gay, and bisexual) people in Wales at Swansea University, and research on sexual diversity and human rights at Universidad Diego Portales, Chile. In 2010, she was awarded the Harold Blakemore prize by the Society for Latin American Studies. Her principal research interests include human rights, LGBTI rights, Latin America, and socio-legal research methods.

Surya Monro is a reader in sociology and social policy at the University of Huddersfield. Her research interests are in the LGBTQI field, specifically in debates concerning citizenship and democracy, intersectionality, and social movements. Surya has published substantially in the fields of gender and sexuality, notably gender politics: citizenship, activism, and sexual diversity and (with Diane Richardson) *Sexuality, Equality and Diversity*. Her forthcoming book *Bisexual Identities* will be published in 2014 by Palgrave Macmillan.

Diane Richardson is professor of sociology at Newcastle University. She has written extensively about gender and sexuality. Her most recent books are *Contesting Recognition*, coedited with Janice McLaughlin and Peter Phillimore; *Sexuality, Equality and Diversity*, coauthored with Surya Monro; and *Intersections between Feminist and Queer Theory*, coedited with Janice McLaughlin and Mark Casey

Erica E. Townsend-Bell is an assistant professor of political science at Oklahoma State University. Her academic interests are comparative racial and gender politics, Latin American politics, and social movements. Her publication "What is Relevance: Defining Intersectional Praxis in Uruguay," *Political Research Quarterly* 64(1): 187–199 (2011), is a one part of a larger book manuscript that she is currently completing, titled *Incorporating Difference: Implementing Intersectionality in Latin America*. Her work is also published in *Signs: Journal of Women in Culture and Society*, and forthcoming in the *Oxford Handbook of Gender and Politics*.

Wendy G. Smooth is associate professor of women's gender and sexuality studies and faculty affiliate with the Kirwan Institute for the Study of Race and Ethnicity at The Ohio State University. Her forthcoming book, *Perceptions of Power and Influence: Race and Gender in American State Legislatures* examines African American women legislators' experiences serving in race and gendered institutions. Smooth has published in journals such as *Gender and Politics* and the *Journal of Women, Politics, and Policy*, as well as numerous book chapters focused on women of color in US politics.

Index

Aguinaldo, Jeffrey 172, 176, 182
Al-Rebholz, Anıl 7, 12, 125, 126, 127, 209
Anderson, Roy 157, 164, 185
Anthias, Floya ii, 17, 38, 107, 127
Arat, Yesim 108, 113, 127

Bazar, Emily 93, 98, 103, 104
Bell, David 199, 200, 204
Benjamin, Harry 134, 135, 136, 137, 141, 151, 152
Berger, Michelle Tracey 13, 37, 38, 40, 61, 172, 182
Bergquist, Kathleen Ja Sook 95, 96, 104
Betteridge, Glen 158, 161, 168, 169, 170, 171, 180, 181, 182, 186
Block, Melissa 98, 103, 104
Bornstein, Kate 69, 86, 147, 148, 149, 152
Brah, Avtar i, ii, 189, 205
Brenner, Bluma 157, 164, 182
Brown, Gavin 191, 199, 205
Browne, Kath 191, 199, 205
Bullough, Vern 134, 137, 152
Burris, Scott 158, 172, 176, 182, 185
Butler, Judith 101, 104, 138, 139, 140, 141, 144, 145, 146, 152

Carabine, Jean 192, 193, 205
Carp, E. Wayne 96, 97, 104

Casey, Mark 163, 187, 199, 205, 206, 210
Cohen, Cathy 22, 38, 151, 153, 183, 185
Cohen, Deborah 137, 138, 153
Colapinto, John 137, 138, 153
Collins, Patricia Hill i, 5, 9, 23, 38, 162, 183
Combahee River Collective i, 19, 39
Combs, Ryan 7, 31, 209
Conaghan, Joanne 25, 39, 190, 205
Connell, Raewyn 73, 74, 77, 84, 86
Cooper, Davina 9, 39, 111, 192, 193, 196, 205, 206
Crenshaw, Kimberle i, ix, 1, 2, 9, 13, 17, 18, 19, 29, 33, 37, 39, 43, 161, 183, 190, 205
Currah, Paisley 65, 76, 84, 86, 153

Davis, Angela 7, 117, 169, 183
Davis, Kathy 7, 16, 30, 39, 43, 60, 127, 128, 189, 190, 205
Denny, Dallas 135, 136, 137, 153
Dhamoon, Rita 44, 60, 160, 179, 183
Diamond, Milton 137, 139, 153

Elliot, Richard 158, 182, 184, 185
Ertürk, Yakin 112, 114, 126, 128

Fausto-Sterling, Anne 138, 148, 149, 153
Ferlatte, Olivier 172, 180, 184, 185
Foucault, Michel 139, 144, 146, 153, 179
Fraser, Christophe 157, 164, 185

Gabe, Jonathan 158, 160, 187
Gilbert, Mark 157, 167, 181, 184
Goffman, Erving 67, 86, 141, 142, 153
Gordan, Linda 16, 39, 96, 97, 104
Grabham, Emily 3, 9, 39, 44, 60, 189, 198, 205, 206
Grace, Daniel 8, 158, 161, 162, 167, 168, 169, 170, 175, 177, 179, 182, 184
Greenberg, Julie A. 70, 76, 86
Grewal, Inderpal 110, 111, 125, 128

Hancock, Ange-Marie 2–5, 9, 20, 24, 31, 32, 36, 37, 39
Hankivsky, Olena 159, 160, 161, 162, 179, 180, 183, 185
Hayes, Richard 157, 164, 185
Hines, Sally 133, 142, 146, 147, 154, 163, 187, 191, 206
Hird, Myra 133, 147, 154
Hirschfeld, Magnus 133, 134, 151, 154
Hollingsworth, T. Déirdre 157, 164, 185

Jordan-Zachery, Julia 23, 37, 39
Juang, Richard M. 65, 76, 85, 86, 153

Kantola, Johanna 3, 4, 9, 44, 58, 60
Kaplan, Caren 107, 125, 128, 129

Kayhan, Fatma 114, 117, 118, 129
Keck, Margaret E. 111, 116, 126, 129
Kessler, Suzanne 132, 142, 154
Kinsey, Alfred 134, 135, 140, 141, 152, 154
Knapp, Gudrun-Axeli 16, 40, 44, 60
Kock, Wendy 93, 98, 103, 104

Lacey, Marc 92, 93, 100, 105
Larcher, Akim 169, 177, 185
Lim, Jason 191, 199, 205
Lombardo, Emanuela 34, 36, 38, 40, 44, 60, 61
Lorber, Judith 143, 147, 154
Luft, Rachel E. 43, 44, 61

MacIntosh, Josephine 161, 167, 168, 170, 175, 180, 184, 185
Manuel, Tiffany 44, 58, 61
McCall, Leslie i, 12, 37, 40, 161, 186, 190, 191, 206
McCann, M. W. 65, 75, 80, 87
Mckenna, Wendy 132, 142, 154
Meyer, Ilan 163, 180, 181, 186, 187
Meyerowitz, Joanne 133, 134, 141, 154
Michello, Janet 147, 151, 155
Miles, Penny 6, 20, 31, 67, 68, 70, 80, 87, 210
Minter, Shannon Price 65, 76, 82, 86, 153
Money, John 137, 138, 139, 140, 141, 152, 154
Monro, Surya 8, 31, 191, 193, 195, 205, 206, 210
Mykhalovskiy, Eric 158, 160, 161, 168, 169, 170, 176, 180, 182, 186

Namaste, Viviane 145, 151, 152, 154
Nash, Jennifer 37, 40, 44, 61, 189, 206
Nousiainen, Kevät 3, 4, 9, 44, 58, 60

Pao, David 157, 164, 186
Parr, Adrian 99, 100, 101, 106
Pattynama, Pamela 2, 9, 22, 40
Phoenix, Ann i, 2, 9, 22, 40, 205

Ravecca, Paulo 52, 53, 61
Richardson, Diane 8, 31, 191, 193, 205, 206, 210
Roen, Katrina 64, 69, 87

Sharpe, Alex 64, 70, 85, 87
Shields, Stephanie A. 16, 32, 40, 189, 190, 206
Siegel, Robert 98, 103, 104
Sikkink, Kathyrin 111, 116, 126, 129
Simien, Eveyln 19, 31, 40
Smooth, Wendy 3, 5, 8, 15, 31, 37, 40, 90, 131, 211
Squires, Judith 33, 34, 35, 41, 44, 58, 61
Strolovich, Dara 22, 34, 35, 41
Stryker, Susan 133, 134, 135, 147, 152, 154

Subedi, Sree 147, 151, 155
Symington, Alison 168, 169, 177, 185, 187

Tausig, Mark 147, 151, 155
Taylor, Yvette 163, 187, 199, 206
Tekeli, Sirin 112, 113, 129
Timmermans, Stefan 158, 160, 187
Townsend-Bell, Erica 6, 8, 34, 35, 47, 61, 210

Valentine, Gill 3, 9, 27, 41, 190, 199, 200, 204, 207
Verloo, Micke 2, 4, 10, 34, 35, 36, 38, 40, 41, 44, 60, 61

Walby, Slyvia 189, 190, 207
Weber, Lynn 90, 106, 161, 187
Weldon, Laurel. S. 2, 10, 24, 25, 31, 41, 44, 61, 190, 203, 204, 207
Whittle, Stephen 133, 135, 146, 152, 154, 155
Wilson, Angelia xi, xii, 36, 205
Wright, Melissa 91, 99, 106

Yuval-Davis, Nira ii, 3, 7, 10, 15, 17, 23, 25, 34, 36, 38, 41, 107, 108, 109, 123, 124, 125, 127, 129, 190, 207

The manufacturer's authorised representative in the EU is Springer Nature Customer Service Centre GmbH, Europaplatz 3, 69115 Heidelberg, Germany. If you have any concerns regarding our products, please contact ProductSafety@springernature.com

Printed and bound by CPI Group (UK) Ltd, Croydon, CR0 4YY
23/03/2026
02076682-0013